LIFE SKILLS COUNSELING WITH ADOLESCENTS

LIFE SKILLS COUNSELING WITH ADOLESCENTS

Steven Paul Schinke, Ph.D.
and
Lewayne D. Gilchrist, Ph.D.
Social Work Research
Child Development and Mental Retardation Center
University of Washington

University Park Press
Baltimore

UNIVERSITY PARK PRESS
International Publishers in Medicine and Human Services
300 North Charles Street
Baltimore, Maryland 21201

Typeset by Brushwood Graphics
Manufactured in the United States of America by The Maple Press Company.
Design by S. Stoneham, Studio 1812, Baltimore.

Library of Congress Cataloging in Publication Data

Schinke, Steven Paul.
Life skills counseling with adolescents.

Bibliography: p. 135
Includes index.
1. Life skills.   2. Youth—Counseling of.   3. Counseling.   I. Gilchrist,
Lewayne D.   II. Title.   [DNLM:
1. Adolescent psychology.   2. Counseling—In adolescence.
3. Life change events—In adolescence. WS 462 S361L]
HQ796.S4138   1983   305.2'35   83-41531
ISBN 0-8391-1795-7

Contents

Preface

"Yesterday a child; tomorrow an adult," "a time of turmoil," "the stormy stormy years," "twixt twelve and twenty," "fifteen, going on thirty-five," and "weird people" are some of the words these authors have heard as descriptors of adolescents and the adolescent development epoch. One clinic where the authors regularly consult last year diagnosed 92% of its several hundred adolescent clients as suffering from "adolescent reaction syndrome." Following a conference presentation not long ago, one of the authors was approached by a colleague who said, "You really work with adolescents? Wow! Nobody works with adolescents. You ought to write a book about it."

In the roles of parent, clinician, researcher, and teacher, the authors daily encounter the *sturm* and *drang* of adolescence. The nine chapters of this volume reflect our personal and professional experiences. Together these chapters offer a comprehensive counseling approach to the life skills children must acquire before they leave home. The skills we discuss are at once separate and interdependent. Thus, thoughts and behaviors involved in peer and family relationships, sex, health, job and career, and societal functioning clearly differ for each of these separate realms of behavior. And yet, the differences are not as great as they may seem. The same fundamental abilities form the requisite skills for success in all important areas of daily existence. These core skills can be learned and transferred to new areas as adolescents grow throughout life.

The book is written to accommodate this flexibility. Human services professionals, educators, health-care workers, and counselors will profit from a cover-to-cover reading of all chapters. Clinicians and students—particularly those with some foreknowledge of adolescence—will be at no disadvantage if they read Chapters 1 and 2, and then move on to the target area that most interests them. In any case, material included in Chapter 9 is intended to permit the necessary tailoring and individualizing to fit life skills counseling into almost any practice setting.

Life skills counseling is not a new psychotherapy. It is not a specialized curriculum for which workshops, continuing education course credit, and certification are given. No one has to do anything out of the ordinary to call herself or himself a life skills counselor. Rather, life skills counseling is a pragmatic approach to professional work with adolescents. Life skills counseling is portable, can be done individually and in groups, and is fun. Most of all, life skills counseling works. Copious proof for these claims is contained herein and need not be reiterated. Skeptics and critics, along with optimists, are encouraged to read on.

Before closing, the authors want to recognize those who taught and continue to teach them the life skills necessary to produce this volume. James K. Whittaker planted the seed, thought up the title, and nurtured the book through its early days. Jim is a considerate, sharing colleague, and is warmly thanked. Lois G. Holt has managed most aspects of the authors' professional affairs for nearly a decade. Lois is a tireless, cheerful associate who, among other things, prevented a thousand problems from ever reaching print. Anna P. Bolstad typed and retyped the manuscript more times than she cares to remember. Without complaint, without error, and with enviable speed, Anna certainly did her part to create a readable manuscript. Cheryl Kelso is the latest member of this production team. Cheryl's editorial expertise and her creative talents appear in several places throughout the book. She, Anna, and Lois made the authors' work look easy and polished.

Jim Pruess edited the manuscript before it was sent to the publisher. Only a few know, and they are sworn to secrecy, how markedly Jim improved the text. He has earned more than a complimentary copy. Beth Bishop did most of the archival work. Beth's familiarity with the literature is exceeded only by her dogged searching of the stacks. Albert Belskie of University Park Press has been a prince. His touch is evident from the front cover to the back, and everywhere in between. Al has served as an able executive, editor, production manager, and marketing specialist. John S. Wodarski is thanked for his role in this project and in the authors' research and careers.

A host of associates at the University of Washington and elsewhere warrant mention and heartfelt appreciation. Dean Scott Briar of the University of Washington School of Social Work has been an unswerving advocate and bellwether throughout the years. Irvin Emanuel and Henry G. Schulte at the University of Washington Child Development and Mental Retardation Center were integral to the writing of the book and to the conduct of the research that went into it. Robert F. Schilling sharpened the authors' thinking in these chapters and in other ventures. Betty J. Blythe, Richard W. Small, Richard P. Barth, Thomas Edward Smith, and Stephen E. Wong collaborated on several of the studies upon which the book is grounded. Deborah Lodish, Josie Solseng Maxwell, Kristine Stewart, Susan Staab, and William H. Snow have further contributed data and assistance to the authors' research with adolescents. Gregory Owen prepared the book's graphics, and Marie Hanak assisted with camera work.

A special kind of inspiration came from those who have unselfishly given the authors life skills counseling over the years. Because the writing of a book invariably means time away from loved ones, these persons get extra credit for understanding and for caring. Thank you Vera and Dorothy; Jim, Hart, and Matthew.

To Edward Paul Schinke and C. Wayne Dorman

LIFE SKILLS COUNSELING WITH ADOLESCENTS

Chapter 1

Adolescence

What is adolescence? Competing perspectives variously define it as a period of physical development, as a specific span of years, as a stage of psychological development, as a sociocultural phenomenon, and as a way of life or state of mind (Rogers, 1972). Whatever the perspective, most observers characterize adolescents in remarkably similar ways. Adolescents are

> . . . In character prone to desire and ready to carry any desire into action. They are changeful too, and fickle in their desires, which are as transitory as vehement. Young people have big aspirations; for they have never been humiliated by the experience of life and are yet unacquainted with its limiting forces. If the young commit a fault, it is always on the side of excess and exaggeration; for they carry everything too far, whether it be love, hatred, or any passion (Aristotle cited in Welldon, 1866, pp. 164–165).

From Aristotle to the latest issues of *Time,* Western culture records the bumpiness of the transition from childhood to adult status and responsibility. Statistics on youthful delinquency, use of cigarettes, alcohol, and drugs, sexual experimentation and pregnancy, accidental deaths, suicides, and homicides depict this transition as tumultuous. Dramatic statistics aside, swings in moods, interests, commitments, and daily behavior are common even among the most stable and well-adjusted youth.

Are these psychological ups and downs an inevitable counterpart of the sweeping physical changes that accompany puberty? Comparison of our own culture with others suggests that, far from inevitable, these psychological events are a product of the way our society is structured.

> In primitive societies, there is no equivalent for our concept of adolescence. In some primitive societies, the transition from childhood to adulthood is so smooth that it goes unrecognized. More frequently, we find that the young person on the threshold of maturity goes through a ceremonial adolescence. Such ceremonial observances are called *puberty* rites. . . . At the conclusion of the puberty rite, the young person is granted full adult status and assumes it without any sense of strain or conflict. Not only is he [sic] officially grown up, but he knows and other people know that he is actually ready for adult activities, including marriage (Stone and Church, 1975, p. 7).

Adolescence as we recognize it, argue Stone and Church (1975) and Phillipe Aries (1962), is the product of an increased delay in the assumption of adult

responsibilities. ''As societies become more complex there develops an inter-
lude of apprenticeship separating biological maturity and adulthood. Indeed, a
long adolescence is a relatively recent phenomenon in our own society'' (Stone
and Church, 1975, p. 8).

In our culture, children reach physical adulthood before they are capable
of functioning in adult social roles (Simmons et al., 1973). In this limbo, and in
the face of many impediments to actual independence, power, and sexual
freedom, young people must learn adult ways. For some, this learning is
lovingly guided. For others, it becomes a scary trial and error process. Failure
to acquire adult competencies and the inability to adopt adult role behavior
might be termed developmental retardation. Youth are developmentally retarded to the degree that they have fallen behind their peers in reaching—
through regular channels of family, school, and community—the milestones
that society expects them to attain as they leave childhood behind. These
milestones or developmental tasks involve moving primary emotional alle-
giance away from the family and choosing new allegiances based on a firm
sense of personal continuity and commitment (identity). Relationships with
family, siblings, friends, and community authorities all change in this process.
Occupational goals and a vocation must be selected. A whole new set of
competencies in the realm of sexual behavior must be acquired. At no time in
the life cycle are internal and external changes in functioning required that are
so comprehensive and so unrelated to previous experience. No wonder that
adolescence in America is stereotyped as a time of clumsiness, bizarre clothing,
fluctuating appetites, extreme tastes in music and literature, 45-minute showers
and telephone calls twice as long, narcissism, lassitude, rudeness, and episodic
depression (McCandless and Coop, 1979). At the same time, young people
appear maddeningly blasé about home and school responsibilities, intellectual
pursuits, money management, vocation, career, and anything that requires
more than cursory attention (Yankelovich, 1974).

For the bulk of young people these patterns are transient. In their late teens
or early 20s, most American youth adopt one of the multitude of life styles
approved by our society and contribute to the common good through work,
community activities, and networks of interpersonal relationships. Still, increasing numbers of adolescents do not negotiate this period of change
successfully—with serious consequences. The self-destruction of youths is
shown by a teenage suicide rate that has doubled in the last 5 years (Holinger,
1979). Over half the fatalities of 12- to 17-year-olds are from suicide, drown-
ing, motor vehicle accidents, and murder (Kovar, 1979). Homicide is the
leading cause of death for nonwhite adolescents in this country (Population
Reference Bureau, 1980). One in four U.S. drug arrests involves an adolescent
(Bureau of Census, 1978). One-third of high school students take illicit drugs
other than cannabis, and 40% use marijuana (Bachman et al., 1981). Ten
percent of all 12th graders get drunk at least weekly (Finn, 1979) and 35%

regularly smoke cigarettes (United States Public Health Service, 1979b). Substance use grows with years, and many Americans are addicted to tobacco, alcohol, prescription drugs, and illegal and deleterious chemicals by age 14 (Jessor et al., 1980; Roush et al., 1980).

Criminal offenses are rife among U.S. adolescents. One quarter of American high schoolers have broken into a home or business, 15% have vandalized school buildings, 10% have intentionally destroyed private property, and 1 in 10 have inflicted medically significant damage on another person (Johnston et al., 1980). The 30% to 40% of young people who shoplift make this the most frequent crime in the United States (French, 1981; Johnston et al., 1980; U.S. Department of Justice, 1978). Every day, $15 million leaves U.S. stores without going through the cash register (Klemke, 1982). Adolescent shoplifters account for an estimated one-third to one-half of this loss (Washington Crime Watch, 1982).

Adolescents' sexual indiscretions are manifest in intercourse at an early age (National Center for Health Statistics, 1982a) and employment as male and female prostitutes (Brown, 1979; Roesler and Deisher, 1972). Venereal diseases are epidemic in youthful cohorts (Center for Disease Control, 1977), and 1.3 million annual pregnancies among U.S. adolescents reflect a soaring number of out-of-wedlock births (Tietze, 1978). Eighty-three percent of Black teenagers bear children outside of marriage (Black and white, unwed all over, 1981). Many of these children are raised in single-parent families. Just 7% of all young mothers relinquish babies for substitute care (Zelnik and Kantner, 1978) and fewer and fewer choose to marry.

Problem behavior considered minor or manageable in childhood can erupt with serious consequences in the crucible of adolescence. Observing a large sample of children, Mussen et al. (1979) report the following:

> Boys who became delinquents were viewed by their teachers as more poorly adjusted than their classmates as early as third grade. They appeared less considerate and fair in dealing with others, less friendly, less responsible, more impulsive, and more antagonistic to authority. In return, they were less liked and accepted by their peers. . . . Peer relations remained significantly poorer among the delinquents in adolescence. The delinquents were less friendly and pleasant toward classmates and, in return, were less well liked and accepted by their peers (p. 354).

As for young women, Mussen et al. (1979) conclude as follows:

> Somewhat similar results were obtained for girls, significant differences between future delinquents and nondelinquents becoming evident by the third grade or earlier. Increasingly it became evident that future delinquents were significantly less well adjusted socially, emotionally, and academically than their nondelinquent peers. . . . They had more difficulty in relating to same- and opposite-sex peers. They were less likely to show respect and consideration for the rights of others and, in return, were less well liked and accepted by others (p. 356).

Substantiating data related problems in adolescence to serious problems in later life, including alcohol and drug abuse (Beachy et al., 1979), arrests (Moore et al., 1979), bad conduct in the military (Roff, 1961), psychological problems, neuroses, and psychiatric referral (Cowen et al., 1973; Kellam et al., 1980; Roff, 1977), schizophrenia (Watt, 1978), marital and family disruptions (Bachman et al., 1978; Janes et al., 1979), and employment difficulties (Ross and Ross, 1976).

THEORIES OF ADOLESCENCE

Psychoanalytic

Early attempts to explain the nature of adolescence and adolescent behavior may be found in the work of Freud and other psychoanalytic theorists. Freud's psychosexual theory of personality development posits an instinctual driving force called the libido that motivates all human behavior. Because of the physical changes of puberty and the wearing out of old childhood defenses against sexual feelings (which protected the child from the full Oedipal drama), libido in adolescence is lodged in complex feelings and behavior centering around the genital organs. The culmination of development—according to Freud—is the undertaking and achievement of full genital sexuality at the end of adolescence. Sexual orgasm is important because it is the best means of releasing libido stored in the id and experienced as tension. ''When a person has regular orgasms in intercourse with one for whom he feels significant liking and respect, the catharsis obtained in this way will reduce his need to rely on defense mechanisms: a proper release of libido means that one doesn't have to guard against it so much'' (Rappoport, 1972, p. 316). In this kind of intercourse, people can express the deepest id-impulses in a way that affirms their sense of being good and worthwhile persons. Energy which has been tied up in controlling inadmissible impulses and feelings then becomes available for a broad range of creative and constructive ventures. In Freudian terms, problems in adolescence arise when libidinal energy cannot find acceptable outlets and the progression toward satisfying genital sexuality is blocked.

Although fundamentally a follower of Freud, Erik Erikson (1968) emphasized the primacy of social concerns over sexual or libidinal impulses in adolescence. Healthy adolescents, says Erikson, develop a dependable sense of who they are and where they are going in terms of the roles and possibilities offered by their society. Settling on a role constitutes the achievement of identity which makes further growth and development possible. Sexuality and vocational choice are the two main foundations of this all-important sense of identity. Failure to achieve identity results in role confusion and stalled development. The requirement that adolescents reorganize their sense of who they are is brought on by physical changes at puberty. If young people ''have an idea of what kind of adult role they want to fill, this can serve as a guide or organizing principle for their emerging sense of identity'' (Rappoport, 1972, p. 319). Youths who have no idea who they want to become have no blueprint for making choices and shaping adult personalities. They spin confusedly from one trial identity to another and do not mature.

Theorists who view adolescence as a battle for control of frightening impulses, an edgy search for ways to discharge libidinal tensions, or as a constant struggle to create a sense of personal identity from the welter of available possibilities depict the period as governed by unseen and uncontrollable forces, storm and stress. As Anna Freud (1958) says, ''The upholding of a steady equilibrium during the adolescent process is in itself abnormal'' (p. 275). Although dramatic and widely publicized, the psychoanalytic *sturm* and *drang* view of adolescence has two major flaws. First, it does not accurately depict the subjective experience of many young people, and second, it does not generate a treatment model that is useful in typical human services settings. Directives to help youth constructively discharge libidinal energies and consolidate stable identities are too vague and diffuse to guide counseling and treatment.

This dark picture of youth torn apart by violent subconscious tensions is strongly criticized by many scholars. In 1962, Daniel Offer and his colleagues set out to improve the understanding of adolescence by directly studying normal adolescents' views of themselves (Offer and Howard, 1972; Offer et al., 1977, 1981b). These researchers developed the 130-item Offer Self-Image Questionnaire (OSIQ). The OSIQ taps adolescents' feelings about five aspects of themselves: psychological, social, sexual, familial, and coping. Data from over 15,000 OSIQs are now available. Offer's major finding is that most teenagers do not see themselves as experiencing the stormy rebelliousness and turmoil often attributed to the adolescent period by mental health professionals and psychoanalytic theorists, in particular. His data support the conclusion that, for a great many young people, adolescence is characterized by good coping, satisfaction with self, and a smooth transition into adulthood. He takes psychoanalytic theorists to task for spinning elaborate theoretical models of adolescence that reflect only adult fantasizing about youth while ignoring the actual experiences of young people themselves.

Sociological

Contrasting sharply with psychoanalytic views, more useful models of adolescence concentrate on social ecology and the social roles of youth. Every society constructs sets of behavioral requirements called *roles*. Individuals who have in common certain age, occupational, sexual, or familial characteristics are expected to behave in socially prescribed ways. These prescribed roles confer status and identity upon the individuals filling them. Several factors complicate the adolescent role in contemporary society. First, the role has no clearly defined end. Entrance into junior high school is generally assumed to be the beginning of adolescence, regardless of puberty (Elder, 1975), and the assumption of adult role responsibilities is the period's theoretical end. But no *rites de passage* exist and numerous ambiguities remain. Adolescents' premature attempts to signal the assumption of adult roles can lead to problem behavior if young people concentrate only on such "adult" role characteristics as drinking, smoking, coitus, and overthrow of established authority (Jessor and Jessor, 1977).

A second complicating factor is the lack of value ascribed to the adolescent role. For American adolescents "opportunities to carry out responsible work outside the home, to engage in efforts that are important to the welfare of others, have been deferred until the end of an increasingly long period of schooling" (Panel on Youth, 1974, p. 129). At the family level, adolescents are not the economic boon they once were. Before the turn of the century, parents who nurtured children to their teenage years strengthened their families by adding powerful family members to help in the struggle for survival. Rather than being important economic assets, today's adolescents are regarded as financial liabilities.

One final factor complicates the current role of adolescents in our society. Adolescents by all definitions are learning how to be grown up. They are dependent upon their families for subsistence; yet the family is no longer the primary agent for transforming children into adults. Society changes so rapidly that a widening gap exists between family knowledge and experience and the requirements of adult life (Elder, 1975). Our urbanized technological culture promotes the fragmentation of families. Bronfenbrenner (1970), Coelho (1980), Lasch (1977), and others document a decline in the amount of time parents and children spend together. Important parenting responsibilities are relinquished to such agents as day care centers, schools, and peer groups. Becoming a mature adult means learning how to love and how to work. But fewer and fewer parents are able to provide adolescents with the crucial emotional and behavioral preparation for these tasks. Adolescents spend much of their time and leisure activities with same-age peers, not parents. "Isolation of the young diminishes the accuracy of adults in taking the role of the young, in knowing how they feel, think and perceive, and in applying this empathic knowledge to guide their own responses in socialization. Physical separation increases adult dependence on the mass-media stereotypes of the adolescent world" (Elder, 1975, p. 12).

Even if adults' understanding of youths' needs, fears, beliefs, desires, and habits were complete, the task of preparing young people for adulthood would not be any simpler. One psychologist summarizes the challenges of such preparation:

In addition to the age-old problems of growing up, finding a mate, keeping body and soul together, we now have the energy crisis, spiraling inflation, pollution of our environment, overpopulation, impending food shortages, and the destruction of time-honored values and institutions. Those who would undertake to direct the young hardly know what directions to give (DiCaprio, 1980, p. vii).

Preparing youths to become effective and satisfied citizens requires dealing with all aspects of contemporary society—even—and perhaps especially—those that seem intricate, ambiguous, and elusive as well as those that are petty and mundane.

Consider what a person has to know to live effectively today: one should know sound principles of money management, of investment hazards and credit risks; one should know something about the various types of savings and checking accounts; insurance is a major area of concern; thus, one should know something about auto, home, life, and health insurance. What about health care? This is a major topic in itself; it includes knowledge of nutrition, medical, and dental hygiene. What are sound principles of self-care, and when should one see a physician? What about the purchase and maintenance of an automobile, a home, clothing, and appliances? (DiCaprio, 1980, p. vii).

These considerations make up the content of daily existence but so, too, do such crucial deliberations as how to disagree with friends and parents without alienating them, how to apply for a job and whether to accept a job offer, how to keep a job, how to get noticed by someone of the opposite sex, when and how to start a sexual relationship, and how to manage feelings of sadness, frustration, anger, or boredom. Growing into adulthood involves grappling with all of these issues.

Cognitive Development

Helping adolescents grow requires understanding not only in what they think but how they think. Piaget's work still provides the best framework for conceptualizing thinking processes and cognitive development (Inhelder and Piaget, 1958; Piaget, 1972). Piaget postulates two critical cognitive processes: assimilation and accommodation. Experiences are perceived and absorbed as they fit into the manner in which the adolescent thinks at that moment. This is *assimilation*. In order to incorporate (assimilate) new or conflicting experience and information, the way the adolescent thinks, the whole cognitive structure, shifts and enlarges. This is *accommodation*. When something too far beyond the adolescent's experience and capacities is presented, it cannot be fitted into the existing organizational framework (assimilated). The information or experience is not understood and is rejected or forgotten. The cognitive framework remains unchanged. No accommodation takes place. The whole assimilation-accommodation process is called *equilibration*. Equilibration is defined as "compensation for external disturbance" (Muuss, 1968, p. 153) and goes on indefinitely throughout life. A state of equilibrium exists when an individual is both modifying new information to fit preexisting mental schema and is adjusting the schema themselves to fit new information (Frieze et al., 1978). This is the process through which adolescents grow to think like adults.

Cognitive maturation through equilibration is not a rapid process. Major improvements in children's cognitive and information-processing capacities begin in early adolescence. In Piaget's theories, thinking (cognition) in childhood is limited by children's inability to mentally symbolize what is not concretely present in their immediate surroundings. In later childhood, boys and girls can perform simple mental operations on bits of experience present in memory rather than the immediate environment. But not until mid-adolescence can they deal with the world wholly in terms of symbols without the need to fall back on actual sensory experience. The adolescent imagination can conjure an infinite variety of hypotheses and possibilities. As one developmental psychologist states, "Many of the stereotyped features of adolescent personality— the romanticism, the moral and social idealism—can be understood as a consequence of the stage of intellectual development reached by the adolescent. [Adolescents are] for the first time able to think in an abstract, broadly theoretical way. And . . . . can thus imagine a family, a society, or a world as it *might* be; an image which is usually preferable to the world as it is" (Rappoport, 1972, p. 69). Cognitively speaking the adolescent is "an enthusiastic nouveau riche" moving awkwardly into "previously unknown domains of thinking, without being much aware of their social-emotional implications" (Rappoport, 1972, p. 325).

Mastery of this kind of thought is uneven. Young people do not apply their new cognitive capacities simultaneously to all areas of experience. Scholars postulate these new cognitive abilities as the cause of such well-observed adolescent characteristics as self-consciousness and needless risk-taking (Elkind, 1967, 1968; Looft, 1971). Elkind (1967, 1981) discusses the egocentrism that accompanies adolescents' new capacity to hypothesize about what others are thinking. One form of egocentrism involves failure to differentiate between their own thoughts and those of others. In Elkind's words youth often "take the other person's point of view to an extreme degree" (Elkind, 1968, p. 153). This leads to adolescents' assumption that all people are as preoccupied with them, as admiring or critical of them, as they are of themselves. "Adolescents thus believe that they are the focus of much attention—as if they operated upon a stage on which they are principal actors and all the world is an audience" (Looft, 1971, p. 489). The feeling of performing for this imaginary audience accounts for adolescents' feelings of self-consciousness.

The other manifestation of adolescent egocentrism, according to Elkind, is young peoples' belief in the uniqueness of their own experiences. Many adolescents are convinced that negative events happen only to other people. Because they believe that they are the focus of so much concern from the imaginary audience, they feel different from others and very special. Unwanted consequences of dangerous actions may disable others, but they themselves have special immunity. For them, driving while intoxicated will get them safely home and unprotected intercourse will never result in pregnancy (Cvetkovich et al., 1975; Elkind, 1981). Risk taking under these psychological conditions seems justified. Both forms of adolescent egocentrism are dissipated by social interaction. Exposure to the beliefs and experiences of others generates a sequence of assimilation and accommodation that eventually shapes a belief system more consonant with reality.

Social Learning Approach

Additional information about how adolescents develop is provided by social learning theorists (see Bandura, 1977; McAlister, 1981). These theorists contend that behavior is the product of a transaction between the internal environment (attentional processes, thoughts, beliefs) and the external environment (events, sensory observations). Development is the continual readjustment—in a process akin to equilibration—of thoughts and actions in response to observations about the real or symbolic consequences of one's own behavior or the behavior of others. People tend to behave in ways they believe will bring reinforcement and avoid punishment. Beliefs about what is reinforcing and what is punishing are shaped by the social environment. What is initially a very aversive experience may be repeated if the adolescent believes it to be socially desirable (McAlister, 1981). For the behavior to persist, however, it must continue to be reinforcing.

In general, according to social learning theory, success in performing some task leads to feelings of mastery, efficacy, self-validation, and self-reinforcement. Recognition of personal efficacy increases willingness to repeat the same behavior again. Repeated practice generates higher levels of skill and more self-confidence in a spiraling learning cycle. Merely observing others performing some action can lead to the initial trial that initiates this cycle. Symbolic, purely cognitive, or imagined representations of a desirable outcome can also provide inducement or motivation to engage in certain behavior even in the absence of prior direct experience.

Such learning cycles can be deliberately accelerated. The life skills training approach outlined in this book rests on this foundation from social learning theory. The skills training approach assumes that problem behavior in adolescents is the result of faulty or incomplete learning, not psychological illness. The next chapter discusses the life skills approach in more detail. Succeeding chapters apply this approach to enhancing adolescents' competence and satisfaction in six important realms—interpersonal relationships with family and friends, sexuality, stress, health, selecting a vocation and getting and keeping a job, and developing responsible citizenship. The last chapter outlines how to organize, implement, and evaluate life skills training programs in community settings.

Chapter 2

The Life Skills Approach

Dramatic, rapid changes in adolescence are good cause for young people to suffer personal and social difficulties. Surprisingly, however, the bulk of American youths finish school, steer clear of drug dependence, unwanted pregnancy, and scrapes with the law, and eventually become responsible, gainfully employed, tax-paying citizens (Bachman et al., 1978; Johnston et al., 1980; National Center for Health Statistics, 1979a,b). The reasons for this outcome are complex.

Early research by Silber et al. (1961) sheds light on why some young people and not others find their way in society with little assistance. Silber and associates went into a suburban high school, drew a sample of college-bound women and men, and asked teachers to assess each student's motivation, industry, initiative, influence, leadership, concern for others, responsibility, and emotional stability. Adolescents who ranked highest were screened and culled from the sample if they seemed troubled, disturbed, or uncomfortable. Individual students in the remaining cohort were interviewed to determine their capacity to complete high school and enter college. The rich yield of these interviews illuminates skills that enable adolescents to gracefully take on adult tasks.

A general characteristic of our students was their tendency to reach out for new experience, a tendency to be active in dealing with challenge and an enjoyment in the sense of mastery. . . . These students developed and maintained an image of themselves as adequate to the perceived requirements of the new situation. Students referred back to analogous situations in the past which had been adequately mastered, thus reassuring themselves about their ability to handle these situations in the future. . . . By seeking out information about the new situation, they reduced some of the ambiguity in it and, in so doing, felt better prepared to deal with it. By role rehearsal they prepared for the new situation by rehearsing in advance forms of behavior which they associated with college students. In addition, they rehearsed behaving more like adults before going off to college. . . . Experiencing anxiety did not in turn signal a feeling of uncomfortable distance from others, but rather as something that was shared. Some students viewed their worrying as something useful, as if worrying extended control over the uncertainties in the unknown situation. . . . Anxiety about some future contingencies could be dealt with also by rehearsing in fantasy how one could deal with that situation ahead of time (Silber et al., 1961, p. 364–365).

INTERPERSONAL COMPETENCE

Other work of this period examined the necessary qualities for people to profitably interact with their environment. According to a 1959 paper, the key was interpersonal competence, defined as "an organism's capacity to interact effectively with its environment" (White, 1959). The results of later laboratory research on the topic developed this insight: "Human competence tends to increase 1) as one's awareness of relevant factors increases (relevant factors are those that have effect), 2) as the problems are solved in such a way that they remain solved, 3) with a minimal deterioration of the problem-solving process" (Argyris, 1965, p. 59). Another statement by the same author puts it more succinctly: "Interpersonal competence is the ability to cope effectively with interpersonal relationships" (Argyris, 1968, p. 148).

The late 1960s witnessed new insights on how people pick up desirable traits. These understandings resulted from a professional concern for increasing clients' positive functioning rather than decreasing their deviant responses (Gladwin, 1967; Maher, 1966), and from advances in social-learning theory and its offshoot, behavior therapy (Bandura, 1969; Ullman and Krasner, 1969). Disenchanted with the "long tradition of defining normality as the 'absence of abnormality,' " Goldfried and D'Zurilla (1969) proposed "a behavioral conceptualization of 'competence'—a conception which, rather than being based on personality characteristics, or underlying dynamics, is defined operationally by the individual's interactions with his environment" (p. 158). In their search, the pair of behaviorists strengthened their conceptualization by juxtaposing young people who were undergoing personal and social problems with those who were faring well.

To their credit, Goldfried and D'Zurilla did not stop with data analysis. They went on to posit that young people learn competence through "a particular *orientation* with regard to problematic situations (designed to encourage independent problem-solving behavior) and a specific *set of cognitive operations* which includes: (a) a careful statement and definition of the problematic situation, (b) a comprehensive search for possible alternative solutions, (c) a 'decision-making' phase, involving the selection of the 'best' alternative based upon a consideration of possible consequences, and (d) the verification of the solution through actual behavior and observation of consequences" (Goldfried and D'Zurilla, 1969, p. 187, italics in original). McFall, writing 13 years later, underscored the value of competence when trying to understand whether adolescents can measure up to adult standards.

> *Competence* is used as a general evaluative term referring to the quality or adequacy of a person's overall performance in a particular task. To be evaluated as competent, a performance need not be exceptional; it only needs to be adequate. The term is used both to characterize past performance (e.g., "This person performed competently.") and to forecast future performance (e.g., "This person is competent to perform that task.") (McFall, 1982, p. 12, italics in original).

LIFE SKILLS COUNSELING

Scientific definitions aside, a semblance of competence is endemic to adolescence. Dependence and naiveté fresh from childhood render adolescents eager to learn (Smart et al., 1978). A congeries of role models means that youths do not have to venture far to see examples of capable adults (McCandless and Coop, 1979). Ideal for practicing new knowledge, adolescence is the time to explore options and take risks (Manaster, 1977). To be sure, parents and professionals may stand idle, letting youths flail and flounder as they pass through the adolescent years. A laissez faire attitude gains credence from psychodynamic theorists who feel that painful trials and errors are unavoidable (Erikson, 1968; Freud, 1958; Kohlberg, 1976; Piaget, 1967).

But a more humane approach, the one argued in this volume, is to deliberately teach adolescents the skills that they must have in order to enjoy happy, prosperous, and healthy lives. Life skills counseling is a proven, cost-effective approach for young people to acquire personal and social competence. The approach is grounded in theory and sanctioned by empirical research. Life skills counseling equips adolescents to handle current problems, anticipate and prevent future ones, and advance their mental health, social functioning, economic welfare, and physical well-being. The life skills are taught by teachers, social workers, psychologists, nurses, psychiatrists, and allied professionals. The following sections outline six components of life skills counseling: information, problem solving, self-instruction, coping, communication, and support systems.

Information

Despite its import, information is frequently misapplied in adolescents' psychosocial treatment. Professionals are largely to blame. Most of them erroneously assume that adolescents automatically know right from wrong. Others transmit information in a dry, unpalatable manner. Worst of all, a few adults exaggerate facts in an attempt to keep young people from temptation (Goodstadt, 1980; Serdahely, 1980). The approach advocated here takes another tack. Whatever its focus, life skills training communicates information with instant meaning. As an example, sexuality counseling for 10-year-olds ought to cover physiology, hormonal vagaries, nocturnal emissions, menarche, and the role of sex in human functioning. With 14-year-olds, such counseling should highlight same-gender relationships, love, and contraception. Older adolescents will want to discuss pregnancy termination, childbearing, single parenting, divorce, and celibacy (Anastasiow et al., 1978; Bongaards, 1980; Saluter, 1979). Of course, professionals will scrupulously avoid misleading young persons when communicating any information.

Anyone charged with information delivery should rank facts having immediate relevance over those bearing long-range or diffuse consequences. For instance, warning teenagers that smoking marijuana may hurt their athletic stamina, mental quickness, peer friendships, and grades has greater weight than telling them about pot's effects on brain tissue, respiratory disease, fetal development, and street crime (Hoyt, 1981; Inciardi, 1980; Kaymakcalan, 1981). For maximum impact, information is conveyed in simple language and stimulating formats. Youth argot ("screw," "clap," "downers," "smoke") and the media of films, videotape, live demonstrations, and cartoons are preferable to adult terminology and written documents (Finn and O'Gorman, 1981; PCP: You Never Know, 1980; Teenage Turn-On, 1978; Tepper and Barnard, 1977). In addition to being understandable, facts that are geared to youthful clients express the commitment of professionals to making skills counseling enjoyable. Information is also maximized by asking young people to put objective knowledge into a personal frame of reference. Thus, "unprotected intercourse may result in unwanted pregnancy" becomes "when Eileen and I have sex without using anything, she could get pregnant."

Problem Solving

Teaching young people to systematically address problems reflects the notion that, although its content changes, the learning process stays the same as youths enter adulthood and encounter the exigencies of daily living (Kendall and Finch, 1979; Little and Kendall, 1979; Meichenbaum, 1978; Williams and Akamatsu, 1978). The validity of linking social competence with problem solving, as in earlier definitions from Argyris (1965), Goldfried and D'Zurilla (1969), Silber et al. (1961), and others, is fortified by more recent research from Freedman et al. (1978). These investigators corresponded differences between deviant and nondeviant teenagers and "requisite skills to deal effectively with the everyday problem situations . . . and [identifying] solutions to such problem situations" (p. 1461). Operationally, problem solving is a tool for breaking formidable dilemmas into small, manageable pieces.

The life skills approach teaches problem solving through a stepwise scheme (D'Zurilla and Goldfried, 1971; Goldfried and Goldfried, 1980; Mahoney, 1974, 1979b; Shure and Spivack, 1978). Reviewing their histories, adolescents learn to expect recurrences of chronic difficulties. They clarify troublesome events by answering a series of questions: "What is the problem? Who has the problem? What will happen if the problem continues? How did you get into trouble? Who can get you out of trouble?" Young persons generate solutions by brainstorming several ways to end their problems. The sole rule for brainstorming is that no solution is too extreme for consideration. Thus, the next time 15-year-old Janet breaks curfew, she can claim amnesia, lose her watch, fake an accident, run away from home, bribe her parents not to ground her, promise never to do it again, or go home, tell the truth, and stoically suffer whatever punishment her parents mete out.

Brainstormed ideas can be listed on a flip chart on chalkboard. Adolescents then can rank each solution relative to its attraction and feasibility.

Attraction is the subjective appeal of a particular course of action. Feasibility notes the solution's payoffs and costs, including its effect on others. For example, despite its attraction, solving an interpersonal problem by punching out an adversary is ranked low on feasibility because the ultimate solution may be a school suspension. Starting with the top-ranked solution, youths try to determine the optimal course of action. If successful, they will implement the chosen solution at the first opportunity. Figure 1 is a flow chart for adolescents to complete as problem-solving homework. Later, they can use the flow chart when solving problems on their own.

Self-Instruction

Developmental theorists have long recognized that inner speech guides behavior (Allport, 1924; Luria, 1961). According to one expert, "children over 5 years of age function and control their behavior primarily by means of verbal mediation" (Mussen, 1963, p. 46). Studies of both disturbed and normal adolescents also indicate that verbal mediation through covert instruction to oneself is central to self-control (Glenwick et al., 1979; Kendall and Wilcox, 1980; McCullough et al., 1977). Finally, research with institutionalized young people shows that, "treatment focusing on . . . internal control of behavior by the use of private speech may be a potent behavior change strategy for aggressive, delinquent adolescents" (Snyder and White, 1979, p. 234). The life skills approach applies these findings in self-instructional counseling through modeling and rehearsal.

Professionals teach self-instruction by basing it on thoughts that accompany daily routines. To get out of bed in the morning, someone may think: "The alarm went off 10 minutes ago and I'm still in the sack. I better get up. I'll start by throwing off the covers. OK, now I'll sit on the edge of the bed. Good. When I stand up, I'll feel more awake. Yup, I was right. Ummm, breakfast sure will taste great!" Youths choose and practice inner dialogues that are appropriate for the decisions they want to make. For example, Al prepares these self-instructions for use when his grandmother badgers him about his dress. "Oh, oh. Here goes Grandma into her 'You look like a bum' speech. But down deep Grandma really likes me. She just says these things because she is used to seeing people who wear suits all the time. Grandma doesn't know everybody goes to school in T-shirts and jeans. Instead of fighting with her, I'll thank her for the advice and talk about something else. I'll ask her about her job at the hospital. She always likes to tell stories about the weird patients and their operations."

Coping

In the course of their lives people discover both adaptive and maladaptive relievers of anxiety, pressure, and the vicissitudes of work and family. These encompass reading the paper, watching television, taking a nap, going for a

SOLVING PROBLEMS

Name _____   Date _____

Step 1: What's the problem?

Step 2: Who's got the problem?

Step 3: What happens if the problem goes on?

Step 4: How did you get into this mess?

Step 5: Who can get you out of it?

Step 6: What can you do to solve the problem? (List everything you can think of.)

Step 7: Order your list into the most and least attractive solutions.

| Most Attractive |
| Least Attractive |

Step 8: Tell what will happen if you use each solution.

Step 9: Predict if you can really carry out each solution.

Step 10: Pick the best solution. Say why you chose it and when you will use it.

Solution	Why	When

Figure 1.   Problem solving flow chart.

stroll, gardening, jogging, chatting with friends, smoking, drinking, and drug taking (Folkman and Lazarus, 1980; Jacobson, 1978). Sadly, maladaptive types of relief enjoy unprecedented popularity in this country. Never before have so many young Americans sought refuge in drugs (Huba et al., 1981; McCoy and Watkins, 1980; Simonds, 1980). Notwithstanding a 22% decline in use during the last 5 years, Valium is still the most heavily prescribed drug in the United States (U.S. Subcommittee on Health and Scientific Research, 1980). Approximately 80 million prescriptions are filled for tranquilizers each year (Radelet, 1981), and stress problems account for over half the visits to primary care physicians in the United States (Mechanic and Cleary, 1980; Rabkin, 1970). Research data attest that once the novelty fades, adolescents continue substance abuse in order to maladaptively cope with stress (Kellam et al., 1980; Van Hasselt et al., 1978).

Teaching youths to cope adaptively requires them to anticipate and prepare for such stressful situations as putting up with unpleasant tasks, overcoming obstacles, and tackling challenges. Regardless of its target, coping training includes both covert and overt mechanisms (Lazarus and Launier, 1978; Roskies and Lazarus, 1980). Rick portrays covert coping with what he will tell himself when tempted to cut 4th period English: "Like, I really want to skip class and have a long lunch. But Ms. Bolstad will flunk me for sure if I miss another one of her pop quizzes. I know, I'll go to English and at the boring parts I'll think about the next record I'm going to buy. Maybe it'll be the new one by Wild Child. The Turkeys have a nice album too. Or, Jim Basnight may still be on sale at Cellophane Square." Overt coping enables young people to symbolically and tangibly reward themselves (Lazarus et al., 1974; Meichenbaum et al., 1982). Rick illustrates: "Halfway through English I'll tell myself I made the right decision by taking a quarter from my wallet and dropping it in my pocket. At lunch I'll spend the quarter for a game on the Space Intruders video machine." Relaxation training rounds out the coping strategy (Benson, 1976; Bernstein and Borkovec, 1973). When Ms. Bolstad's class grows too painful, for instance, Rick settles back, breathes deeply, and relaxes muscles in his feet, legs, trunk, hand, arms, neck, and jaw.

Communication

Both nonverbal and verbal behavior are integral to academic and career achievement, friendships, and intimate relationships. Adolescents who communicate well earn respect, become leaders at school, and successfully compete as adults (Michelson and Wood, 1980; Trower, 1978, 1980; Van Hasselt et al., 1979). Youths who interact badly are often depressed, socially disordered, isolated, alcoholic, and drug dependent (Bornstein et al., 1977; Ollendick and Hersen, 1979; Reardon et al., 1979). To illustrate the interpersonal behavior of some adolescents, there are findings that juvenile delinquents frequently make aggressive remarks (Phillips, 1968), use threats, frowns, and sneers when talking with peers and adults (Buehler et al., 1966), and speak disparagingly about themselves (Schwitzgebel, 1967). These youths also show low rates of laughing, smiling, and verbal statements of reinforcement, sympathy, positive regard, and compliments (Beuhler et al., 1966; Schwitzgebel, 1967). Mussen et al., (1979) relate adolescent interactions to adult functioning:

> The role peers play in adolescence is an . . . important one for a variety of reasons. For one reason, relations with both same-sex and opposite-sex peers in this period come closer to serving as prototypes for later adult relationships. The young man or woman who has not learned how to get along with others in a work setting, how to relate socially to others of the same sex, and how to establish satisfactory heterosexual relationships—ranging from friendship to love—is likely to have difficulty in later social adjustment (p. 304).

Teaching adolescents to communicate takes into account postures, facial mannerisms, gestures, voice inflections, and words that unambiguously express personal resolve (Bornstein et al., 1980; Trower et al., 1978; Twentyman and Zimering, 1979). Depending on setting and format, youths can watch effective communicators on videotape, live, or in role play. Adolescents pick communication styles that are closest to their personalities and practice communicating in archetypal situations. These practices optimally occur in small groups of three or more persons so that professionals and peers can act as coaches, offering feedback and reinforcement while youths interact with each other. The dialogue below portrays communication practice with teenagers dealing with alcohol-related problems.

Ms. Kelso (a social worker): "Lois, let's practice how you're going to tell your friend you don't want to go drinking with her. Remember to be positive and firm. Don't worry about making a mistake; we're not going to criticize you. All set?"

Lois: "I guess so."

Ms. Kelso: "Anna, you be Lois's friend. Keep in mind what she said about her friend being 'pushy.' You and everyone else should be ready to tell Lois how she did. Rob, you be the coach. Stand by Lois and whisper suggestions if she needs them. Pretend like it's after school and Anna comes up to Lois at her locker."

Anna: "Hey Loie, want to get high? I stashed a 12-pack of Oly at home. My mom works late, she won't be there."

Lois: "Uh . . . I don't know. I'm kind of tired."

Rob (sub voce): "Fine so far, Lois, but try to speak up."

Anna: "Tired! You're never too tired to toss down a couple. Come on, let's go."

Lois: "Gee Anna, I don't think I want to."

Rob (sub voce): "Good. Suggest another activity."

Anna: "What gives? I thought you liked Oly. I got it on ice."

Lois: "Let's do something else, like going to Winchell's and listening to the juke box."

Anna: "Winchell's is a drag. We can listen to records at my place. What's wrong with you?"

Rob (sub voce):   "You're doing swell, Lois. Hold your ground."

Lois: "Anna, I don't want to go to your house and drink. Let's you and me go to Winchell's, or I'll go by myself."

Ms. Kelso: "Great!" We'll stop here and give Lois our feedback. You start, Debbie. Comment on the good things Lois did; then suggest how she could improve."

With increasing comfort and ability, youths can practice more difficult situations. When viable, videotape equipment is drawn into the teaching of communication techniques. Videotaping and playback give young people a glimpse at how others see them, assist professionals in feedback, reinforcement, and coaching, and contribute an extra novelty to life skills counseling.

Support Systems

Anecdotal and empirical studies signify that support systems based upon the resources of self, others, and the environment nurture and sustain adolescents' growth and long-term habits. According to Gottlieb and Todd (1979), "There is increasing evidence that social support mediates life stress (Cobb, 1976), and it is likely that the vitality, richness, accessibility, and sensitivity of natural support systems have significant impact on personal and collective adaptation" (p. 183). Survey data provide some of the evidence: "Life event stress, adverse first childhood experience and poor social support were related to both physical and psychiatric illness . . . [and] twenty percent of the physical illness and thirty-seven percent of the psychiatric impairment could be attributed to the presence of social factors" (Andrews et al., 1978, p. 27). Another investigator surmises that, "support buffers the effects of life stress . . . [and] these and other study findings demonstrate the exacerbation of life stress by a low sense of social support" (Gore, 1978, p. 157). Research on adolescent drug abuse reaches this conclusion: "Correlations between [youths'] and mother's and friends' use further underscore the necessity to consider social networks in explaining this type of health behavior" (Radelet, 1981, p. 171).

Building young persons' support systems is an important feature of life skills counseling. By dint of using relevant information, problem solving, self-instruction, coping, and effective communication, adolescents can construct cognitive, interpersonal, and environmental systems of support. Cognitive supports are thoughts that foster sound decision making. Interpersonal support systems of family, peer, and community relationships expand youths' ability to effect permanent changes in behavior and outlook. Environmental supports are alterations in routine or setting that encourage beneficial lifestyle adaptations. Fearing her parents' divorce will split her loyalties, Beth, as a cognitive system of support, recalls once a day each parent's positive attributes. Her interpersonal supports are interactions with her mother or father that neither malign nor praise the absent parent. Beth also experiences face-to-face support during chats with a favorite teacher who lends an empathic ear. The young woman's environmental supports are realized in resolutions to rise sooner, kill less time at the local hangout, and learn city bus routes so that she can weekly visit her mom who resides in a distant neighborhood.

The likelihood of adolescents changing their thoughts, interactions, and surroundings increases once they participate in advance rehearsals and develop homework plans. Rehearsals physically engage young people, allow them to polish cognitions and actions, and inure them to the travails of lifestyle modifications (Haynes and Avery, 1979; Robin, in press). In rehearsing the ways they intend to shape their everyday worlds, youths are exposed to feedback, social reinforcement, coaching, and prognostic questions (Schinke, 1981c). Are adolescents' goals realistic? Can their objectives be accomplished quickly, or will changing old habits require time and patience? How will they handle others' reactions to their new behavior?

To answer such questions, life skills participants detail their plans on a homework form like the one in Figure 2. Homework forms indicate the day, context, and main characters for each planned change. Youths specify an intended plan of action along with a backup contingency. They also identify immediate and tangible rewards they can give themselves when the plan of action has been accomplished. For example, a reward is earned when the homework is done, regardless of whether it met with success. Afterwards, youths arrange to tell someone else (professionals, concerned friends, or relatives interested in a young person's welfare) that their plan of action has been completed. Adolescence and professionals review, discuss, and (if necessary) renegotiate homework plans the next time they get together.

SUMMARY

Adolescence brings a mix of excitement and tragedy. Although most young people pass from childhood to adulthood unscathed, a growing number of them demand special attention. The previous sections have sketched the life skills approach to dealing with the deficits and potentials of adolescents. Six counseling strategies provide methods for youths to grapple with their troubles and to promote their futures. Taught by mental health professionals and educators, the strategies of using relevant information, problem solving, self-instruction, coping, communication, and using support systems mutually advantage adolescents and their friends, families, and communities. The following chapters apply life skills counseling to adolescents' peer and familial relationships, sexuality, psychological stress, health, vocational and career goals, and societal adaptation.

HOMEWORK

Name _____ Date _____

I agree that on this day _____ and date _____

when at this place _____

and with these people (use initials only _____, _____,

_____, _____. I will _____

_____

_____

If something goes wrong, my backup plan is _____

_____ .

After I do what I agreed, I will reward myself by _____

_____ .

I will contact _____

and tell what happened by phone _____ or in person _____ at this

time _____, day _____, and date _____ .

_____

My signature

_____

Professional's signature

Copies to: Client

    Professional

Figure 2. Planning sheet for homework.

Chapter 3

Enhancing
Interpersonal Relationships

I'll get by with a little help from my friends
Lennon and McCartney*

For adolescents more than any other age group, the Beatles' lyrics capture a fundamental truth. Adolescence, that sustained withdrawal from benevolent adult protection (Konopka, 1973), may at times be bearable only if shared with friends who understand. Through peers, adolescents learn about life outside their families. Peers are their bridge to a wider world. Peer groups offer adolescents the chance to experiment with new roles, different identities, and behavior not possible at home. Young people gradually gain a realistic sense of who they are by constantly evaluating what they do in terms of whether it is better than, as good as, or worse than what other adolescents do (Santrock, 1981). Research has at last validated a phenomenon that has always been clear to parents. Childrens' progression from birth to adulthood begins in strong conformity to parents, moves to equally strong conformity to peers—peaking about the ninth grade—and finally, for normal adolescents, to conformity to self and the self-governing maturity and independence of adulthood (Berndt, 1978). In their classic text on adolescence, Douvan and Adelson (1966) limn the primacy of friendship in teenagers' development.

> Friendship engages, discharges, cultivates, and transforms the most acute passions of the adolescent, and so allows the youngster to confront and master them. Because it carries so much of the burden of adolescent growth, friendship acquires at this time a pertinence and intensity it has never had before nor (in many cases) will ever have again (p. 174).

Although they are all-important, satisfying interpersonal relationships in adolescence are neither smooth nor automatic. Lacking in skill, youths often make mistakes that disrupt or destroy their friendships. Albert and Beck (1975) found that their seventh and eighth graders overwhelmingly named social relationships as the source of their most serious problems. Often, youth are not clear about what to expect from a friendship. Intimacy, if defined as the capacity to

---

take chances with one's identity in sharing deeply with another person, can be threatening to many young people. Open interactions with others can erode cherished beliefs and produce profound discomfort. Psychologist John Mitchell (1976) and others have outlined the consequences of the self-protective strategies that adolescents use to guard themselves from possible rejection and loss.

> Adolescence is the period in the pre-adult cycle where social masks are devised to keep others at a distance. . . . The distancing games devised to keep inner feelings intact sometimes backfire. Youth become so proficient at keeping their distance from others that they lose their ability to discard their masks when necessary; for some, the distinction between real-self and pretend-self becomes so blurred and confused that the person never knows for sure when he is being himself and when he is merely acting out an image of himself. Once this confusion takes place, the capacity for genuine intimacy is reduced for the simple reason that the honesty required of authentic intimacy is not to be found. One cannot be honest about something one does not know (p. 277).

Sexuality, too, enters into and confuses adolescents' understanding of intimacy. Many teenagers believe that sexual intercourse *is* intimacy and are deeply disillusioned when sexual encounters bring only a sense of shallowness and exploitation.

FAMILY RELATIONSHIPS

In counterpoint to friendships with peers, relationships with family members also have a special salience for adolescents. Interactions between teenagers and their parents change dramatically during the adolescent period but, in contrast to the stereotypic parent-adolescent wars often depicted in the popular media, most adolescents maintain fairly cordial relationships with their parents and siblings (Bandura and Walters, 1959; Santrock, 1981). Forty years ago it was axiomatic that parents teach, shape, and socialize their children. Today it is clear that the socialization process is reciprocal and that adolescents shape their parents as much as their parents shape them (Shostrum, 1972). All families develop repetitive patterns for managing day-to-day interactions and, particularly, conflict. Even well-functioning families can benefit from examining and improving outmoded strategies for making important decisions, solving problems, and settling disagreements. When counselors have access to whole family units, this examination and improvement process is relatively straightforward. Often, however, life skills counselors must teach individual adolescents how to cope alone with their parents' faulty communication patterns. In many instances, with careful planning, teenagers can initiate changes that strengthen their entire family.

This chapter first outlines components of interpersonal competence and then, how counselors can assess and teach these components in a variety of contexts.

INTERPERSONAL COMPETENCE

What makes interpersonal or social relationships smooth and satisfying? Answers have ranged from "Damned if I know," to:

> A repertoire of verbal and nonverbal behaviors by which children affect the response of other individuals (e.g., peers, parents, siblings, and teachers) in the interpersonal context. This repertoire acts as a mechanism through which children influence their environment by obtaining, removing, or avoiding desirable and undesirable outcomes in the social sphere. Further, the extent to which they are successful in obtaining desirable outcomes and avoiding or escaping undesirable ones *without inflicting pain on others* is the extent to which they are considered "socially skilled" (Rinn and Markle, 1979, p. 108, italics in original).

Comparing the performances of more and less competent individuals, early social skills researchers isolated several discrete verbal and nonverbal behavioral strategies that seemed to increase performers' chances for effective interpersonal interaction. Good eye contact, a firm handshake, smiling (neither too much nor too little), using voice volume appropriate to the situation (neither too loud nor too soft), relaxed body posture free of distracting twitches and mannerisms, the ability to make firm and convincing refusals, and the tactic of beginning disclosures of feelings with "I want . . ." and "I think . . ." rather than the blaming "You always . . ." and "You never . . ." are all behavioral skills that have been taught in countless assertive training programs for young and old alike (cf. Alberti and Emmons, 1970; Gambrill and Richey, 1976; Lange and Jakubowski, 1976; NiCarthy, 1981; Osborn and Harris, 1975; Schinke et al., 1979b).

Just knowing these simple and discrete skills, however, is not the sum of interpersonal competence. Curran (1979b) argues persuasively that socially competent individuals are those who are able to assess conditions in a given social situation and flexibly moderate, sequence, and time their behavior to fit those conditions. One of the authors learned about the importance of such timing and moderation early in her career when she designed an experiment to pinpoint the social skill deficits of a group of adolescent boys in an outpatient clinic for learning-disabled and delinquent children. Wishing to contrast these boys with socially successful counterparts, she asked teachers in a local private school to identify same-age boys in their classes who were popular with both peers and adults and could serve as examples of socially skilled adolescents. The skills assessment protocol required boys in both groups to enact three situations in front of a video camera with a male teenager who had been trained to respond identically to each subject. Raters then counted the frequency with which each boy employed a number of discrete skills and awarded each participant a general score for the overall quality (i.e., social competence) of his performance.

Results were not as expected. Far from exhibiting specific skill deficits, the delinquent group outperformed the socially competent group on many counts of discrete skills and on several overall competency ratings. Subsequent assessments revealed that in their natural environments, the delinquent boys often failed to behave appropriately—but not because they didn't know or couldn't perform the necessary behavioral skills. In circumscribed situations such as the authors' role-played test, the behavior required of them was simple and clear and they produced it. But in the distracting, multifaceted, ambiguous world outside the clinic's video lab, standards of appropriateness are not so transparent. Complex real world interactions require accurate, flexible, and sustained sensitivity to cues coming from interpersonal partners and situational requirements. Also required is the ability to continuously monitor and adjust one's performance, control nervousness and anxiety, and rapidly make choices that have positive long-term consequences. The secret of the socially competent boys' interpersonal success clearly lay in this realm and not in the percentage of time they engaged in eye contact while making requests.

A comprehensive list of discrete interpersonal skills applicable for all adolescents under all circumstances will never be devised. Human behavior is simply too varied and too complicated. Understanding of the general requirements for competent social interaction, however, can guide counselors' assessment of adolescents' specific strengths and weaknesses. At the broadest definitional level, social competence encompasses two complementary dimensions. The active or instrumental dimension includes the ability to forthrightly express wants and needs and to initiate transactions with others to achieve desired ends. The passive or receptive dimension—sometimes called empathy—involves the ability to assume another's point of view, to listen carefully, and to react with respect for others' feelings and beliefs. Exemplifying these dimensions, Klos and Paddock (1978) identify three more circumscribed interpersonal capacities that promote social growth and harmonious relationships, especially with parents. These are the ability to engage in constructive confrontation with others to resolve interpersonal tension, the ability to tactfully self-disclose opinions and feelings despite risk of disapproval, and the ability to learn from interpersonal experience through receptive listening to constructive feedback from others.

For almost 20 years, Spivack, Shure, and their colleagues have collected evidence supporting a special class of problem-solving skills that are critical for interpersonal competence (Shure, 1981; Shure and Spivack, 1972; Spivack et al., 1976). Skills for solving interpersonal problems include the ability to recognize the actual or potential existence of an interpersonal problem. This involves "a willingness to see at any given moment that a human interaction has gone sour and that something has been done or said by one or another person that has altered the situation—an ability to look at how one relates to others and an ability to examine self in relationships to others right now" (Spivack et al., 1976, p. 5). A second critical skill is the ability to generate more than one possible solution to an interpersonal problem. When adolescents have an array of options to examine, chances increase that they will choose an optimal, high-quality resolution for an interpersonal dilemma rather than having to act on the only option that comes to mind. A third crucial skill is that of articulating a step-by-step plan to resolve or carry out the solution to an interpersonal problem. To do this, adolescents must recognize realistic obstacles that they must overcome to achieve their goal.

A fourth necessary skill is the ability to consider the consequences of social actions—to oneself and to others. Adolescents who constantly need to apologize have no trouble knowing what they want and how to get it, but do have difficulty foreseeing the impact of their actions and the reactions of others. The final skill in Spivack's and Shure's schema is the ability to recognize the reciprocity of social relationships. Adolescents must appreciate that how they feel and act may have been influenced by and may in turn influence how others feel and act. Such appreciation is a form of causal thinking: ''I am unhappy because he is irritated with me. But maybe he is irritated with me because I ignored him today'' (Spivack et al., 1976, p. 7). These five interpersonal problem-solving capacities are learned through experience with others and are only loosely related to general intelligence. A specific adolescent may thus have a measured IQ of 145 but, because she has not mastered or fails to use interpersonal problem-solving skills, may be judged socially incompetent and unpopular.

The best articulated model of social competence comes from Richard McFall (1982). He makes a useful distinction between social competence and social skills. *Competence* refers to the adequacy of an individual's overall performance in a given social situation. *Skills* are the specific abilities required to perform competently in that situation. The appropriateness or competence of adolescents' social behavior can never be evaluated in the abstract. McFall summarizes a consistent finding of social researchers, namely that social performance can be judged only with reference to a particular situation or task. ''To assess how adequately a person has performed a particular task, one must understand these important features of that task: its purpose, its constraints, its setting, the rules governing task performance, the criteria for distinguishing between successful and unsuccessful performance, and how the task relates to other aspects of the person's life-system. In effect, one must conduct a task analysis, assessing the task from a systems perspective'' (McFall, 1982, p. 16).

McFall emphasizes social skills as the specific abilities necessary to receive incoming stimuli or social cues, interpret and process these cues, and transform the interpreted cues into a behavioral response that fits the situation or task. To accomplish this transformation, skills are required in each of three distinct personal response systems: physiological, cognitive, and overt behavioral. Physiological skills include sensory processes and regulation of physical arousal. Teenagers who are unable to control their anxiety or over-excitement on a date, for example, will most likely not interact with their partners in a very satisfying way. Cognitive skills, similar to those identified by

Spivack et al. (1976), encompass information-processing abilities such as generating a number of potential responses, evaluating the appropriateness of each, selecting one as optimal, and planning the timing and implementation of that response. Overt behavioral or motoric skills are verbal and nonverbal expressive actions that communicate personal choices, needs, desires, opinions, and beliefs to others. Adolescents may know cognitively what a given situation requires—an apology, for example—and know when and where this response should be made. They may also successfully control their anxiousness about apologizing but still not be able to orchestrate words, facial expression, and eye contact to transmit an effective apology.

Helping adolescents improve their interpersonal relationships is obviously not a simple, cut-and-dried application of a few succinct rules of thumb. Bellack (1979b) identifies four questions that counselors need to answer in order to plan treatment programs to enhance adolescents' interpersonal relationships: 1) Does the adolescent manifest some dysfunctional interpersonal behavior? 2) What are the specific circumstances (i.e., situations) in which the dysfunction is manifested? 3) What is the (probable) source of the dysfunction? and 4) What specific social skills deficits does the adolescent have? In some cases, the answer to question 1 is no or at least, not yet. Preventive life skills counseling is an efficient way to stave off problems and prepare teenagers for impending difficulties and transitions to new social settings. Often, life skills counselors must proceed on the basis of what they think may go wrong when adolescents face a social situation completely new to them—confronting a teacher with evidence of unfairness, refusing peer pressure to drink, or asking someone for a date, for example. At other times, counselors will be treating youth, self-referred or referred by adults concerned about their social behavior, who have clear and ongoing social problems. The next section discusses methods for pinpointing adolescents' social skill deficits and the sources of social difficulties they may be experiencing.

ASSESSING SOCIAL SKILLS

A comprehensive picture of how adolescents manage social relationships ideally should involve counselors' unobtrusive observations of youths' physiological, cognitive, and motoric responses during actual occurrences of problematic or targeted social situations. This goal is not merely difficult—with the cognitive response system in particular—it is impossible. Life skills counselors must find ways of making the best possible inferences on the basis of incomplete information about what's going on during adolescents' social interactions. A number of tools exist for this purpose. As long as counselors appreciate the limitations inherent in each assessment tool, these information gathering procedures can provide reliable guidelines for responsive treatment.

Assessment procedures cluster into four general categories: self-reports, where adolescents comment on their own behavior; role play tests, where adolescents enact a contrived scene with someone who has been briefed to respond in a predetermined manner; naturalistic observations, where counselors watch and rate adolescents' real interactions; and significant-other reports, where individuals in an adolescent's environment—parent, siblings, peers, teachers, dating partners, for example—are polled regarding their observations of the subject's social behavior. Each of these methods has advantages and drawbacks for aiding understanding of physiological, cognitive, and motoric responses involved in adolescents' social actions.

Measuring Physiological Skills

Objective data on blood pressure, stomach muscle contraction, perspiration, muscle tension, heart beat, body and skin temperature, and breathing delineates adolescents' ability to control physiological arousal (Schinke, 1981c). When these physiological processes are under control, cognitive and behavioral life skills are easier to acquire (McCullough et al., 1977; Schinke, 1981c). Chapter 5 discusses procedures for helping adolescents control arousal so that additional learning can take place. Nevertheless, practitioners typically do not have access to biofeedback equipment that constitutes state-of-the-art technology for physiological measurement. Physiological skills are thus the least studied of all aspects of social competence. Another still useful, though less objective method for judging physiological skills involves asking adolescents for verbal reports of their somatic responses before, during, and after social encounters. Such responses may include sweaty palms, shortness of breath, stomach "butterflies," dry mouth, and so on. Some teenagers, however, are not accurate self-observers or are not skilled in describing clearly what they feel. Counselors may need to supplement youths' self-reports with their own observations of youths' somatic reactions (e.g., flushed or white face, frequent wiping of palms, rapid breathing) and with reports of such reactions from significant others.

Measuring Cognitive Skills

Until telepathy becomes a common communication technique, counselors will have to rely on asking individuals to self-report their thoughts and information processing strategies. A number of standardized self-report questionnaires are available for assessing attitudes, beliefs, and thinking processes relevant to social performance. These include the Social Anxiety and Distress Scale (Watson and Friend, 1969), the Fear of Negative Evaluation Scale (Watson and Friend, 1969), the UCLA Loneliness Scale (Russell et al., 1978), the Assertiveness Self-Statement Test (Schwartz and Gottman, 1976), the Interpersonal Reactivity (Empathy) Index (Davis, 1983), Social Self Scale of the

Offer Self-Image Questionnaire (Offer et al., 1981a), the Expectation of Social Efficacy Scale (Moe and Zeiss, 1982), and the Cognitive Assessment of Social Anxiety Scale (Glass et al., 1982).

Branden (1983) has developed a sentence completion technique for assessing irrational social cognitions. Counselors ask adolescents to finish such sentence stems as "If I express my anger honestly and straightforwardly. . . ." Although it is not widely available, Jones' (1968) instrument for examining irrational cognitions has had the most extensive validation (Sutton-Simon, 1981). Sutton-Simon (1981) presents a useful transcript outlining an interview method for assessing interpersonal cognitions. The methods she outlines can easily be adapted for adolescents. Cacioppo et al., (1979) developed a thought-listing procedure for tapping the cognitive activity of subjects who were waiting for a social interaction to occur. In their research, socially anxious people spontaneously generated more negative and self-deprecating thoughts than nonanxious people. Berlin (1981) asked her subjects to keep a running record of self-critical thoughts, and the time of day and environmental conditions under which each self-criticism occurred. Sophisticated compendia of additional cognitive assessment techniques are Meichenbaum (1977), Meichenbaum and Jaremko (1983), Kendall and Hollon (1981b), and Glass and Arnkoff (1982).

Interpersonal problem-solving processes and the ability to anticipate the consequences of social actions are the focus of measurement procedures designed by Platt and Spivack (1972, 1975). The Means-Ends Problem-Solving Procedure (MEPS) taps social problem solving (Platt and Spivack, 1975). Counselors supply adolescents with the beginning and the end of a social situation and youths must detail what happens in the middle. Youths' responses are scored for realism, interpersonal sensitivity, recognition of possible obstacles, and for how well and how directly they are able to link the beginning and the end of the story. An example adapted for our research on adolescent dating behavior illustrates Platt's and Spivack's (1975) means-ends procedure:

> *Here's the beginning* There is a boy/girl in your speech class that you like but you know that he/she spends a lot of time with an opposite sex friend who is class president and captain of the track team.
> *Here's the end* You and the boy/girl from your speech class are dating. You like each other a lot and you are happy with your relationship.
> *You make up the middle of the story.*

This assessment procedure may be given in either written or oral form. Platt's and Spivack's (1975) method for assessing youths' ability to anticipate consequences of social actions involves a similar technique. A written or verbal prompt from the counselor outlines a situation containing a temptation (e.g., the opportunity to divulge a friend's secret to get desired attention). Adolescents are asked to list everything that might be going through their minds while they decide what to do, what they choose to do, and what happens. Reports by Butler and Meichenbaum (1981) and D'Zurilla and Nezu (1982) are useful references for counselors who wish to know more about assessing interpersonal problem-solving skills.

As a general aid to understanding social cognition, Kendall and Hollon (1981a, b) and Kendall and Korgeski (1979) provide excellent discussions of other techniques such as postperformance questionnaires, thought listing, think-aloud procedures, and thought sampling that can be used to assess the covert internal dialogue we all maintain as we monitor our own experience. Counselors with the goal of improving family relationships can get access to family members' varying perceptions of the parent-adolescent relationship with the Parent-Adolescent Communication Inventory (Bienvenu, 1969), the Moos Family Environment Scale (Moos, 1974), and the Family Adaptability and Cohesion Scales (Olson et al., 1979; Olson et al., 1979; Russell, 1980).

Measuring Behavioral Skills

An exhausting overload of research documents the popularity of assessing behavioral skills (see, for example, Bellack, 1979b; Ciminero et al., 1977; Cone and Hawkins, 1977a; Curran, 1979a; Curran and Mariotto, 1980; Foster and Cone, 1980; Foster and Ritchey, 1979; Haynes and Horn, 1982; Johnson and Bolstad, 1973; Jones et al., 1975; Schinke and Rose, 1976; Schinke et al., 1979; Wasik and Loven, 1980). The most desirable—but least practical— approach is simply to follow a teenager through a typical week of social interactions and record strengths and weaknesses. Patterson and his colleagues (Jones et al., 1975; Patterson, 1982; Patterson et al., 1975) have developed the most advanced applications of this technique in their work on family relationships. Observers enter a home at dinner time and, using a detailed coding scheme (Patterson et al., 1975), record interactional behavior. Prinz and Kent (1978) have developed a similar, less complex but still useful, scheme for coding and understanding parent-adolescent interactions. The problem with the naturalistic observation method is, of course, that all individuals change their behavior when they know they are being observed. Therefore, even though observations are done in the real environment, the validity of the assessment findings is still in question. Making observations secretly is usually not feasible. Most counselors find it ethically dubious as well as logistically frustrating to make detailed observations of clients who are unaware that they are being watched.

Role-play tests, usually done in front of a video camera in the counselor's office, are an expedient alternative to naturalistic observation. Such tests have been widely used (Schinke, 1981c). The following is an example of one such test situation.

Counselor: "In this scene, I'll play the part of your date. You are at a party with me but you don't know me very well. The party is at somebody's house; their parents are gone for the weekend. There's a lot of beer and drugs around. Couples are going upstairs to the bedrooms to make out. You don't like the looks of things and would really rather leave. You and I (remember, I'm your date) are going to have a conversation now that I'll start. You respond with whatever you think you'd really say.''

Counselor (in role):   "John and Sue have gone upstairs."
Adolescent:
Counselor (suggestively):   "It's real nice up there. Let's go."
Adolescent:
Counselor: "Come on . . ."
Adolescent:
Counselor: "You're going to spoil my evening."
Adolescent:
Counselor (sarcastically):   "Bill said you'd be like this."
Adolescent:
Counselor: "You'll have to find somebody else to go home with."
Adolescent:

From adolescents' responses in such role plays, counselors can gain understanding of youths' ability to make effective and persistent refusals, to make direct, clear requests, to negotiate, to offer compromises or alternatives to unwanted requests from others, and to use voice, facial expressions, posture, and eye contact appropriate to the message they want to communicate. Role-play tests can be specifically tailored to unique individuals and problems. They can easily be adapted to assess family interactions. Typically, counselors select a task or situation that is currently causing tension and ask a family to enact the methods they use to talk about and cope with the situation.

The drawback of the role-play method is its "as if" quality. There is evidence that role-played responses differ from actual behavior (Bellack et al., 1979; Mungas and Walters, 1979; Wessberg et al., 1979). Youths may be more—or markedly less—relaxed than they are in real life and therefore respond differently. This chapter opened with an account of one author's experience with this very problem. Although it is useful for assessing discrete behavioral components such as eye contact, the format of these tests is too short and too restrictive to tap more complex interactive behaviors.

The third assessment method available to counselors is simply to ask adolescents and those who know them to report on how they act in social situations. Self-report scales for measuring assertiveness are available (Connor et al., 1982; Gambrill and Richey, 1975; Lowe and Cautela, 1978; Rathus, 1973). In addition to its utility as a self-report measure, Lowe and Cautela's (1978) instrument is suitable to give a parent, teacher, or friend to rate an adolescent client's behavior. The work of Klos and Paddock (1978) provides a sophisticated measure of family interactions and relationships. Their instrument requires adolescents to react in writing to hypothetical situations involving another family member. The following is an item for assessing youths' skill in constructive confrontation.

> Ever since Mom's heart attack two years ago, she has more than followed her physician's advice to get neither upset nor tense. Indeed, she is quick to remind the family that emotional upset will harm her health. Over the last few months, Mom has developed the habit of opening your mail, and this continually irritates you. You have asked her not to do this, but she persists saying, "Oh, I forgot" or "We shouldn't have secrets in this family." You feel very angry but are concerned about the consequences to her health of confronting Mom. Imagine that you are in this situation now, and write what you *actually would* do (Klos and Paddock, 1978).

Youths' responses are rated on a scale from 0 (Ineffective) to 10 (Very Skilled). Other test items measure youths' ability to listen to and heed constructive feedback and to disclose unpopular preferences. Counselors working with adolescents with low academic skills may adapt this assessment strategy to require oral rather than written responses. Spoken responses should be audio-taped for later rating. The limitations of self-report measures are essentially the same as those for role-played tests. They are restricted to narrow, hypothetical samples of social behavior and scores on these measures do not always correspond to or summarize actual performance (McFall, 1982).

Multimodal Assessment

Before launching treatment related to social skills, life skills counselors must grapple with three fundamental questions: What does the problematic or target social situation require? How does the adolescent client react when in that situation? and What is going on when the adolescent performs poorly in that situation? The most useful answers emerge when counselors select two or more target situations and measure adolescents' performance in terms of all three response channels. Results from this multicomponent or multimodal assessment can then be integrated into a performance profile for each youth that will serve as the basis for comprehensive treatment planning (McFall, 1982).

ENHANCING SOCIAL SKILLS

Once a careful assessment of situational requirements and individual abilities is done, counselors must translate assessment findings into responsive counseling programs. Useful models of well-designed interpersonal skills programs for adolescents are available focusing on shyness (Jackson and Marzillier, 1982), conversational skills (Minkin et al., 1976), empathy and self-disclosure Haynes and Avery, 1979), anger control (Feindler and Fremouw, 1983; Kaufman and Wagner, 1972; Kolko et al., 1981), dating and heterosexual relationships (Gilchrist, 1981a; Gilchrist and Schinke, 1983b; Jaremko, 1983), job-related behavior (Braukmann et al., 1975; Sarason and Sarason, 1981; Schinke et al., 1978), dealings with adult authorities such as teachers and police

(Sarason and Sarason, 1981; Werner et al., 1975), and conflict with parents (Alexander and Parsons, 1973; Ginsberg, 1977; Guerney et al., 1981; Kifer et al., 1974; Robin, 1981; Robin, et al., 1977). Resources with general information on designing and implementing programs for enhancing adolescents' interpersonal skills are Gilchrist (1981b), Goldstein et al., (1980), Kelly (1982), Kendall and Hollon (1979), Kraus (1980), Schinke (1981c), and Schrader (1979). In planning, counselors must decide whether to work with adolescents individually, with whole family units, or with groups of adolescents (Gilchrist, 1981b). Usually, the circumstances under which counseling occurs dictate one format as best. Interpersonal skills enhancement programs are generally organized around three phases: recruitment and preparation, skills acquisition, and skills practice.

Recruitment and Preparation

It comes as a surprise to many youths that interpersonal success is not an inborn trait to which they will never have access. The idea that good interpersonal relationships are built on skills that they can observe, practice, and learn for themselves needs to be stressed again and again to create motivation to enter and complete social skills enhancement programs. Most youths can benefit from initial training in observing and describing verbal and nonverbal behavior in concrete, specific terms. Skills acquisition proceeds rapidly when youth can analyze the specific components of a model's good performance. When working with groups, counselors should early teach group members how to give constructive feedback to each other. Comments such as, "Boy, that was pitiful," following practice role plays should be transformed into suggestions for future practice preceded and followed by several positive comments—for example, "Your facial expression was very good and you spoke up loud and clear. Next time try looking her in the eye. Overall, though, I think you got your message across."

Skills Acquisition

Bandura's (1977) work on modeling provides the theoretical underpinning for teaching new skills to youths. Counselors first arrange for adolescents to view a model who is performing adequately or well in a targeted social situation. Discussion picks out the critical features of the good performance and then—to the extent feasible—counselors help youth duplicate the modeled performance. A good bit of research underscores the importance of providing models that are adequately but not superlatively skilled lest adolescents despair of ever attaining such a high level of performance themselves (Perry and Furukawa, 1980). Models may be filmed or videotaped; they may be other members of skills training groups or counselors themselves; or, counselors may request adolescents to identify useful (i.e., successful) models to observe outside the counseling sessions. When discussion has identified the crucial elements of the modeled performance, counselors discuss each of the elements in more detail and then arrange role plays so that every youth has a chance to try out the target skill or sequence of skills. Counselors and training group members offer constructive feedback regarding youths' initial attempts and discuss and counter anxiety reactions and negative cognitions that may be inhibiting good performance. Youths engage in additional role plays and receive feedback until they feel at ease with the skill and are judged by others to be performing competently.

Interested counselors may wish to examine the ASSET program available commercially from Research Press (Hazel et al., 1981). This program package includes films of models giving positive and negative feedback, accepting negative feedback, resisting peer pressure, making conversation, negotiating, following someone else's instructions, and solving a social problem. Such materials are helpful but not necessary in setting up opportunities to acquire new skills. Creative counselors can draw upon other means for acquainting adolescents with good social performance—movies, direct observation of good models while on field trips, scenes from plays, and the like. When motivation to learn is low or adolescents belong to a different racial, ethnic, or socioeconomic group than the counselor, it is helpful to invite high status members of adolescents' particular subculture—community or other well-known figures or older youths—to model appropriate skills (Gilchrist, 1981b).

Skills Practice

After adolescents are acquainted with and can perform isolated skills, they need considerable practice to make these skills a permanent part of their behavioral repertoires. Practice exercises should require flexible application of skills and mastery of increasingly complex interactions. Typically, two kinds of practice occur in social skills enhancement programs. One kind makes use of role plays, games, and other simulations of social encounters. The other involves contracting to perform target skills in real encounters in the natural environment. Both kinds of practice are necessary. Flowers' and Booraem's chapter (1980) contains useful descriptions of a variety of simulation methods. In addition to supervising role-played practice, counselors can devise jobs or tasks requiring real cooperative interaction among adolescents (Gilchrist, 1981b). As the task progresses, counselors offer coaching and feedback to shape adolescents' social behavior and use of target skills.

Some commercially available games are helpful for skills enhancement. Blechman (1975, 1978, 1980; Blechman et al., 1981; Blechman et al., 1981) has developed board games which lead youths and families through strategies for effective negotiation. Players learn to resolve issues that concern them with attention to consequences that are agreeable to all group members. The Ungame Company[1] produces the Ungame which requires cooperative non-

---

[1]The Ungame Company, 1440 South State College Blvd., Building 2-D, Anaheim, CA 92806.

competitive collaboration among participants to complete and the Roll-A-Role game in which dice are rolled to establish a social setting and the identities of two role players. A randomly drawn card gives the players an issue to discuss and resolve *in role*. This latter game is especially useful for teaching empathy and respect for others' points of view.

A major goal of skills practice exercises is the transference of skills learned during counseling sessions to the natural environment. A wealth of literature establishes the fact that skills do not automatically transfer from one setting to another (cf. Stokes and Baer, 1977). Counselors will need to plan specific skills application exercises for adolescents to perform on their own. Youths' reports of successes, hitches, and failures in applying skills under real conditions should form the content of the last stage of skills enhancement programs. Chapter 2 outlines a contracting procedure for initiating this transfer of skills into the real world. Behavioral skills literature also shows that without counselors' encouragement and coaching, adolescents may not persevere in applying new skills after the skills enhancement sessions are over (Schinke, 1981a). When feasible, counselors should plan to implement booster or review and trouble-shooting sessions at regular intervals for up to a year after completion of the concentrated program.

SUMMARY

Interpersonal relationships are the vehicle by which adolescents test themselves and grow into adulthood. Social interaction forms the core of most aspects of daily existence; social skills and life skills are synonymous in many ways. The past decade and a half has witnessed burgeoning interest in defining and describing interpersonal competence and in developing methods for assessing and teaching skills to enhance social relationships. Although a number of guides and tools now exist to aid counselors, human social behavior is complex enough to require hard work and constant creativity in making skills enhancement programs meaningful and useful to young people. The payoff for such effort is great. Improved interpersonal relationships alter an adolescent's entire life context, sense of self, choices, and commitments. Good interpersonal relationships are the foundation for a satisfying life.

Chapter 4

Coping with Sexuality

BACKGROUND

In the United States today, 5 million adolescent women and 7 million adolescent men are sexually active (The Alan Guttmacher Institute, 1981). Sexual activity most often begins before the 16th year. Many youths sexually debut before they are 13 (Baldwin, 1981b). The mean age of first intercourse is dropping—especially among ethnic-minority groups. For example, in 1971, black women reported starting regular intercourse at an average of 15.9 years; 5 years later, the mean age was 15.6 years, whereas in 1979 the mean for this group was 15.5 years of age (Zelnik and Kantner, 1978, 1980).

Contraceptive use has not kept pace with adolescents' coital activity. Ten percent of all sexually active U.S. adolescent women regularly used contraceptives in 1976 (Zelnik et al., 1979). The 1979 rate of birth control use for these women was 13.5% (The Alan Guttmacher Institute, 1981). Experts in the area recount another disturbing trend: "Even though more teenagers are using contraceptives, and more of them are using birth control methods consistently, pregnancy rates have continued to climb. In part, this seems to be a result of the decline in popularity of the most effective method of contraception, the pill, and the substitution by many adolescents of one of the least effective methods, withdrawal" (Zelnik and Kantner, 1980, p. 237). Gerrard (1982) similarly summed up her data: "If this trend continues, both physicians and clinicians can expect to see more unmarried women with unwanted pregnancies not because they choose not to use birth control but because they choose not to use the most effective methods of birth control" (p. 156). The reasons for adolescent failure to practice are disquieting (Zelnik and Kantner, 1979). Nine percent of one sample who had had premarital intercourse without birth control said they were trying to get pregnant; 41% had experienced unprotected sex because they believed they could not conceive. Of the remaining 50% who knew they were at risk, most had coitus without contraception because the sexual encounter was not expected (DeAmicis et al., 1981).

Increasing rates of unprotected intercourse result in 1.33 million adolescent pregnancies each year (Hofmann, 1982; Tietze, 1978). Most of these conceptions are unintended and unwanted (Dryfoos, 1982; National Center for Health Statistics, 1978). After the 1973 Supreme Court legalized abortion, the incidence of abortions among adolescents more than doubled, and now exceed one-half million each year (Forrest et al., 1979; National Center for Health Statistics, 1980). The 36% of young women who elect this option account for a third of all U.S. abortions (Burnham, 1982).

Population Changes

Sexual trends among adolescents are best appreciated in light of changes in U.S. demography (Baumrind, 1981). Between 1960 and 1970, the country's population rose from 179 million to 203 million, a 13% increase (Ventura, 1977). But the number of Americans aged 15 through 19 years increased by 35% from 7 to 10 million (Baldwin, 1981a). As they comprise more of the population and as their birthrates climb, adolescents deliver disproportionately greater numbers of babies. Teenagers were responsible for 14% of live deliveries in 1960, 17.5% in 1970, 19.3% in 1975, and 16.1% at present (Baldwin, 1981b; Eckard, 1982). American adolescents give birth to 600,000 babies each year (National Center for Health Statistics, 1983).

Parenthood

Following the lead of older Americans, adolescent mothers often remain single. Rates of nonmarital childbearing have increased 42% since 1972, and just 4% of all teenaged mothers relinquish their children for adoption and substitute care (Chilman, 1979b; National Center for Health Statistics, 1982a). Pregnant adolescents have multiple medical problems. Early intercourse and pregnancy are linked with cervical cancer and with uterine complications (Koepsell et al., 1980; Marano, 1977). Infant deaths are twice as likely for babies born to adolescents as for those born to mothers beyond the teen years (New York State Department of Health, 1980). Adolescents risk having low birthweight babies (National Center for Health Statistics, 1981). Infants of adolescents more than those of nonteenagers are subject to congenital malformations, developmental disabilities, behavior disorders, school problems, and low intellectual functioning (Belmont et al., 1978; Finkelstein et al., 1982; Gunter and LaBarba, 1980).

Young parents experience social, legal, psychological, educational, and economic adversities. Their marital troubles and divorce rates are greater than those of older couples (Baldwin, 1980). Adolescent childbearing may result in larger families than parents desire (Card, 1981; Jekel et al., 1979; Koenig and Zelnik, 1982a; National Center for Health Statistics, 1978; Trussell and Menken, 1978). In contrast to youngsters of adult mothers and fathers, adolescents' children spend a greater share of their lives in one-parent homes and themselves are at high risk for precocious pregnancy (Baldwin and Cain, 1980). Young parenthood sets the stage for child abuse and neglect (American Humane Association, 1978; Herrenkohl and Herrenkohl, 1979).

Adolescent pregnancy is the most common reason for youths to quit school; seldom do they recapture these lost years of education (McCarthy and

Radish, 1982; Moore and Waite, 1977; Zellman, 1982). Adolescent mothers are wont to suffer isolation and depression (Hardy, 1982; Kellam et al., 1982). Early parenthood frequently results in young mothers' and fathers' prolonged unemployment (Bureau of Labor Statistics, 1980b), reduced income (Hofferth and Moore, 1979), and dependence on public welfare (Mott and Maxwell, 1981). Adolescent mothers fall below federal poverty lines at twice the rate of women who initiate childbearing after the teen years (Borker et al., 1979; Clapp and Raab, 1978). According to the latest figures, "It has been demonstrated that women who bear their first child at a very early age may face a lifetime of economic stress and limited opportunities" (Dillard and Pol, 1982, p. 257).

ETIOLOGY

The etiology of adolescent problems with sex lies in three areas: developmental dissonance, social standards, and family and peer relationships.

Developmental Dissonance

As outlined in Chapter 1, adolescents develop cognitive and behavioral skills at disparate points in time. A lack of synchrony in sexual and psychosocial development allows youths to be physically equipped for sex in advance of being able to emotionally and socially commit themselves to responsible sexual relationships. Half of all U.S. females menstruate before their 13th birthday, and most American males have seminal emissions around age 12 (Anastasiow et al., 1978; Masters et al., 1982). On the other hand, median ages at first marriage are 22 and 24 years for women and men, respectively (National Center for Health Statistics, 1979b). The decade between biological and social maturity gives adolescents opportunities to risk pregnancy, venereal diseases, and sexual exploitation (Bell and Bell, 1982).

Social Standards

Sex in America is tinged by a gender-specific double standard. One survey of sexually active teenaged women found 70% were of the opinion that "I feel I shouldn't have intercourse at all, so I wouldn't plan ahead to do it or use birth control" (Goldsmith et al., 1972). Another, similar teenaged sample revealed 71% of the women agreed that "If a girl uses birth control, it makes it seem as if she were planning to have sex" (Sorensen, 1973). The majority of adolescent males in a third study believed that "Birth control is for girls only" (Hale, cited in Ingersoll, 1981). Eighteen percent of the young men agreed that "A guy should use birth control whenever possible"; and 70% held that "It's okay to tell a girl you love her so you can have sex with her."

Societal standards concerning adolescent sexuality are in a state of flux (Greydanus, 1982; Schinke, in press-b; Shornack and Shornack, 1982). According to a review of 140 years of literature on sex education in the home,

"Parents have had many divergent opinions sent their way, and the present atmosphere in the United States is especially filled with contradictions and differing points of view as to how to best deal with their children and their sexual development. . . . But the direction seems obvious, the trend is toward a lessening of parental restrictions and a helping attitude to assist children to develop in the style that has many options open to them when they reach adulthood. This trend in all likelihood will apply to the area of human sexuality" (Swan, 1980, pp. 9–10).

A social evolution is reflected in commentaries on the sexual values faced by two generations of adolescents. "We are adrift on a sea of sexual permissiveness. We have changed from a somewhat sex-denying to an openly sex-seeking culture. Sex is becoming larger than life itself: One of the new half-gods in America today" (Hoyman, 1967, p. 28). A similar observation came 13 years later. "Society's mixed message to the young has left them with a mixed blessing. They have more choices than their elders ever had, but no guarantees that they will choose wisely. And that has left many of them with an equivocal appreciation of the benefits of sexual emancipation" (Gelman et al., 1980, p. 53).

Family Relationships

Adolescents generally do not learn about sex from their families. In one investigator's words, "The data from this study seem to support findings from prior studies which have consistently indicated that children get little sex education in the home" (Bloch, 1974, p. 11). According to another author, "A girl cannot readily ask her parents about birth control. They are usually ambivalent about, if not downright opposed to, premarital sex. Even in families that have a permissive attitude toward premarital sex, parents are not able to help their daughters plan for birth control in concrete terms. When it comes to what to do, where to go, and which method to use, the family doesn't tell and the girls don't ask" (Lindemann, 1974, p. 29). A later study found the same phenomenon: "Families head off discussion of sexual matters through a conspiracy of silence. Neither adults nor offspring really want to know what the other is doing. The parents, particularly, may suspect the worst, but they'd rather hope for the best" (Pocs et al., 1977, p. 56).

Rothenberg's (1980) research revealed that less than one in five parents told their teenaged children about intercourse or birth control or provided them with sex education literature. After studies of adolescent women and their mothers, Fox and Inazu (1982) concluded that "The mother's presence as a role model for her daughter, both in terms of her salience as a significant other in her daughter's life and in terms of her own nonmarital sexual experiences, was significantly related to daughter's sexual status, even after controlling for relevant background variables. By far the strongest predictor of sexual experience was the daughter's report of her relationship with her mother; the more favorable the relationship, the less likely was she to have had sex'' (Inazu and Fox, 1980, p. 98).

Fox (1980) bemoaned the neglect of sex-related communications between mothers and daughters: "It would appear that there is not a lot of communication within the home. . . .only one-third to one-half of the children had been told anything by their mothers about intercourse and even smaller numbers had been instructed by their mothers about birth control. Clearly, not many children receive much direct information about sexuality, sexual intercourse, or fertility regulation from their mothers'' (p. 25). Other researchers show the lack of parent involvement in adolescents' decisions about abortion (Rosen, 1980; Rosen et al., 1982).

Peer Relationships

Peers are the driving influence upon sexual attitudes and behavior in adolescence. One researcher found youths "most likely to communicate about sex and birth control with friends, with whom they may well have exchanged misinformation'' (Rothenberg, 1980, p. 49). Adolescents note peers as responsible for their knowledge of masturbation, ejaculation, petting, intercourse, prostitution, homosexuality, and contraception (Thornburg, 1981a). Peers give out wrong information in many cases. Friends powerfully determine adolescents' sexual activity. For women, prevalence and incidence of sexual intercourse may be as much learned by role modeling from girlfriends as by social pressure from boyfriends. According to one study, "Peer contraceptive use [was] positively and significantly associated with regularity and effectiveness of the subject's contraceptive use'' (Jorgensen et al., 1980, p. 151). Other teenaged women report having had sex because they felt unable to say "no,'' wanted to please their partners, or saw intercourse as expected (Cvetkovich and Grote, 1980). An adolescent may agree to make love, incorrectly assuming that the partner will be responsible for contraception (Francome, 1980; Thornburg, 1981b). Many youths begrudgingly have sex, find no enjoyment in it, and deny their very participation (Cvetkovich et al., 1975; Oettinger, 1979). A pregnant teenager told one interviewer: "I was trying so hard to think I wasn't fucking that the thought I might get pregnant never entered my mind'' (Sorensen, 1973, p. 324).

Several factors have an impact upon adolescent sexuality. Developmental discrepancies and gender-specific sex roles affect youthful attitudes and behavior in this area. American societal standards push young people toward sexual responsibilities they may not want. Adolescents are unprepared to handle their bodies and feelings. Rarely are youths well-informed by their parents. Peers may be inchoate, biased sources for the facts of life, birth control information, and sexual decision making.

PAST COUNSELING

Deviancy Perspective

Much human services counseling has regarded the sexual behavior of young people as somehow deviant. Studies have searched for an underlying pathology to explain adolescents' masturbation (Katchadourian and Lunde, 1975), vulnerability to intercourse (Goldfarb et al., 1977), risk of pregnancy (Cherry, 1980; Rosen and Ager, 1981), incidence of abortion (Dworkin and Poindexter, 1980; Rothstein, 1978), and choices concerning childbearing and parenthood (Perlman et al., 1981; Schaffer et al., 1978). The results of such work provide little backing for the deviancy perspective (cf. Crosbie and Bitte, 1982; Gilchrist, 1981a; Gilchrist and Schinke, in press-c; Litt et al., 1980; Olson, 1980; Protinsky et al., 1982; Rogel et al., 1980; Schinke, 1979). Programs based on the view of adolescent sexuality as pathology have been less than successful. Scare tactics, information-only strategies of sex education, and the hope that pregnant young women will realize their mistake and seek abortions have but marginally altered adolescents' behavior (Amonker, 1980; Dryfoos and Heisler, 1978; Kirby, 1980; Luker, 1975, 1977; Mindick and Oskamp, 1979; Reid, 1982; Smith and Gorry, 1980; Zelnik and Kim, 1982).

Adult Perspective

A second approach embodies the idea that young people with objective facts about sex will integrate and apply the knowledge. Counseling programs with this perspective lean toward adult rather than adolescent concerns (Kirby and Alter, 1980). Such programs tend to emphasize anatomy, physiology, dating, masturbation, necking, menstruation, nocturnal emissions, virginity, marriage, reproduction, illegitimacy, and extramarital relations. Although these matters deserve attention, their coverage should not exclude information that adolescents want to know. What sexual topics do youths find meaningful? Adolescents identify such nontraditional subjects as sexual enjoyment, guilt about sex, love, fear of sex, abortion, sexual offenses, prostitution, rape, cunnilingus, and fellatio (Hacker, 1981; Schinke, in press-b). Mirroring changes in society, young persons often are uninterested in the basics and more curious about the emotional side of sex, disturbing sexual feelings, lesbianism, male homosexuality, the feminist movement, gay liberation, and sex-role differences (Block and Block, 1980; Cammaert and Larsen, 1979; Chng, 1980; Grady et al., 1979; Loewenstein, 1980; Norman and Mancuso, 1980; Rubenstein et al., 1976; Seaman and Seaman, 1977; Weinberg and Williams, 1974; Zukerman, 1979).

Other programs with an adult perspective focus on sexual values clarification. Implicit is the notion that young persons who resolve their value conflicts will make sound choices (Ross, 1979). Values programs are distanced from sex education programs, and can attract young people who might not otherwise participate in the latter because of possible negative connotations (Gingerich et al., 1982). But trying to clarify adolescents' values seems a circuitous way to approach sexual counseling. The data suggest that values clarification is benign in terms of youths' self-esteem, interpersonal behavior, sexual values, attitudes, and relationships (Lockwood, 1978).

Normalcy Perspective

A third way to look at sex in adolescence comes from Cvetkovich and Grote's (1981) work on teenage pregnancy: "This view asserts that teenagers are placed at contraceptive risk not by any pathology, personal, moral or otherwise, but by a unique convergence of factors that are normal to the lives of many adolescents" (p. 212; cf. Cvetkovich and Grote, 1979a, 1979b; Cvetkovich et al., 1978). The normalcy perspective is relevant for all adolescents—not just a special high-risk group. This perspective also broadens the material appropriate for sexual counseling (Chesler, 1980).

Normalcy-oriented programs are more likely to include males (Earls and Siegel, 1980; Gordon, 1981; Robinson and Barret, 1982; Shapiro, 1980). Adolescent men are not easy to involve in sex counseling. They become sexually active on the average of 2 years before young women (The Alan Guttmacher Institute, 1981); they will often be 2 or more years older than their partners (Zelnik and Kantner, 1980). American men will never fully appreciate pregnancy and childbirth (Namerow and Jones, 1982). Nevertheless, as parents, they will experience what it means to bring up a child, and may be taking a larger share of childrearing duties. Households including minor children with a man as the sole parent increased 65% during the last decade in this country (United States Bureau of the Census, 1980). In addition, the social and political advancement of women is having an effect on male responsibilities for family planning (Blechman, 1981). Some programs are now convincing young men to accept their roles in sexual counseling (Gumerman et al., 1980; Hendricks, 1980; Rappaport, 1981; Smith et al., 1982; Wagner, 1980).

LIFE SKILLS COUNSELING

The collective evidence points to a cognitive-behavioral approach for professional counseling on all facets of adolescent sexuality. According to one review, "There is certainly a lack of information given to adolescents. However, there is also indication that more or improved information alone may not change behavior. When information and methods of birth control are available, they often remain unused, distorted, or denied. It appears that information, cognitive-emotional development, and sexual identity are inextricably intertwined" (Dembo and Lundell, 1979, p. 661). More support for life skills counseling issues from the suggestion that "adolescents are being required to make a decision about contraceptive use at a time when they are sexually undifferentiated and perhaps unprepared for such analytical thinking'' (Cvetkovich et al., 1975, p. 266). Adolescents' lack of problem-solving creativity (Little and Kendall, 1979; Smith et al., 1982) and their inaccurate assessments of others' reactions to their decisions (Rogel et al., 1980; Schinke, 1981c) further indicate the need for the counseling approach advocated in Chapter 2 of this book.

In addition, the suitability of life skills counseling in this area is underscored by the correlation between poor interpersonal behaviors and youths' problems with sex (Campbell and Barnlund, 1977). Elsewhere, the present authors summarized the literature germane to this relationship: ''These findings imply that unwanted and unprotected intercourse sometimes occurs because adolescents lack social and communication skills. Lack of interpersonal skills also appears to result in the poor use of contraceptives, even when knowledge of birth control is adequate'' (Schinke et al., 1980, p. 55).

Applications

The authors have used life skills counseling to focus on adolescent sexuality in several applied programs (Barth and Schinke, in press; Barth et al., in press; Blythe et al., 1981; Gilchrist and Schinke, 1983a, b; Gilchrist et al., 1979; Schinke et al., 1981; Schinke et al., 1981; Schinke and Gilchrist, 1977). The first group to be counseled consisted of 10 high school students (nine female, one male), with the mean age of 16.8 years. Once they and their parents and legal guardians gave informed consent, the students completed a brief measurement battery. Group counseling through interpersonal communication training is illustrated by the following dialogue from one of four, 2-hour sessions.

Counselor: ''Let's think of problems with dating that make you uncomfortable. The problem doesn't have to be about sex, but it should be something that will happen again. Melinda, you seem to have something on your mind. Want to talk about it?''

Melinda: ''Gee, it's hard to explain. You see, I like this guy and I know he likes me. But he's going out with someone else.''

Counselor: ''O.K. Tell us some more.''

Melinda: ''Well, I know he and I could be friends, but he always acts scared when I'm around.''

Counselor: ''What do you mean, 'scared'?''

Melinda: ''Well, he comes up to me in the hall and smiles and acts like he wants to talk. Then, all of a sudden he says he's got to go, he splits. Once, after we had talked he asked me to call him. So I did. He wasn't there, but his brother knew it was me. He said he'd tell Terry, that's the guy's name, and he'd call. But he never did call me.''

Counselor: ''He seems to run hot and cold.''

Melinda: "Yeah."

Counselor: "How does that make you feel?"

Melinda: "It makes me feel really stupid. I wouldn't have called him if he hadn't asked me to. I know from the way he looks at me and talks to me that he likes me. Shoot, I don't like that kind of hassle from nobody."

Counselor: "Sounds like it makes you angry."

Melinda: "Yeah, you know it! We can't go out because he's got a girlfriend. He's a lousy friend; yet I like him."

Counselor: "What do you want? To go out with him or be friends?"

Melinda: "I'd settle for anything."

Counselor: "So your problem is that you like him, sometimes he acts like he likes you, sometimes he acts like he doesn't, and it all kind of makes you mad. Do you want to clear up the situation? In other words, do you want to decide whether you are friends with him or whether you will go out with him?"

Melinda: "Yeah, that's it. I just want him to make up his mind."

Counselor: "Let's role play how you might be able to do that and to tell him how you feel. Pretend you're at school and Terry walks up to you and goes into his 'hot and cold' routine. What might you say?"

Melinda: "Uh . . . well . . . uh . . . (breaking role). What can I tell him? How am I supposed to start talking about it?"

Janie: "You want her to do your talking for you? Just tell him what you want!"

Arnetta: "Tell him you want to be friends. But your friends don't treat you like trash."

Maggie: "Yeah. Ask him why he wants you to call him if he can't call you back." (Group members make several additional suggestions).

Counselor: "Those are good suggestions. Let's role play the scene for a few minutes. Dawn, would you play Terry's part? I want to coach Melinda." (Counselor moves next to Melinda to give her feedback and instructions.)

Melinda: "Terry . . ."

Counselor (sub voce): "Look him in the eye."

Melinda: "Terry, I like you but sometimes I think you don't like me. . . ."

Counselor (sub voce): "Good! Don't play with your hair."

Dawn (as Terry): "What do you mean?"

Melinda: "Well, like when you asked me to call and didn't call me back."

Counselor (sub voce): "Keep looking him in the eye. Talk a little louder."

Dawn (as Terry): "Uh. . . . To tell you the truth, I was really home but my girlfriend was over. I didn't want her to know you had called. So I grabbed my brother and told him to keep it to himself when it sounded like he was talking with you."

Melinda: "Umm . . ."

Counselor (sub voce): "Don't stall. Tell him what you want."

Melinda: "Is there some reason your girlfriend shouldn't know that we're friends?"
Counselor (sub voce):   "Great! Specific and clear."
Dawn (as Terry):   "Yeah, she'd get jealous."
Melinda: "She doesn't have to (frowning). If you want, we can just be friends. I'd like that O.K."
Dawn (as Terry):   "Oh, all right. . . . (breaking role). Hey, you mean business."
Kelly: "Terry won't know what hit him. I liked it!"
Counselor: "Very nice. You were firm and reasonable."
Maggie: "I couldn't hear her sometimes."
Counselor: "O.K., let's try it again. This time, Melinda, try talking louder and slower. Don't lose eye contact even when he does."
Melinda: "O.K. That wasn't bad. I don't mind it at all. It's kind of fun."
(Melinda continues to practice.)

After all group members role played similar interactions, they took a battery of posttests. Analyses of pretests and posttests indicated that the adolescents had learned relevant overt behaviors, but that they did not have the cognitive abilities to use their skills in pressure situations. The authors interpreted their findings as follows: "Our interpersonal-skills program was as remiss as earlier reductionistic efforts: Where previous research focused on reproduction and contraceptive information input, interpersonal-skills training concentrated on behavior-change output. For effective pregnancy prevention training, information input and behavior-change output both must be considered. More important, training must address influential intervening variables—cognitive processes mediating the understanding and use of information in decision making" (Schinke et al., 1979, p. 84).

Life skills counseling in line with this interpretation was tested with a group of 18 female high school students. The students were enrolled in a continuation program for teenage parents and parents-to-be. Their ages ranged from 14 to 17 years. Eleven young women were black, five were white, and two were Hispanic Americans. Six students were pregnant at the time of the counseling program. The rest were teenaged parents. Rather than nulliparous adolescents, these young women were selected for counseling because the host school had been experiencing a high rate of repeat unwanted pregnancies among the student body (cf. Schinke, 1978, 1979, 1982, 1983b). The adolescents and their parents and legal guardians gave their written informed consent as requested. The youths were pretested, and one-half of them were given life skills counseling. The other half were assigned to a discussion group. Young women in life skills counseling met for 10 1-hour weekly sessions with two group leaders who covered sexual information, attitudes, and communication. The adolescents suggested problem situations concerning dating, sex, and use of birth control. They put objective facts in their own words. Thus,

"Unprotected intercourse leads to pregnancy," for one young woman became, "If Charlie and I do it and we don't protect ourselves, we'll both be sorry." The youths role played and practiced new patterns of interactions. Data analyses revealed that the young women who received life skills counseling possessed better self-images, greater perceived control over their lives, and more persuasive interpersonal skills than their peers in the discussion group.

Based on the results of these two studies, life skills counseling was refined, then evaluated with 36 sophomore students. The mean age of the group of 19 women and 17 men was about 16 years. No adolescent reported prior involvement with a pregnancy. After completing consent statements and obtaining the same from their parents and legal guardians, the youths submitted to a battery of measurement instruments. Half of the group received life skills counseling, while the other half remained in a test-only control condition. Counseling was implemented in 14 50-minute small group sessions led by two graduate social workers.

The counseling included age-relevant information on reproductive biology and on contraceptive techniques. Group leaders discussed value and emotional issues related to sexual activity. Supplementary materials came from presentations by nurses and family planning counselors and from audio-visual aids (cf. Tepper and Barnard, 1977). The leaders taught the youths problem-solving techniques outlined in Chapter 2. The group members specified sex-related problems, generated solutions to them, judged the payoffs of each solution, and selected the one that seemed best. The youths applied problem solving to sex-related conversations with parents, teachers, siblings, and peers; choices about birth control use; and such issues as gender preferences, sexual relationships, and decisions about intercourse, pregnancy, childbearing, and parenthood.

As in previous programs, the youths practiced both nonverbal and verbal communication. They discussed future interpersonal problems. Dyads and triads of adolescents assisted one another, and the counselors rotated among the subgroups to provide individual attention. At the close of the counseling sessions, all adolescents in both conditions completed posttest measures. Data analyses indicated greater pretest to posttest improvements for adolescents given life skills sexual counseling than for youths in the control condition on measures of knowledge, cognitive abilities, and behaviors in face-to-face peer interchanges (cf. Schinke et al., 1981). At follow-up and contrasted with control condition youths, adolescents in the counseling condition were more habitually using birth control, had employed more effective methods of contraception during the last time they had intercourse, reported fewer instances of unprotected sex at any time, and were better disposed toward family planning for themselves and for their future partners.

The experiences and findings from earlier programs helped to upgrade the counseling procedures that were next used with a group of 53 nulliparous high school sophomores and juniors. After they and their parents gave written permission, the youths were assigned to one of the following conditions: pretest, counseling, and posttest; counseling and posttest; pretest and posttest; and posttest only. Adolescents in the first two conditions participated in 14 1-hour counseling groups and completed pretests and/or posttests as required. As before, a team of female and male counselors discussed physiology, contraception, and pregnancy resolution options. They also presented and rehearsed problem solving.

The counselors demonstrated interpersonal communication components such as eye contact, gestures, voice volume, and inflection. The youths practiced using these in interactions that required them to listen, recapitulate what they had heard, ask for clarification, and state their own opinions (cf. McFall et al., 1982). The adolescents' increased competence during structured situations enabled them to move on to practice personal interactions. For example, one of Ted's goals was to discuss the use of birth control with his girlfriend. He and his peers identified the necessary communication elements, and Ted practiced how he could broach the topic when he was in an appropriate situation. Ted: "Carol, I've got something on my mind I want to talk about. We just can't keep going all the way without using some kind of birth control. Neither of us wants you to get pregnant. I really don't want to have sex again unless it's safe. Let's talk about the kinds of things we can use. We can get hold of something before the next time so we'll be O.K. Maybe you feel weird talking about it like this, but it's better to hash it over now than being sorry if something happens."

At the end of each counseling session, the youths devised contracts to apply their knowledge and skills to everyday situations (cf. Kazdin and Mascitelli, 1982; Martin and Worthington, 1982; McFall, 1982). In contracts similar to the one described in Chapter 2, the young people anticipated forthcoming problems concerning sex, specified how they might respond, and planned alternative actions. Ted had contracted to arrange with his girlfriend about birth control protection. He agreed to obtain some condoms and spermicidal foam for them to use on a trial basis. According to the contract, he was to go to a downtown drug store, find what was available, select a small package of condoms and foam, and purchase them. If rebuffed because of his age, Ted's contingency plan was to try to buy the items at two other drug stores. Three failed attempts would trigger a backup plan for Ted to call another group member who had bought over-the-counter contraceptives and to decide upon his next move. All of the adolescents discussed their accomplishments, replicated one anothers' contracts, and set new objectives for themselves as counseling progressed.

Analyses of posttests revealed no differences between pretested and nonpretested adolescents. Posttest scores on a measure of reproductive and contraceptive knowledge were higher for youths given sexual counseling than for those who received no counseling. (Miller and Lief, 1979). The former were much better able to specify problems, to identify obstacles in solving them, and to find alternative solutions for sexual problems (Glass and Arnkoff, 1982; Shure, 1979; Shure and Spivack, 1978). Objective ratings on behavioral performance tests were more positive for adolescents who received counseling than for those who did not; these measures rated eye contact, assertiveness, refusals to act against one's interests, and requests that sexual partners take equal responsibility for birth control (Gormally, 1982; Schinke and Smith, 1979). During follow-up assessments 6, 9, and 12 months later, the young people who received counseling, more than their control-condition peers, reported fewer incidences of unprotected intercourse, greater habitual use of birth control, and more positive attitudes toward delaying pregnancy.

Anonymous feedback sheets (Lloyd, 1983) contained such comments as, "This is super!" "Hearing other guys have a hard time talking about sex is neat." "I like play acting." "Let's keep doing like you have to do on dates when guys throw the make on you." "I really think what we talk about is good. I tell my sister about it." The mother of an adolescent who received life skills counseling forwarded a note that said, "I'm delighted with what happens in the groups [youth's name] goes to. He tells me things he never used to dare mention. The other day he nonchalantly mentioned he was 'redecorating' his room. When I saw a sexy poster had replaced the Seahawks line-up I was inwardly pleased at his openness." Sophomore and junior class advisers at the host school put up on the faculty lounge bulletin board a letter that included this passage: "Thanks to you, our students have discussed their anxieties about sex and other personal topics. Please accept our thanks."

A replication of the counseling methods confirmed previous findings. The latest program involved 107 informed and consenting female ($n = 42$) and male ($n = 65$) high school students (mean age = 15.65 years). About one-third of the adolescents had been exposed to sex education; five youths reported a prior experience with pregnancy. After they took pretests, the adolescents were assigned to life skills counseling ($n = 54$) or to wait-list control ($n = 53$) conditions. A pair of graduate social workers, each with a group of 27 young people, conducted 10 50-minute counseling sessions. Counseling condition youths learned reproductive and contraceptive facts, problem solving, and communication skills. They implemented outside homework assignments, and reported back on their experiences.

At posttest, compared with adolescents in the wait-list condition, those who were given life skills counseling knew more about human sexuality, had better attitudes and intentions toward future use of birth control, and were more effectively able to raise and to discuss sexual and contraceptive matters with an opposite-sexed partner. These youths, in contrast to their wait-list counterparts, were more subjectively comfortable and more objectively competent during archetypal pressure situations (Chiauzzi et al., 1982). Self-reports and obser-vations of individual adolescents negotiating birth control decisions under stressful circumstances with an opposite-sexed confederate showed adolescents who got life skills counseling to be more mature, empathic, and assertive than young persons who did not get counseling. Consumer feedback from both adolescents and their parents and teachers was laudatory.

THE FUTURE

Two million sexually active adolescents in the United States today are denied access to sexual counseling and family planning services (The Alan Guttmacher Institute, 1980). Because minors are not supposed to engage in sexual intercourse, the availability of responsive services for them poses a moral dilemma for social welfare and health-care providers. In addition, American free enterprise excludes those who cannot pay for private counseling and medical assistance relative to sexual issues (Jones et al., 1982). Appropriate sexual resources for youths and adults alike are absent in many counties and states (Foster, 1981). Sex-related programs for adolescents are impeded by young people's ignorance about their rights and by questions about the legality of providing them with sexual counseling (The Alan Guttmacher Institute, 1978; Henshaw and Martire, 1982). Only 13% of all American teenagers are able to approach physicians for birth control services (Chamie et al., 1982). Few social and health clinics target adolescents. Most that do ask for parental permission before giving youths contraceptive devices and prescriptions (The Alan Guttmacher Institute, 1979).

Politics severely hamper sexual counseling with adolescents (Beck et al., 1982; "Should Parents be Notified?," 1982). While he was Secretary of the Department of Health and Human Services, Richard S. Schweiker said that he "did not think his department should promote sex education and that doctors treating poor, unmarried teenagers under Medicaid should not be permitted to prescribe contraceptives" (Rosenbaum, 1981, p. 1). Mr. Schweiker's successor, Margaret Heckler, appears to be staying the course; however, by one account, "Mrs. Heckler has been a quiet supporter of family planning in the past" ("Change in DHHS Leadership," 1983, p. 3). Notwithstanding the lack of hard data to back his assertion, a member of the Senate Human Resources Committee claimed, "Increasingly, it appears that family planning clinics are serving teen-agers in the absence of their parents' advice and counsel and in contradiction of laws concerning sexual conduct in many of their own states" ("Family Planning Funds Hit," 1981, p. A4).

Marjory Mecklenburg (1982), Deputy Assistant Secretary for Population Affairs, has noted, "About half the teens who get prescription contraceptives from clinics never return . . . for follow-up attention. The result? Not being mature enough to use certain contraceptives properly, young teens have an extremely high failure rate" (p. 6). Jeremiah Denton (R-Ala.) and Orrin G.

Hatch (R-Utah) responded to conservative fears about the carnal behavior of American youth with a Senate amendment "to promote self-discipline and chastity, and other positive, family-centered approaches to the problems of adolescent promiscuity and adolescent pregnancy" (97th Congress, 1st Session, 1981, p. 1). In 1983, the Department of Health and Human Services now attempted to require social and health agencies that receive Federal funds to notify parents whenever minors are prescribed contraceptives (Kenney et al., 1982).

Regardless of any required parental involvement, public schools are ideal places for sexual counseling. Sex education in schools is of higher quality and less controversial than it once was (Gallup, 1978; Gilchrist and Schinke, in press-c). Public outcry is seldom heard when educators introduce sexual counseling into their schools (Mahoney, 1979a; Scales, 1979; Zellman, 1982). An exemplary program in St. Paul, Minnesota, shows what the future might hold if school-based sexual counseling were done on a national scale. The St. Paul program employed social workers, nurses, and physicians to provide students with pregnancy diagnosis, venereal disease screening, birth control, nutrition counseling, and appropriate prenatal care (Edwards et al., 1980). Over 75% of all enrolled students requested such services, and one in four asked for sexual counseling or birth control assistance. Three years later, 90% of the students served by the program were regularly using contraceptives, and there had been a 49% drop in adolescent pregnancies at the host schools.

Other school programs (including one with a sexual counseling and pregnancy prevention curriculum designed by a group in upstate New York) suggest that responsive services for adolescents can be delivered by classroom teachers within the instructional routine (Shapiro, 1981; Shapiro et al., 1979). Even schools that lack resources can at least expose their students to presentations and materials from family planning providers and sexual counseling services. Teachers and counselors ought to be acquainted with referral sources so they could direct students toward professional and community services that deal with all areas of adolescent sexuality (Ebaugh and Haney, 1980).

SUMMARY

Along with acquiring other life skills, learning to cope with sex is a haphazard process for adolescents. Young people teach themselves about sex through trial and error, undergoing experiences either vicariously or directly with sometimes painful consequences. This unsystematic learning leaves both young women and young men vulnerable to problems with peer relationships, venereal diseases, sexual acting out, and unplanned pregnancies. In scope alone, the latter problem justifies concern. For example, 780,000 girls who turn 14 this year will become pregnant as teenagers. Over 300,000 of them will receive abortions. Nearly all the babies conceived by the others will be unwanted, born out-of-wedlock, or raised by single mothers. When the females mature, they themselves are highly likely to become pregnant during adolescence.

Life skills counseling is logical, efficient, nonjudgmental, and effective for lowering the chances of adolescents' problems with sex. The ability to regard sexual concerns in adolescence as normal enables life skills counselors to provide all young persons with pertinent information and advice. Individuals are not singled out as deviant or needy. Group counseling gives adolescents an opportunity to discuss previously forbidden topics, and to find out from each other what sexual behavior is normal and expected. They learn to adaptively interact with peers, family members, and partners in regard to sex-related matters. Life skills counseling teaches youths to objectively analyze the societal factors that influence their sexual decisions.

The test scores of adolescents who have received life skills counseling document multiple benefits. In contrast to youths in control groups, these adolescents have gained knowledge, cognitive abilities, and communication skills. The impact and longevity of sexual counseling can be measured by youths' positive attitudes toward family planning and their regular practice of contraception. Consumer data from adolescents, parents, and teachers validate life skills counseling as a sound professional investment to prevent serious troubles with sex in adolescence. Life skills counseling also offers promise as a strategy to prepare young persons for the trials of adult sexuality as they mature and face novel situations.

Chapter 5

Managing Stress

The popular press daily documents the fact that stress is related to a multitude of social, physical, and mental problems. Practitioners in many disciplines are called upon to recognize and treat symptoms of stress. Yet our understanding of the nature, causes, and treatment of stress is by no means clear or complete. Researchers attempting to define stress usually emphasize it as the outgrowth of a mismatch between individuals and their context or environment. Stokols (1979), for example, describes stress as "a state of imbalance within an organism that (a) is elicited by an actual or perceived disparity between environmental demands and the organism's capacity to cope with these demands and (b) is manifested through a variety of physiological, emotional, and behavioral responses" (p. 27). Psychologist David Elkind conceptualizes stress in terms of extraordinary demands on available energy. "Stress . . . is any unusual demand or adaptation that forces us to call upon our energy reserves over and above that which we ordinarily expend and replenish in the course of a twenty-four hour period" (Elkind, 1981, p. 144).

Whatever the formal definition, stress for adolescents can mean sleepless nights, nervousness, tension, anxiety, inability to concentrate, weight loss, disturbed interpersonal relationships, and the condition known as anhedonia— the inability to enjoy anything. Stress can also mean physical illness. "Of all the risk factors in cardiovascular disease prevention, the most pervasive is stress" (Farquhar, 1978, p. 58). Stress alters the human body in ways we are only beginning to chart. "Stress and anxiety responses do share a common underlying set of changes in body chemistry: increases in blood levels of lactate (a substance derived from muscle contraction) and of adrenalin and nor-adrenalin (hormones released during stress and activity which speed up the heart rate and constrict blood vessels)" (Farquhar, 1978, p. 59). The list of medical conditions attributable to psychosomatic origins and stress grows yearly: peptic ulcer, mucous colitis, ulcerative colitis, bronchial asthma, atopic dermatitis, angioneurotic edema, hay fever, arthritis, atherosclerosis and its sequelae, angina and myocardial infarction, Raynaud's disease, hypertension, hyperthyroidism, amenorrhea, enuresis, paroxysmal tachycardia, migraine headache, impotence, general sexual dysfunctions, sleep-onset insomnia, alcoholism, and a wide range of neurotic and psychotic disorders (Elliott and Eisdorfer, 1982; Pelletier, 1977)—and this listing is conservative.

As the dean of stress researchers, Hans Selye, noted a decade ago, virtually all human activity involves stress (Selye, 1974). Challenging new tasks and pleasurable sexual activity are stressful, but in positive ways. Stress becomes harmful—or in Selye's terms "distressful"—when the states of arousal are of such duration, intensity, or frequency that individuals are overwhelmed and cannot find the means to restore their sense of balance and control. Given the classical picture of adolescence as full of turmoil, sweeping changes, and psychodynamic strife, practitioners might expect a natural concentration of research on stress reactions in adolescence. In fact, little empirical work in this area is available. This chapter outlines the beginnings of a knowledge base regarding sources and results of stress for teenagers, the nature of coping and stress management, and methods and practical applications for life skills counselors and human services practitioners interested in treating and preventing stress in adolescence.

SOURCES OF STRESS

As previous chapters indicate, almost every aspect of life undergoes major alteration during the adolescent period. The chapters of this book outline areas where sweeping changes and potentially high stress levels occur. Simply growing can create enormous strain. The physiological changes that herald puberty, for example, tax all youths' adaptive resources but none more so than those of teenagers who experience these changes too early or too late relative to their peer group (Hamburg, 1974). The pressure to achieve both socially and academically sharply escalates in adolescence. A recent study of high school students' perceptions of peer pressure revealed strong feelings of coercion during these years to be socially active, to have steady opposite-sex relationships, and to get good grades (Brown, 1982).

Parents, too, exert increasing pressure on teenagers to prepare themselves—vocationally and psychologically—for adulthood. Parents' own middle-aged crisis—often culminating in divorce, depression, job change, or relocation—add to the stress of the changes confronting adolescents. Jobs produce new kinds of stress. One group of researchers studying adolescents who work recently concluded, "Time spent in the workplace is significantly predictive of psychological distress, somatic symptoms, school absence, and the use of cigarettes, alcohol, and marijuana" (Greenberger et al., 1981, p. 696). Initiation of dating and sexual activity does not come easily to most young people, and the extraordinary stresses surrounding such events as an unplanned pregnancy or contracting venereal disease can be devastating (Brown, 1981; Gilchrist and Schinke, 1983b).

Even if physiological and social changes were minimal, adolescents' new cognitive capacities alone have the power to generate psychological discomfort and stress reactions. As mentioned in Chapter 1, youths' mastery of formal-operations thinking—the ability to think about their own and others' thinking—leads them to construct what Elkind (1967) calls the "imaginary audience." Adolescents tend to confuse what they are thinking about with what other people are thinking about, leading to the hyperself-conscious belief that other people are as concerned or preoccupied with them as they are (Elkind, 1967; Elkind and Bowen, 1979). Younger adolescents are especially vulnerable to the disquieting belief that everyone knows their private thoughts, acts, wishes, dreams, and family secrets best left unrevealed. Constant exposure to scrutiny from such an "audience" can be stressful indeed.

RESULTS OF STRESS

Adolescents' manifestations of stress are as varied as youths themselves. For example, academic underachievement and dropping out of school are also related to chronic stress (Berzonsky, 1981; Santrock, 1981). Fear of academic failure can create stress reactions strong enough to paralyze even able students on examination days (Santrock, 1981). In order to lower such anxiety and help maintain a sense of personal control, some adolescents may adopt the strategy of simply giving up, refusing to compete, or risking an unsatisfying performance.

Physical illness and deviant behavior can be viewed as responses to chronic stress. Psychosomatic reactions linked to stress, such as migraine headaches and bronchial asthma, are relatively common among teenagers (Labbé and Williamson, 1982). Research on the self-perceptions of a huge, multinational sample of young people revealed that physically ill, psychiatrically disturbed, and delinquent youth, when compared with normal adolescents, much more often appeared taxed beyond their resources and overwhelmed by their environment. Youth in the deviant groups were far more likely than normal teenagers to report that they give up easily, often feel confused, at times believe that they would rather die than go on living, find it hard to establish friendships, and often find life "an endless series of problems without solutions in sight" (Offer et al., 1981a, p. 77; see also Berzonsky, 1981; Gibbs, 1981). Even for normal, competent youth, depression during adolescence is not uncommon (Teri, 1982). In a study of seventh and eighth graders in surburban Philadelphia, one-third of the youths reported experiencing moderate to severe depressive symptoms and 35% reported current thoughts about suicide (Albert and Beck, 1975).

Suicide rates among American adolescents 15 to 19 years old are currently higher than ever recorded (Holinger and Offer, 1982). Jacobs' (1971) model of suicide-prone teenagers as youths who have exhausted other options for coping with their environment is supported in a recent study: "Suicide attempts of children in this study, when understood in the context of their dynamic biographics, represent active coping efforts to counteract the sense of helplessness they felt in being unable to effect changes in the stressful, chaotic conditions of their families'' (Cohen-Sandler et al., 1982, p. 184). In this study, suicide-prone youths' parents, although not suicidal themselves, modeled coping styles that were impulsive, ineffective, or harmful. Compared with other families, these parents, ''Abused alcohol and/or drugs more often and engaged in earlier and more frequent marital unions and separations. . . . [They] present to the potentially suicidal child an example of interpersonal conflict, avoidance, impulsivity, and lack of more adaptive coping skills'' (Cohen-Sander et al., 1982, p. 184).

Suicide is not the only potentially fatal response to stress in adolescence. A series of studies show that the Type A behavior pattern—a recognized risk factor for cardiovascular disease—is acquired early (Berenson et al., 1980; Matthews and Angulo, 1980; Siegel and Leitch, 1981; Wolf et al., 1982). The Type A pattern is characterized by a strong sense of time urgency, competitiveness, impatience, and easily aroused aggressiveness and anger (Friedman and Rosenman, 1974). Type A adolescents go all out and put a lot of energy into everything they do (Voors et al., 1982). Often, they interrupt while others are speaking, talk rapidly and loudly, eat, drink, and walk quickly, find it hard to wait, lose their tempers and get into fights easily, have few hobbies, like to boss others around, and have a strong need to be leader (Wolf et al., 1982). Although the specific ways in which the Type A behavior pattern interacts with physiological processes and increases the likelihood of cardiovascular damage are not yet understood, the fact that adults who experience such damage are often Type A is well established.

The links between the experience of stress and Type A behavior are clearer. A growing number of studies support the view of Type A behavior as a coping style aimed at maintaining and asserting control over stressful aspects of the environment (Brunson and Matthews, 1981; Glass, 1977; Matthews, 1979; Vickers et al., 1981). It appears, in fact, that among Type A individuals, the poorer the overall level of coping skills, the greater the risk of heart disease (Vickers et al., 1981). There is great need for research that will demonstrate whether or not teaching adolescents new coping strategies will reduce Type A responding and, ultimately, heart disease.

THE NATURE OF COPING

As with the term *stress* references to ''coping'' appear widely in professional and popular literature. The nature of coping, however, is complex and difficult to pinpoint. According to one group of well-known researchers, ''Coping is defined as efforts, both action-oriented and intrapsychic, to manage (that is, master, tolerate, reduce, minimize) environmental and internal demands, and conflicts among them, which tax or exceed a person's resources'' (Cohen and

Lazarus, 1979, p. 218). Coping is best thought of as a process, not a discrete behavior (Wrubel et al., 1981). "Coping is not a single act but rather a constellation of many acts and thoughts, triggered by a complex set of demands that change with time" (Cohen and Lazarus, 1979, p. 225). Two decades ago, Murphy (1962) captured some of the diverse tactics that adolescents have drawn upon to deal with problems and demands that threaten to overwhelm them.

> [The adolescent] may attempt to reduce the threat, postpone it, bypass it, create distance between himself and the threat, divide his attention and the like. He may attempt to control it by setting limits, or by changing or transforming the situation. He might even try to eliminate or destroy the threat. Or he may balance the threat with security measures, changing the relation of himself to the threat or to the environment which contains it, but which also includes sources of reassurance. Instead of dealing with the actual threat itself, he may deal primarily with the tension aroused by the threat: discharging tension by action, or by affect releasing displacement into fantasy, dramatizing activities, or creative work. Or he may attempt to contain the tension via insight, conscious formulation of the nature of the threat, defense maneuvers such as being brave, reassuring himself that he would be able to deal with it. . . .(p. 277).

Anesthesia through alcohol or other drugs is, of course, a coping strategy relied upon by some youths, as are other compensatory activities such as smoking and overeating. This raises the issue of maladaptive versus adaptive means for reducing or controlling stress. Some strategies to reduce stress and restore self-esteem—such as drinking or daredevil behavior—can result in permanent disability, even death. Much coping behavior takes place in a social context where youths' actions have impact on or are evaluated by others. It is clear that the consequences of some stress management or coping strategies— such as verbal or physical assaults on others or prolonged social withdrawal— are counterproductive and harmful to youth in the long run. Good or adaptive coping consists of strategies that: "(1) contain distress within tolerable limits; (2) maintain self-esteem; (3) preserve interpersonal relationships; and (4) meet the conditions of the new situation" (Hamburg et al., 1982, p. 75). Researchers have persuasively demonstrated that adaptive stress management consists of a set of learnable skills. The next section outlines approaches to helping adolescents acquire adaptive stress management skills.

STRESS MANAGEMENT SKILLS

Skills for coping with stress differ, depending upon whether the cause of stress is anticipated or immediate, chronic or acute. Good stress management consists of three stages that are loosely related temporally: cognitive preparation, skills acquisition, and application and practice of skills under less and less controlled circumstances (Meichenbaum and Novaco, 1978).

Cognitive Preparation

Simply knowing about stress and being able to identify it is surprisingly helpful for managing stress reactions. Many young people, however, need help in recognizing and correctly labeling bodily manifestations of stress—pounding heart, sweating, chills, stomach "butterflies," dry mouth, rapid breathing, throat "lumps," or chronic feelings of exhaustion. Our clinical experience has revealed that even those adolescents who pay attention to these somatic messages very often mislabel them as embarrassing indicators of cowardice, or lack of ability and requisite "cool." Teenagers can readily understand explanations of the physiological changes that ready the body for fight or flight in the face of dangerous or difficult circumstances. Knowledge that all human beings experience such bodily changes involuntarily can reduce self-blame and focus counseling on that aspect of stress reactions that is most amenable to change—namely, the cognitive processes that accompany physiological arousal.

Research has emphasized two related models to explain stress reactions (cf. McKay et al., 1981). In the first model, a stimulus in the environment triggers the physiological fight or flight arousal which the individual then attempts to understand by constructing an explanation for it. If this explanation reflects badly on the individual and the probable outcome of the arousal episode ("I must be scared. Only losers are scared in these situations, so I know it's not going to go well."), negative emotions and distress follow. In the second model, the environmental stimulus triggers negative thoughts ("I knew a setback like this would happen. I'm no good at this sort of thing."). The emotions that follow this negative evaluation then begin the physiological arousal process and the experience of tension and distress occurs. In both models, thoughts that interpret the stimulus or situation as threatening, dangerous, or unfair contribute heavily to the experience of stress. It follows, then, that by changing their thoughts about events, individuals can control stress responses.

This sort of information about the nature of stress and stress reactions can help adolescents see that stress management is not simply desirable but feasible and achievable. Counselors can then more easily engage youths in self-monitoring assignments to identify when and where their stress reactions occur, and practice can begin on employing specific techniques to alter stress-producing cognitions.

To be most useful, cognitive preparation for stress management must be expanded from helping adolescents understand stress in general terms to helping them identify specific elements of their personal environment that trigger their stress reactions. These elements may be a class of situations (resisting peer pressure to drink, asking girls for dates), specific individuals (a parent, a teacher), or internal worries about more global concerns (grades, college admission, job or occupational choices). Checklists, informal discussions between counselors and adolescent clients, and self-monitoring assignments are all useful tools for identifying sources of stress. The most important aspect of the cognitive preparation phase is giving adolescents a plausible conceptual framework that will lead naturally to the practice of specific cognitive and behavioral coping techniques. It is worth counselors' time, therefore, to help youths define the origin of their stress in concrete, specfic terms.

Skills Acquisition

Coping with stress is a process and not a discrete act, therefore, youths will need a variety of skills to apply differentially under changing circumstances— "a sort of cafeteria array of procedures from which participants [can] pick and choose" (Meichenbaum and Novaco, 1978, p. 327). The most important aspect of the skills acquisiton phase in learning to deal with stress is that it conveys to youth a sense of control, a sense that there are concrete masterable steps to initiate that will lead to favorable outcomes. For some time, researchers have noted that recognition of the availability of coping responses reduces stress. "The degree to which a person experiences psychological stress is determined by the evaluation of both what is at stake (primary appraisal) and what coping resources are available" (Coyne et al., 1981, p. 440; see also Lazarus, 1966; Meichenbaum, 1975; Roskies and Lazarus, 1980; Rotter, 1966).

Recent data show a majority of youths coping with stress passively through such sedentary activities as watching television, listening to music, being alone, or being with friends (Nader et al., 1982). When adolescents know that they have a variety of concrete ways for dealing with tension and unpleasant feelings, their outlook changes from one of "learned helplessness" to "learned resourcefulness" (Meichenbaum, 1975). With this change comes increased motivation to employ stress-moderating techniques. Youths experience success in consciously controlling threatening events and feelings, which leads to increased motivation and further successes in an upward spiral. Specific stress management skills fall into three general categories: voluntary muscle relaxation techniques, cognitive coping techniques, and behavioral coping techniques.

Relaxation Techniques   Most stress management programs begin with methods for quelling physical tension and discomfort and mustering enough calm to proceed with other coping strategies that require more concentration. Youths are asked to breathe slowly and deeply and to mentally repeat the command, "Relax," every time they exhale (Smith, 1980). For some youths, pairing the image of a tranquil, pleasant scene with deep breathing exercises enhances results. Teenagers are asked to call into mind either independently or with the aid of the counselor's verbal descriptions a relaxing scene (seashore, moonlit lake, meadow, aspen grove) or image (black velvet, running water) and to concentrate on it to the exclusion of everything else.

Some young people are so chronically tense that they simply cannot recognize the state of true relaxation. For these youths, Jacobson's (1938) progressive muscle relaxation exercise is useful. In sequence from head to toes, groups of muscles (e.g., shoulders, jaw, hands) are deliberately tensed, slowly relaxed halfway, and then just as slowly relaxed completely (Everly and Rosenfeld, 1981; Smith et al., 1978). With this kind of practice, youths can begin to discriminate and describe the relaxed end state. Breathing is slow and regular, hands and feet feel warm or hot, and all body parts are at rest and feel relatively heavy but move without resistance.

Exercising is also a good method for reducing physical tension (Kobasa et al., 1982). Help in planning when and where to jog, swim, or practice tennis, basketball, or soccer skills will give some adolescents a very effective stress-reducing strategy. Exercising, however, does not appeal to all teenagers. It appears most attractive to middle- and upper-middle-class youth—usually boys. Chapter 6 discusses means for helping other, less interested groups increase physical activity.

Cognitive Coping Techniques   Meichenbaum's (1975, 1977) work in self-instructions provides the basis for cognitive coping skills training. Adolescents can be taught to "talk themselves through" stressful episodes. This approach focuses on the development of specific task-relevant self-commands that can be used in relevant situations. Examples of such commands are: "Don't think about fear; just think about what you have to do; one step at a time. Develop a plan to deal with it; and take a deep breath and relax" (Smith, 1980, p. 273). Youths can be encouraged to construct their own personalized "self-talk" to help them manage tension and deal effectively with environmental demands. Self-talk can also be tailored to specific situations. Recent work has identified numerous self-statements that are helpful at different points in the coping process (Meichenbaum et al., 1975). Examples of self-talk that prepare youths for future stress are: "I'm going to map out a plan to deal with it; I have a lot of different strategies that I can call on; I won't worry—worrying doesn't help anything." Other statements help young people confront and manage immediate stress: "I can handle it; Relax; I'm staying calm; I'll just take it one step at a time; I'll just think about what I have to do." It is clear that those who cope most effectively are individuals who reward themselves verbally or tangibly for good performance. In the authors' experience, however, even highly competent adolescents need practice in reviewing past stressful episodes and giving themselves positive messages about how they coped. Examples of such self-reinforcing messages are: "Good, I did it. I handled it well. I knew I could do it. Wait until I tell other people how I did it."

Training in self-talk also increases the likelihood that adolescents will engage in systematic problem solving when confronting stress. Knowledge about a series of steps for solving a problem is not the same as actively using the steps to achieve a desired goal. Distressed adolescents who merely have information about the problem-solving process very often cannot apply this information. Counselors should provide young people with frequent and varied opportunities to verbalize—first overtly and then covertly—each step in the problem-solving sequence. With this practice, youths are much more likely when under stress to initiate and maintain resourceful adaptive searches for stress-reducing solutions (Gilchrist and Schinke, in press-a; Gilchrist et al., in press).

In addition to training in straightforward self-instruction, some—particularly older—adolescents may benefit from a more comprehensive examination of the explanatory messages they are giving themselves about their feelings and behavior. With practice, they can learn to recognize the stress-producing and self-limiting internal dialogue. Dysfunctional self-talk may include direct negative self-criticism—"You dummy, you blew it again." Dysfunctional self-statements may also be less overtly negative but indicative of underlying irrational beliefs that are the true bases for recurring stress reactions. Often only half-conscious, examples of such beliefs include, "I must have the complete approval and love of everyone who matters to me; it is a terrible catastrophe when things are not the way I demand them to be; I must do this right in order to be worthwhile." (Smith, 1980). Such disabling self-talk needs to be identified, rationally evaluated, and replaced with internal dialogue that facilitates active adaptive coping—for example, "Don't overreact, I may not like this but I can certainly live with it; I can do no more than the best I can; I'm still the same person whether I succeed or not." (Smith, 1980; see also Ellis and Harper, 1975; Goldfried and Davison, 1976; Lazarus, 1972).

Behavioral Coping Techniques   The behavioral techniques for reducing stress that are of the most value to adolescents are usually interpersonal skills that allow them to successfully confront, hold their own, and get what they want from their environment. Such skills include making effective requests and refusals, negotiating and bargaining, and expressing feelings accurately and appropriately. Youths' knowledge that they have the skills to manage an upcoming risky or potentially unpleasant event diffuses much anticipatory discomfort. Throughout Chapter 3 are examples of stressful interpersonal encounters that daily confront adolescents. That chapter, too, details behavioral skills that smooth and facilitate good personal relationships.

The acquisition of appropriate self-assertion and other social skills is uneven. Some young people will lack necessary behavioral skills in all situations, regardless of the participants involved. Others, although appropriately assertive generally, will need new skills to reduce stress when interacting with specific individuals—a particular teacher, or a perceived rival, for example—or in specific situations—dating or job interviewing. Finally, we have seen a surprising number of youths who appear skilled in many situations but are still experiencing stress because they remain unconvinced of their own good performance. In this case, role playing, demonstrating skill, and receiving positive feedback, especially from an admiring group of peers, has usually been reinforcing enough to overcome doubts and induce self-confidence.

Skills Application and Practice

Both group and individual training sessions are useful for the cognitive preparation and skills acquisition phase of stress management counseling. But for lasting behavior change to occur, adolescents must be helped to apply their new learning flexibly with varied and real everyday problems. Often, multiple opportunities for role playing stressful encounters during counseling sessions desensitize adolescents to the point that they are able to confront and manage formerly stressful situations without discomfort. Chapters 2 and 3 detail exercises and activities that have proven successful for moving into the skills application phase where new learning is applied in the natural environment. Young people may contract with the counselor or with each other to tackle difficult situations during the coming weeks and report results at future counseling sessions. The recent book by Meichenbaum and Jaremko (1983) is a good resource for counselors wishing to expend their knowledge of stress reduction and prevention techniques.

If possible, parents, siblings, teachers, coaches, or best friends should be recruited to help particular youths practice good stress management outside the counseling sessions. These recruits can provide ongoing, immediate feedback and booster sessions or skills review as needed. The opposite approach— assigning adolescent trainees to help improve their families' and friends' stress management—is also useful for expanding and solidifying youths' flexible application of newly learned skills (Nader et al., 1982). Modifying the whole family's approach to stress and coping provides the best possible means for ensuring permanent skill maintenance.

SUMMARY

Although many young people appear stressed throughout their adolescence, little detailed research directly addresses stress-management techniques for this age group. Jaremko (1983) and Feindler and Fremouw (1983) are welcome exceptions. Counselors can benefit from understanding the nature and consequences of stress reactions. Inability to control stress underlies numerous social and health problems encountered in adolescence and adulthood. Effective stress management is a key life skill that provides the foundation for prevention and treatment of difficulties in virtually all areas of youths' functioning.

Chapter 6

Promoting Health

For many individuals, events occurring in adolescence—choices made and habits acquired—have permanent consequences that affect their health and well-being for the rest of their lives. Now that the disease consequences of smoking are well documented (United States Public Health Service, 1979a), all health professionals express concern over young peoples' adoption of this hard-to-break habit. Each day about 4,000 adolescents start smoking cigarettes (United States Public Health Service, 1979a). Young people experiment with smoking at earlier ages than ever before, and the percent of 12- to 14-year-old female smokers increased eightfold in the last decade (National Cancer Institute, 1977). Teenage smokers now number over 6 million and about 100,000 preteenagers smoke cigarettes (Pinney, 1979).

As they exit from childhood, young people try other health-compromising substances too. Seventy percent of 12- to 17-year-olds have consumed alcohol, and 37% regularly drink (Fishburne et al., 1979). One-fourth of all American teenagers say they took 5 to 10 drinks during a single day during a given month (Finn, 1979). Statistics on marijuana and hashish show a third of 12- to 17-year-olds routinely using these substances (Fishburne et al., 1979). Thirty percent of American teenagers intentionally inhale fumes from gasoline, glue, paint, and cleaning fluid (Barnes, 1979; Watson, 1980). Barbiturates are taken by 20% of high school students (Kandel et al., 1976; Single et al., 1975). Better than one in four young persons ingest a hallucinogen before age 20 (Fishburne et al., 1979). Cocaine sniffing among U.S. 12- to 17-year-olds has multiplied by three in the past 5 years (Feldman et al., 1979). As for heroin, youthful addicts are at greater risk of permanent harm from this and other opiates than are older abusers (Johnston et al., 1980). The permanent physiological consequences of experimentation with alcohol and drugs are still under investigation. Nonetheless, no one questions the vastly increased risk to teenagers of serious injury and accidental death while under the influence of these substances. Motor vehicle accidents, many of them drug and alcohol related, are the leading cause of death among young people (Kovar, 1979). For every young American killed in an auto accident, approximately 43 others are injured—some permanently (Califano, 1978).

Other threats to health emerge in adolescence. Biological maturity brings the opportunity for sexual experimentation. Although sexual activity unquestionably can be positive and pleasurable, many youths do not know how to protect themselves from such negative consequences as unwanted pregnancy and venereal disease. In Chapter 4 we examined in detail adolescent sexuality and the cognitive and behavioral skills necessary to manage sexuality without risking physical or mental health. Several of the threats to health dealt with in the present chapter are problem behaviors that are likely to elicit social sanctions from adults. These behaviors—smoking, drinking, and drug use— are not restricted to some small subgroup of so-called "problem youth" but are prevalent to a substantial degree among today's adolescents. As one authority notes, "The argument can be made, in fact, that *coming to terms with alcohol, drugs and sex has emerged as a new developmental task that all adolescents face as part of the normal process of growing up in contemporary American society"* (Jessor, 1982, p. 297, italics in original).

Not all health compromising behavior involves socially proscribed actions. Some impediments to good health are quite ordinary but magnified by the sweeping physical and social changes of adolescence. Rapidly growing adolescent bodies require better than ordinary nutrition. As one professional states, however, "Adolescents provide one of the nutritionalist's greatest challenges because of their unique social and psychological needs" (Cordrey, 1979, p. 26). Others concur: "Adolescence is notoriously a period of dietary excesses and deficits, from junk food addiction to adolescent obesity to anorexia nervosa. . . . The consequences in later life include adult obesity, hypertension and its own fatal consequences, and oral diseases which account for $9 billion annually in health care costs" (Califano, 1978, p. 11). Envious adults who sometimes view teenagers as concentrations of boundless energy encased in bodies that are firm, healthy, and almost carelessly perfect, may be surprised by data from the President's Council on Physical Fitness and Sports. One out of every six adolescents is weak or uncoordinated enough to be classed as physically unfit. "Each year the schools discover countless apparently healthy teenage girls who cannot run a city block without stopping to rest; a similar number of high school boys cannot chin themselves even once" (Califano, 1978, p. 11). Only about a third of all 10- to 17-year-olds participate in daily school physical education programs and that proportion is declining (United States Department of Health and Human Services, 1980).

Adolescents' emerging adulthood requires that they assume responsibility for their own health and for obtaining health care when they need it (Green, 1981; Horn, 1976). This is a difficult task. Young people have less control over their environment than adults and have restricted access to health resources. As with adults, health status among adolescents is significantly linked to psychosocial factors. The more stressed and depressed adolescents are, the more health problems and poor health habits they have (Gad and Johnson, 1980; Kaplan et al., 1980). As Kovar (1978) states, "Adolescents often have health problems related to stress and unevenness of growth and development, to the difficulties inherent in being neither adult nor child, and to behavior that can lead to serious medical problems but may not pose an immediate health or medical burden (i.e., smoking). The picture is of a group of young people who think their health is good but who report feelings of anxiety and nervousness, who are frequently dissatisfied with their appearance, who report medical problems, but are unlikely to seek medical care'' (Kovar, 1978, p. 31).

For inexperienced young people, negotiating for health services without the aid of parents can be confusing, frightening, embarrassing, and sometimes—as in the case of sex-related services—legally impossible. Even when they recognize and acknowledge the onset of illness, few adolescents seek out readily available medical care in their own behalf (Radius et al., 1980a, b). The self-treatment preferred by the majority is simply hoping that a worrisome condition will go away. Many conditions, of course, do not. Untreated acne, tooth decay, and abnormalities in hearing and vision can have permanent undesirable consequences. About 1 in 20 teenagers has significant cardiovascular problems, and 8% of adolescent males and 4% of adolescent females have elevated blood pressure (Kovar, 1978).

In summary, the potential for lasting damage exists if youths do not acquire skills for making and acting upon health-promotive decisions. In this chapter we first examine influences on adolescents' health-related attitudes and behavior and present general guidelines for professional intervention. Then we examine specific threats to health commonly encountered in work with adolescents, along with appropriate treatment strategies.

INFLUENCES ON HEALTH

Kreuter and Christenson (1981) suggest that influences on adolescents' health behavior fall into three categories: predisposing influences, reinforcing influences, and enabling or facilitative influences. Predisposing influences are those factors within individuals which render them susceptible or resistant to health risks. These factors include attitudes, beliefs, and the stage of cognitive and social development attained by the still-growing adolescent. The second category, reinforcing influences, are factors external to adolescents that promote or discourage healthy behavior. Such factors include the attitudes and actions of parents and peers, representations of habits and health practices by the media, and behavioral norms that prevail in the regional and ethnic subcultures to which the adolescent belongs. The third category, enabling or facilitative influences, consists of those factors which help adolescents act in health-promotive ways. These factors include possession of accurate, relevant information about health risks, easy access to health-related services in the community, and acquisition of a set of cognitive and behavioral skills necessary for controlling one's impulsive behavior, planning ahead, resisting peer pressure, and obtaining needed assistance. Effective intervention and life skills counseling must recognize and address all three categories of influences on youths' health-related decisions and behavior.

Predisposing or internal influences on health decisions are inextricably related to developmental processes. Adolescents often understand the whole notion of health differently than adults do. To many young people, health means "the ability to be active, the capability to do what I want" (Green, 1981, p. 111). Bodily functioning is taken for granted. The egocentrism of this developmental period (Elkind, 1967) instills feelings of personal invulnerability and special protection from injurious consequences that incapacitate others. Health-compromising behavior such as smoking, drinking, and drug use have symbolic importance and many youths adopt these behaviors to announce formal transition from childhood to adult status (Jessor and Jessor, 1977). In the necessary attempts to separate from parents and establish an autonomous identity, "health-compromising behavior can represent a way of gaining control over the environment, a learned way of coping with failure or frustration, and 'acting out' against conventional society and the family, or perhaps a way of achieving an alliance with peers" (Green, 1981, p. 113).

These developmental factors that predispose adolescents to unhealthy behavior combine in some young people with a passive attitude, akin to learned helplessness, that they do not have the power or the skill to influence what happens to them. In terms of cognitive development, youths in early adolescence think in terms of the concrete here and now. Abstract and long-range consequences of present actions are difficult to contemplate. Exhortations such as "developing good health habits while you are young helps prevent future heart attacks" are meaningless. Emphasis on the immediate, concrete, personal impact of health-compromising actions must be the focus of life skills and other health-related interventions.

Developmental and attitudinal factors have other important implications for health promotion with adolescents. Because they do not have a strong future time orientation, many youths do not understand the concepts of probability and prevention (Baizerman, 1979). They do not see health promotion efforts as beneficial to themselves in the long run but as merely obstructive of present desires. Teenagers' cost-benefit analyses favor concrete, immediate gains (the admiration of peers) over nebulous, uncertain future ills (cancer, heart disease). Young people also discount health information if it appears contrary to personal experience—for example, "My brother smokes dope and nothing bad has ever happened to him. There's nothing wrong with dope." Most adolescents hear advice about reducing risks to their health as moral messages from adult authorities who are trying to limit their hard-won independence and freedom of choice (Baizerman, 1979). Because of adolescents' strong interest in developing personal power and control, effective health promotion emphasizes these elements ("Be the best you can be"; "Take control"; "Learn to be lucky"; "Why do you think they call it dope?"). Emphasis on prohibitions, limitations, and negatives ("Don't smoke, don't drink, don't eat junk food, don't, don't, don't. . . .") is counterproductive.

Reinforcing factors, the second category of influences on adolescents' health decisions and behavior, are part of the sociocultural context in which the adolescent operates. This context consists of networks of peers and adults who provide social and moral support, the sense of belonging, and the behavioral norms and standards that reinforce or furnish important incentives to young people to act in certain ways. Unfortunately, various supports in an individual adolescent's sociocultural world often reinforce different and mutually exclusive health choices. The classic admonition of parents to be careful, thoughtful, and law abiding clashes with peer culture values that reinforce rule flouting and risk taking. Adult role models are often absent or inconsistent in providing examples of health promotive behavior. And media representations of "ideal" masculine and feminine behavior are often unrealistic and swayed by commercial interests that profit from condoning and promoting unhealthy choices.

Good health promotion programs for adolescents should make young people aware of the influences that shape and control their actions and decisions. Health professionals should seek ways to strengthen social supports that reinforce health promotive choices. Working with groups of young people rather than individuals can accomplish this goal. If a group norm endorsing no smoking, for example, is established, health professionals have created an incentive powerful enough to keep many young people away from cigarettes. Professionals can also focus efforts on parents to more consistently demand and model responsible health behavior. Participation in consumer protection and youth advocate groups also helps create a positive, health-reinforcing environment. The construction of a reinforcing environment that supports health promotive decisions is no mean feat, especially in the face of developmental factors that predispose adolescents to ignore health information and overvalue risky peer culture norms.

The third and last set of influences on healthy behavior—the enabling or facilitative influences—has been the focus of the most successful programs to date. Facts about health risks are important but useless unless youths have the ability to act on this information. Adolescents need well-developed communication skills to resist dares and challenges and to propose less risky alternatives without losing peer group status. They also need techniques for recognizing and controlling their own emotions and impulses before such feelings overwhelm rational decision making. Enhancing these skills and techniques is the goal of most of the life skills counseling methods emphasized in this chapter. The following sections examine specific health issues, pertinent research, and techniques for helping adolescents adopt health-promotive habits.

NUTRITION AND EXERCISE

Rapid growth in adolescence requires nutritional fuel. Peak nutritional requirements occur in the year of maximum growth during which young peoples' body mass almost doubles. This growth period usually occurs between ages 10 to 12 for girls and ages 12 to 14 for boys (Whaley and Wong, 1979). Surprisingly, adolescents' specific nutritional requirements are not well known beyond the increased need for protein, calcium, and iron due to rapid muscle and soft tissue growth in both sexes and the onset of menstruation in girls (United States Public Health Service, 1979b; Whaley and Wong, 1979). In their increasing separation from parents, adolescents eat more and more meals away from home and away from family-controlled food consumption patterns. Despite the popular stereotype that depicts teenagers subsisting solely on Coke and french fries, most youth get at least minimally adequate nutrition though their diets may be unusual by adult standards (Caghan, 1975; Cordrey, 1979; Whaley and Wong, 1979).

When it does occur, substandard or inadequate nutrition is not usually the result of a lack of information but of adolescents' failure to put into practice knowledge that they already have. Some adolescents are too sleepy to eat breakfast and experience morning fatigue and inability to concentrate to the detriment of their school work. Most teenagers choose snacks on the basis of availability, not nutritional value. Junk food is all too visible in ubiquitous vending machines. In addition, teenagers' social activities often center around meetings at fast food restaurants and impromptu gatherings where potato chips and soda pop are the main fare. Dental problems are the frequent result. By age 17, the average American has decay in at least six permanent teeth (United States Public Health Service, 1979b).

Ill-advised food choices usually mean that adolescents consume more fat and more sugar than is healthful. Elevated blood fat levels and full-blown coronary arteriosclerosis are turning up in seemingly healthy older teenagers (United States Public Health Service, 1979b). This evidence, plus the fact that, once established, childhood eating habits are very hard to change, means that today's youth will be particularly at risk for heart disease as adults.

In several recent studies, professionals have tested methods for lowering cardiovascular risk by teaching youth new eating and exercise habits. For example, Coates and his associates developed a health education program for elementary students that was designed to decrease consumption of fat, cholesterol, sodium, and sugar, increase habitual physical activity, and generalize these changes to other family members (Coates et al., 1981). Fourth and fifth grade students received reinforcement in the form of praise and special stickers whenever the lunches they brought from home passed the "Healthy Heart" inspection. The concrete immediate rewards for appropriate behavior and the skills counseling strategies that influenced major segments of the youths' total social environment were noteworthy features of this study. The students gave their approval to the importance of healthy lunches at school. This group norm acted as an incentive to them to persuade their parents to provide varied and more nutritious sack lunches.

Practitioners should note that, although sophisticated and energetic, the Healthy Heart program did not increase youths' exercise or activity levels. Stronger incentives are required for shaping skills related to regular physical exercise. Many adolescents find exercising per se (jogging, skipping rope, swimming) lonely and boring. Contracting with teenagers to gradually increase the number of minutes per day that they exercise can sometimes be made more palatable if the exercise activity itself is novel or perceived as exotic. Adolescents who won't jog or involve themselves in team sports may be more attracted to belly or aerobic dancing, fencing, weight lifting, trampoline workouts, or karate or other martial arts instruction. There are several life skills goals that are served by enhancing exercise. Adolescents feel better, are more productive, and less at risk for serious disease when they exercise (U.S. Department of Health and Human Services, 1980). Important for both adolescents and adults is a sense that diligence and effort result in skill acquisition, mastery, and personal competence. For many adolescents, sports and physical activities provide the best—sometimes the *only*—arena for such learning. As books on organizational psychology and business management point out, the social and self-control skills acquired through participation in competitive sports are highly rewarded in the business world. Such skills involve learning how to win and how to lose, how to cooperate with others in a team effort, and how to plan and pace strategies to accomplish a desired goal (Harragan, 1977).

By far the biggest problem related to nutrition and exercise in adolescence is obesity. As one textbook succinctly states, "There is probably no problem related to adolescence that is so obvious to others, is so difficult to treat, and has such long-term effects on psychologic and physical health status as obesity" (Whaley and Wong, 1979, p. 754). Estimates identify 15% to 30% of all adolescents as obese. More than 80% of these youths will perpetuate their obesity into adulthood (Whaley and Wong, 1979).

The most successful approach to treating adolescent obesity combines control of diet with behavior therapy that emphasizes the identification and elimination of inappropriate eating habits and physical lassitude. But even superbly designed programs cannot work miracles. Adolescent obesity remains difficult to treat (Harris et al., 1980). Excellent programs are available to guide teenagers' dieting (see Egger et al., 1980). Nevertheless, most dietary programs do not give health professionals a realistic view of resistances they will encounter when implementing the programs. Weight loss takes considerable time. Teenagers are typically present oriented and want rapid, easy results. They become impatient and discouraged and drop-out rates are high (Harris et al., 1980; Langford, 1981). Groups for obese young women have successfully used contracting and rap-group style attention and supportive discussion to increase motivation to remain with the program (Langford, 1981).

Problem solving is important for identifying a range of behavioral alternatives that promote program objectives and do not involve eating. For example, when cold weather intervened to make an outdoor exercise program unpleasant, one dieter simply gave up exercising. Another dieter in the same program used problem solving to identify a feasible way to continue exercising—she went to a nearby gym (Gormally and Rardin, 1981). As with other addictive behaviors, most dieting slip-ups occur because of failure to cope with day-to-day emotions and stress (Gormally and Rardin, 1981). Accordingly, weight-loss programs should teach cognitive and behavioral strategies for dealing with feelings. Obese adolescents often have very negative self-images (Langford, 1981). Training to reduce self-criticism and increase self-praise is helpful. One now classic study found that people who were able to praise and reward themselves were far more successful at losing weight than their self-critical counterparts (Rozensky and Bellack, 1974).

Increasing teenagers' ability to self-praise and self-reward generally requires teaching them how to set realistic and attainable goals. Setting and reaching these goals provides frequent opportunities for success, positive self-evaluation, and self-reward. Research shows that setting a lengthening series of small scale, attainable subgoals is far more conducive to long-lasting behavior change than aiming all efforts at long-range, distant goals (Bandura and Schunk, 1981; Bandura and Simon, 1977; Mahoney and Arnkoff, 1979; Marlatt and Gordon, 1980). If the loss of 30 pounds is set as the goal for an overweight adolescent, that young person must wait a long time to merit reward for goal attainment. On the other hand, if not eating between-meal snacks on Tuesday is the goal, legitimately earned rewards can be claimed on Wednesday morning with accompanying feelings of accomplishment and efficacy. Failure to set realistic subgoals may deprive adolescents of self-rewards and feelings of self-satisfaction. This leads to the perfectionistic ''saint or sinner'' syndrome or the ''abstinence violation'' effect where one slip of the diet brands the entire weight loss effort a discouraging failure and a full-blown eating binge and return to old habits occurs (Mahoney and Arnkoff, 1979; Marlatt and Gordon, 1980).

Discouraged and diffident teenagers are usually giving themselves a stream of covert negative messages—for example, ''You're too weak-willed to be skinny,'' ''You're too unlovable, too pitiful,'' ''You're just a dumb fatty.'' Adolescents need to become aware of the self-critical messages they give themselves; they must learn to accurately evaluate the validity of their self-criticism; and they must know how to substitute positive self-talk in place of negative self-criticism (Berlin, 1981). Professionals can help young people generate a list of true, favorable statements about themselves that they can repeat when they feel self-critical. Self-talk in the form of self-instructions is incompatible with self-criticism and has proven useful for initiating and maintaining many types of self-control (Mahoney and Thoresen, 1974; Meichenbaum, 1977). Self-instructions might begin, for example, with "Stop— take a deep breath—you can handle this," or "You need to problem solve. What's the first step?"

SUBSTANCE USE AND ABUSE

There is probably no activity of greater concern to adults who care for and care about adolescents than drug use. A rainbow array of exotic substances—yellow jackets, bennies, reefers, blue devils, gold dust, horse, and acid—is frequently depicted as all too readily available in countless community parks, shopping centers, and schools. Ironically, the two psychoactive drugs most commonly used and abused by adolescents—alcohol and nicotine—are not usually considered drugs at all although their physiological and psychological effects in no way differ from those of acknowledged "hard" substances. Approximately 22% of all U.S. adolescents smoke regularly (Santrock, 1981) and about 6.1% of all high school seniors consume alcohol on a daily basis (Office of Drug Abuse Policy, 1978). The vast majority of teenagers drink some kind of alcoholic beverage at least once a month (Hawkins, 1982). Although rates for consumption of cigarettes and alcohol among young men began to level off in the late 1970s, increasing numbers of young women have taken up these substances (Ensminger et al., 1982; Hawkins, 1982; Johnston et al., 1980). Rates for use of other substances by American teenagers dropped slightly in the early 1980s (except for cocaine use) but significant numbers of young people (about 3%) still use some form of stimulant, sedative, opiate, hallucinogen, or tranquilizer at least once a month (Jalali et al., 1981). One in seven 14- to 15-year-olds smokes marijuana once a month (Santrock, 1981).

Reasons adolescents give for getting high by whatever means include curiosity, exploring and testing new areas of experience, relieving boredom, imitating someone they like or respect, marking an important transition away from childhood, conforming to peer pressure, and escaping from anxiety and stress (Jalali et al., 1981; Jessor and Jessor, 1977; Meyers, 1979). Numerous researchers have tried to distill a consistent psychosocial profile for identifying adolescents most likely to become substance users. No consensus, however, has emerged. There appears to be no simple pattern of factors that explains or predicts adolescent drug use. Recent studies recommend that use of drugs and alcohol by adolescents be viewed as a complex phenomenon greatly influenced by psychosocial contexts (Finn, 1979; Jalali et al., 1981). Particularly for adolescents, the line between substance use and substance abuse is vague. Professional judgments about how (or whether) to help a specific young drug user must consider the context in which the young person gets high. In behavioral terms, professionals must uncover the antecedents and consequences of drug use episodes for that individual. Finn (1979), for example, lists questions that help evaluate the seriousness of an adolescent's drunkenness:

a. Are his or her drinking practices having any immediate harmful effects? How severe are these consequences? Are they temporary or permanent?
b. Does the drunkenness take place in a relatively safe environment or where there may be dangerous consequences during or after drinking?
c. Is the frequency of his or her episodes of intoxication increasing, decreasing, or remaining stable?
d. Is getting drunk an accepted social behavior in his or her peer group? What are the other youngsters in the group like?
e. Is the youngster normal in other areas of his or her life, including social activities, recreation, employment, family life, and school work?
f. Is the youngster deriving any benefits from getting drunk? (p. 830)

With the exception of cigarette smokers, the majority of adolescent drug users are experimenters who in time discontinue use of drugs without difficulty (Jalali et al., 1981; Plant, 1976; Wurmser, 1972). An important goal in designing drug-related programs for adolescents is to distinguish between the experimenter and the compulsive user (Wurmser, 1978). Experimenters use drugs socially to relax, have fun, and feel part of a peer group. Compulsive users consistently rely on drugs to relieve unpleasant emotions and to cope with a host of ongoing life problems. Young compulsive users have psychological difficulties beyond those normally encountered in adolescence and may require long-term professional help. This special group comprises less than 10% of all youthful drug takers (Coombs et al., 1976; Jalali et al., 1981; Schnoll, 1978; Wurmser, 1978). Treatment programs for these youths must be complex, individually tailored, and carefully designed to impact social, emotional, familial, and—if they are physiologically addicted—biological spheres. Frequently, substance abusers require extensive help in learning new skills to enhance interpersonal relationships and to cope with stress and manage feelings. Many of the techniques described in this chapter and in Chapter 3 on enhancing interpersonal skills and Chapter 5 on managing stress may be adapted for helping individual adolescents who are drug dependent. The remainder of the present discussion focuses on prevention efforts with youths who are potential or occasional users of psychoactive substances.

Prevention of drug use and drug problems is understandably a popular goal among human services workers (Klein and Goldston, 1977). But definitions of prevention vary. Some professionals see total and lifelong abstinence as the only appropriate target for prevention efforts. Because drug use serves a variety of important functions related to adolescent development and prevalence data indicate that sooner or later most adolescents will try one or more drugs, professional intervention is unlikely to succeed with the abstinence interpretation of prevention. A more realistic and useful set of treatment goals is proposed by Richard Jessor (1982). These overlapping goals are minimization, insulation, and delay of onset. The minimization goal seeks to limit adolescents' involvement in drug use to exploration or experimentation and to a controlled, "responsible" level of use. The treatment focus is building constraints against heavy, chronic, or frequent drug use. The insulation goal seeks to protect the experimenting adolescent from serious, irreversible, or long-term negative consequences. An emphasis on how to avoid driving while intoxicated is one example of an insulation strategy. The delay of onset goal directs efforts toward postponing initiation of drug exploration until young people are more mature, more skilled, and more likely to handle the experimentation responsibly. The best existing programs help adolescents recognize pressures that tempt them to try various substances, and teach them skills for resisting such pressures. These programs also focus on constructing a reinforcing environment for trying out and repeating needed skills. The following sections summarize treatment strategies to accomplish these general goals. Although commonalities exist in the antecedents and consequences of all drug use regardless of the substance involved, each of the next sections examines strategies that have been empirically validated as effective with a particular substance.

Cigarettes

Some time ago researchers concurred on the ineffectiveness of programs that simply gave out information on the harmful effects of smoking. Although some of these ventures appeared to change participants' knowledge and attitudes, few had any impact on smoking behavior (Andrus, 1964; Bradshaw, 1973; Evans, 1979; Jones et al., 1970; Merki et al., 1968; Piper et al., 1970, 1974; Tennant et al., 1973; Watson, 1966). As Redican and his colleagues note, many youths are "not likely to have personal values opposed to smoking, nor does [this] social environment lend support to non-smoking behavior" (Redican et al., 1979, p.56). Indeed, recent work illustrates that 60% of preschoolers think they will smoke as adults (Shute et al., 1981). Until very lately, smoking has been not simply an accepted behavior, but a socially desirable one in many subcultures (Nuehring and Markle, 1974). A national survey found that 83% of a large teenaged sample indicated that they usually thought of their teenager peers as smokers rather than nonsmokers (Fishbein, 1977). Richard Evans and his colleagues have developed and tested a series of programs to minimize the effects of prosmoking social pressure on teenagers. This work is based on social inoculation theory from social psychology research (Evans, 1976; Evans et al., 1978). Social inoculation is analogous to biological inoculation whereby a person is exposed to a small dose of an infectious agent in order to develop antibodies, thereby reducing susceptibility to subsequent exposure (Flay et al., 1981). Applied to smoking, this theory suggests that resistance to social pressures to smoke will be greater if young people have developed and then refuted arguments in favor of smoking cigarettes. "Such experience with counterarguments inoculates the individual against pressures in similar real-life situations'' (Flay et al., 1981, p. 69). Evans' group used films to show adolescents how three major social influences—parents, peers, and the media—work to promote smoking. Young people discuss these films and learn ways to counteract the effects of peer and parental modeling, advertising, and other prosmoking social influences. Evaluations of programs emphasizing this approach show lower rates of onset of smoking among trained youth.

Several other investigators have built upon the inoculation foundation. Hurd et al. (1980) expanded Evans' work to include specific suggestions to adolescents on how to refuse cigarettes and in requiring them to publically commit themselves to not smoking. McAlister (1979; McAlister et al., 1979; McAlister et al., 1980) added other innovations such as slightly older peers to lead the inoculation groups and role plays for youths to act out situations requiring resistance to social pressure. Over 2 years of follow-up, McAlister and his group showed that their training significantly reduced the number of students who began smoking when they were compared with a group of untrained students. Jason and his associates also employed role-playing temptation situations (Spitzzeri and Jason, 1979) and asked youth to imagine withstanding a variety of pressures related to smoking (Jason, 1979). The short-term result of this refinement was positive.

This expansion of life skills counseling to include cognitive techniques for changing behavior is the basis of ongoing work by the present authors (Gilchrist et al., 1979; Schinke and Blythe, 1981; Schinke and Gilchrist, in press; Schinke et al., 1983). Our life skills approach emphasizes problem-solving techniques that youth can carry with them into situations involving cigarettes and other drugs to help them flexibly generate means for avoiding harmful substances without alienating friends or reducing their own self-esteem. Practice in self-instruction gives adolescents a framework for guiding themselves through high risk situations. Finally, instruction in assertive communication enables them to exert control over environmental events that might lead to smoking. In addition, adolescents receive information about physiological effects of smoking, methods of advertising and other social pressures that promote smoking, and the emotional sources of urges to smoke. Figure 3 is an overview of one 8-session curriculum currently in use in a longitudinal study of health hazard prevention.

The curriculum is designed for sixth grade students. Two group leaders introduce the sessions by covering ground rules and goals and leading get-acquainted exercises. Group members watch and discuss films giving the pros and cons of smoking. They acquire systematic steps for making decisions about how to handle difficult situations and use case examples and their own personal experiences to master steps of defining a difficulty clearly, generating a variety of possible solutions, selecting one, and planning its implementation. In role

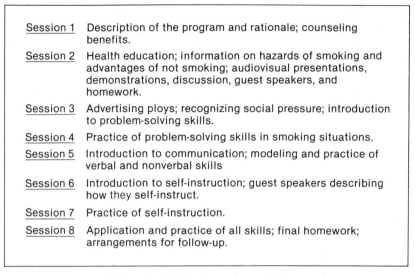

Session 1	Description of the program and rationale; counseling benefits.
Session 2	Health education; information on hazards of smoking and advantages of not smoking; audiovisual presentations, demonstrations, discussion, guest speakers, and homework.
Session 3	Advertising ploys; recognizing social pressure; introduction to problem-solving skills.
Session 4	Practice of problem-solving skills in smoking situations.
Session 5	Introduction to communication; modeling and practice of verbal and nonverbal skills
Session 6	Introduction to self-instruction; guest speakers describing how they self-instruct.
Session 7	Practice of self-instruction.
Session 8	Application and practice of all skills; final homework; arrangements for follow-up.

Figure 3.   Smoking prevention curriculum.

plays while leaders and peers offer feedback, reinforcement, and coaching, students use self-instructions and assertive communication skills to practice sticking to tough decisions, dealing with risky situations and influential people, and using self-control. Figures 4 and 5 illustrate representative skills practice exercises. Practice progresses until students feel confident of their ability to withstand prosmoking pressures, urges, and temptations. Specific exercises are designed to carry this training out of the classroom into youths' everyday environments. Students implement homework requiring them to obtain additional information about tobacco, observe tobacco use in various settings, leave places where others are smoking, refuse to smoke, ask peers not to smoke, and proselytize the advantages of not smoking to classmates and adults. Students turn in written descriptions of completed homework encompassing the time, place, people involved, and each person's comments and response. Evaluation favors this cognitive-behavioral skills counseling approach over attitude modification and no-treatment control approaches.

Marijuana

Programs developed to prevent or reduce marijuana consumption follow much the same format as other smoking control programs. Because adolescents who are drawn to regular use of marijuana typically are involved in a range of other problem behaviors (truancy, delinquency, conflicts at home), prevention programs may need to be longer and more structured than those focused on other substances. Schrader (1979) provides a useful outline of one such program. Teenagers attend the group sessions once a week and earn points for

Imagine yourself in the following situation and use good problem solving to get through it. Write your answers in the space below each question.

Here is the situation:
You and your best friend had a fight and your friend ended up calling you "Chicken." The next day you see your friend with someone else and they're both smoking. Your friend says, "Come on over, or are you too chicken?"

—How do you want this situation to turn out?

—Write everything you can do to make the situation turn out the way you want.

—Which of these things is best?

—Why is this the best solution?

Figure 4.   Problem-solving practice exercise.

attendance and participation. These points are exchangeable for money, goods, field trips, and other reinforcers. Exercises focus on building group cohesion and on two clusters of basic skills: assertive communication and problem solving. A third set of group sessions teaches youth job-related skills such as job hunting, filling out job applications, interviewing, and handling on-the-job problems. These job skills enable many adolescents to move away from a peer group environment that condones or requires marijuana use.

Alcohol

Because alcohol consumption is so prevalent and so readily condoned in our society, abstinence does not appear to be a realistic emphasis when teaching adolescents about alcohol. Reduction of alcohol abuse and insulating youth from permanent injury due to drinking are better targets for life skills counseling. The best alcohol abuse programs (like the best substance use programs, generally) focus on communication, problem-solving, and decision-making skills; aid in reassessing and clarifying personal values; expand adolescents' recognition of responsible options when they feel pressures to drink; and provide experiential skills-practice exercises. One school-based program with this focus reported a 95% drop in the number of at-school drug and alcohol offenses over a 4-year period (Hawkins, 1982). The U.S. Department of Transportation publishes an excellent booklet, *You . . . Alcohol and Driving* (U.S. Department of Transportation, 1977) that serves well as the nucleus for life skills counseling groups. The booklet succinctly summarizes crucial information on the physiological effects of alcohol. It also presents a number of

Role play the following situation with your partner. Remember to use good eye contact, to be clear about what you want, and to be assertive. The first time you practice, say out loud all the instructions you are giving yourself to help you handle the situation. Then practice a second time. Say the same instructions to yourself but silently inside your head. After you have practiced this scene twice, switch roles and let your partner practice. Do the best you can.

Here is the situation:
You are in line at the movies. A person your age right behind you is smoking and blowing a lot of smoke at you. Act out what you sould say to yourself and what you would do in this situation. You speak first.

You:
Other person: "Huh."

You:
Other person: "What do you mean?"
You:

Other person: "What's the matter with you?"
You:

Other person: "Are you a weirdo!"
You:

Other person: "Grow up. I don't have to do what you say."
You:

Other person: "Leave me alone."
You:

Other person: "Oh, all right."
You:

Figure 5. Role play and self-instruction practice exercise.

realistic drinking-related situations that adolescents must learn to manage. Figure 6 illustrates two of these. In small groups, students can discuss and role play such situations and receive coaching and praise from peer and adult leaders.

A different approach to teaching adolescents life skills for prevention of alcohol and drug problems focuses on stimulating parents' involvement in establishing health promotive environments. The National Institute on Drug Abuse and the National Institute on Alcohol Abuse and Alcoholism in recent years have been extremely supportive of mutual support groups springing up among parents all over the United States (Cohen, 1982). Well over 900 such groups in 48 states are now in existence. Many are affiliated through the

---

Exercise 1

Annie had been home all week with a cold. She went to school Friday so she could go to a party that night. She was known around school as "Six-Pack Annie." Annie and her six-pack always got a big laugh at parties. Somebody always made sure she finished it. On her way to the party, Annie realized she was still feeling pretty weak. At the party, Annie kept feeling worse and worse. As the party started to break up, she felt nauseated. When she picked up her jacket to leave, Joe laughingly teased her about finishing only four beers and said she was losing her touch.

—What should Annie do?

—What shoud she have done?

Exercise 2

You drink too much while partying at a friend's house. In fact, you feel a little sick. To make matters worse you promised to be home with the car by 9:00 p.m. It is already 9:30 p.m. To top it off, your parents told you not to drink.

—What are your alternatives to driving?

—What is your best alternative?

—Which alternative would be most difficult for you to carry out?

—What will you say to your parents when you get home?

(Adapted from U.S. Department of Transportation, 1977.)

Figure 6.   Skills integration exercises.

National Federation of Parents for Drug Free Youth. These groups help parents strengthen communication within their families, clarify values, and design and implement effective disciplinary and guidance strategies for their children. Together, parents explore ways to combat pro-drug messages in the community. Telephone or neighbor coffee networks are used to disseminate information, problem solve, and organize for action. Many parent groups use human services professionals as information sources and consultants for drug prevention projects. Life skills counseling in this instance consists of teaching parents how to teach their children. When it works, this approach can be more effective than professional work directly with young people themselves. Teaching parents new skills permanently modifies the environment in which the adolescent lives. Skilled parents can adopt life skills teaching to the immediate needs of their adolescent over the whole course of the youth's development—a potentially much more powerful prevention or insulation strategy than a single time-limited contact between professional and adolescent.

SUMMARY

Developing good nutrition and exercise habits, and learning to deal with alcohol, smoking, and drugs are tasks faced by all adolescents in our society. Life skills counseling can ameliorate eating and exercise problems and prevent or minimize harmful substance use. Social pressure to engage in substance use and other risky behavior is strong. Counseling must provide youth with cognitive and behavioral strategies to counter this pressure.

Chapter 7

Anticipating Employment

The passage of a young person from adolescence to adulthood is marked by a number of events. Of these, none is more important than the young person's finding work and becoming economically independent. Today in the United States, this transition is often painful and frustrating, and large numbers of youth are failing to achieve it. For such youth, the reality is a desire for a meaningful job that goes unfulfilled because there is no such job, or because the young person's skills are not sufficient to obtain such a job, or because there is a failure of the job and the person to come together. For the society the reality is crime, violence, drug use, health problems, and a sense of alienation and despair on the part of a large segment of the nation's youth (Dayton, 1981, p. 321).

Dayton's summary of youth employment and the consequences of unemployment is supported by contemporary research. Employment status greatly determines Americans' mental, social, and physical functioning, and, of course, their economic stability (United States Department of Labor, 1979). The causal relationship between job and personal well-being, however, is not known. Thus, teenage pregnancy, drug addiction, and psychiatric disorders at once antecede and follow joblessness (Dayton, 1978; Presser and Baldwin, 1980; United States Department of Labor, 1980). A more potent variable to predict and explain life problems is the level of income. Personal earnings affect an individual's self-esteem, diet and exercise, friendships, marital discord, familial harmony, and health care (United States Department of Labor, 1979, 1980). In short, research data and anecdotal observations leave little doubt that money buys happiness.

Job satisfaction is another variable in the life-work equation. As borne out by rapid turnover rates, especially among young cohorts, many workers are displeased with their first, second, or umpteenth job (United States Department of Labor, 1980). Teenagers and young adults are prone to switching positions often and abruptly (Dayton, 1978; United States Department of Labor, 1979). Employment changes are frequently not for the better in terms of hours worked, wages, and job title. National surveys uncover extreme job dissatisfaction for women and men in the teens and 20s (Dayton, 1981). Only one in four young people are highly satisfied with their job. Ethnic-minority persons are most dissatisfied at work. Just 10% of Hispanic women are happy with their employment; two-thirds of black men are very unhappy, moderately so, or neutral about their job. This chapter addressed these and other variables in the world of work by applying life skills counseling to help adolescents choose careers and get jobs.

CHOOSING A CAREER

The career track is prepared so early that many young people seem innately able to enter any given field or profession (Hollmann, 1972). Even though motoric, sensory, and mental abilities may limit or expand youths' career options, changing mores, legislated guidelines, and expanding work opportunities in certain fields mean that genes are less important in determining who enters what career (Bergland and Lunquist, 1975). Developmental and social learning factors are more important influences on career choice (Peng, 1977). Early perceptions and goals about work are molded by parents, siblings, friends, relatives, and teachers. One of the authors recalls his mother's response to various career decisions: "When I grow up I'm going to be a policeman." "Umm hmm." "Or, maybe a fireman." "Is that so?" "Well, maybe I'll be a doctor." "Really? That would be wonderful! Doctors make lots of money and are important people. What kind of doctor will you be?" "Umm, what kind make the most money?" "Surgeons. They are always rich; especially brain surgeons." "Gee, maybe I'll be a brain surgeon." "Terrific! Wait till I tell Gramps you're going to be a brain surgeon. Won't he be surprised!"

By adolescence, youths have ingrained impressions about the career path (Farmer, 1983). Some of these are not malleable. But the bulk of young people alter their aspirations and preparations, often to their parents' chagrin (Haldane et al., 1976). "And how's your son, the one who wants to be a brain surgeon?" "Oh, he's fine. Except now he's going to be a teacher." A few adolescents appear to intentionally thwart parental wishes by selecting careers antithetical to their upbringing (Shedd, 1978). Other youths act contrary to their interests by choosing a route beyond the ken of their experience—the graduating senior who decides to be an engineer after foregoing the high school prerequisites, for instance. A growing number of young people, perhaps misguided by adults, drift through adolescence waiting for natural talents to spring forth until they inadvertently close off their options (Gardner et al., 1981). Such indecision indicates that many careers come about by accident.

Systematic Training

Adolescence is the time to map out an array of career possibilities. Adolescents can select from these options and can verify the wisdom of their choice by taking the initial steps along their career course (Lieberoff, 1978). Training for career decisions begins by informing young people of their choices. Because adolescents are daily exposed to conventional and traditional careers, life skills counseling introduces a panoply of job titles and roles. Programs in restricted or homogeneous settings take extra care to provide a balanced selection of available careers (Rabinowitz et al., 1979). Thus, a program at a residential center includes careers in life sciences and business as well as the human services professions whose representatives young residents routinely see. Likewise, adolescents in an upper-income suburb need to hear about trades and crafts that they might not witness in their rarified environment.

Films are handy and lively tools for delivering career information. Guest speakers can concretely describe their career experiences for adolescents. Field trips can associate abstract job titles with the conditions, surroundings, and operational definitions of real work. A visit to a bank, for example, removes the stereotype of bankers as people who just count money. Homework provides adolescents with opportunities for observing the duties of various careers. Youths can watch people at work, and they might note how jobs are dramatized in the written and electronic media. By comparing and discussing their observations, young people erode the mystique that glamorizes or maligns some occupations.

Professionals must conscientiously avoid identifying sex roles with particular careers (Lang, 1978). A good start is to use neutral job titles—police officer, not policeman; actor, not actress; weather reporter, not weatherman; nurse, not male nurse; flight attendant, not stewardess; sculptor, not sculptress; homemaker, not housewife; comedian, not comedienne. Judicious use of feminine, masculine, and plural pronouns also reflects professionals' sensitivity: "the doctor . . . she"; "the nurse . . . he"; "the research scientists . . . they." Career options should never be depicted as exclusive to either women or men. Here, resource persons who belie sex-role archetypes are invited to training sessions—a woman army sergeant, a man kindergarten teacher, and so on. To the same degree, young persons deserve to know if their career choice is dominated by one gender and if this tradition may work for or against them (Clemson, 1981).

Problem solving enables adolescents to sort out appealing careers. Small groups speed the process, yet individual formats and even large groups are conjointly beneficial as long as every young person has time to brainstorm all possible employment choices. Regardless of format, brainstormed lists are boundless (Bolles, 1978). Youths are free to list any legitimate career. Professionals stand watch over the problem-solving process and refrain from limiting the realm of possibilities. The authors once worked with a young woman who quit high school and wanted to be a psychiatrist. Rather than disparaging the client's goal, damaging her ego, and ruining our objectivity, we did not relate the adolescent's current state to her future plans. Meanwhile, the young woman explored the necessary preparations for her choice and in so doing ruled out the option altogether and made several community contacts.

After adolescents list their career choices, they rank them and select the three top candidates. Picking several careers is important because some may not be viable. Furthermore, a single career choice is dangerous when many variables are not under youths' control—being accepted to the vocational school or college where specialized training is offered, for example. A dossier of job titles permits independent problem solving when the decision point draws near. Before choosing their careers, adolescents should commit themselves to prepare for their goal. Even a tentative commitment reduces the likelihood of prematurely discarding one career choice for the next that catches the eye and will in turn be discarded later on. Not only is it unhealthy during adolescence, but career indecision may foster jumping from job to job in adulthood (Rothstein and Jackson, 1980). An early commitment may provide young people with an opportunity to learn that a career is or is not for them. If so, the exercise of ranking and selecting career options can be repeated with different careers to help youths recognize their values and interests (Minor and Minor, 1978).

Most adolescents use the exercise to gather data on other people's responses to their choice and on what they must do to get ready for the career. With professional assistance, youths assemble a chain of preparations, resources, and events that must be linked together to achieve their objectives. Thus, being an accountant requires going to college and that takes good grades in high school, respectable SAT scores, and lots of studying and money. Predictions about the future throw light on the confluence of youths' present behavior, preparations to date, and career choice. If they have studied the area or have related work experience, the desired career may seem logical. Youths may have excelled in junior high courses that anticipate curricula they will experience in high school and college. Just as well,they may have had part-time or summer work that resembles the jobs sought. On the other hand, if they have had little or no prerequisite experience, one ought to question the soundness of the career choice. To determine its feasibility, young people get a taste of the career path by sitting in on a cognate class or spending a day with someone who works at the position they seek.

Supplementary information relevant to job choice comes from adolescents' self-study of noncareer goals (Kirn and Kirn, 1978). Perhaps for the first time, young people systematically fantasize about their ideal place of residence, material acquisitions, intimate relationships, families, friends, spiritual development, physical fitness, political involvement, and recreational pursuits. The awesome task can be done with checklists of the myriad achievements that fill a person's life (Bolles, 1978). Calendars of major life events and imaginative diaries for days decades hence are other means to crystal ball gaze (Kirn and Kirn, 1978). Another way adolescents imagine their future lives is by writing personal epitaphs. The exercise can begin with humorous examples: "Penelope Sullivan, 1969–2044. She always punched in on time." "John S. Herbert, 1970–2032. He was nice." "Carolyn Miller, 1968–2020. She paid her taxes and had good insurance." When so disposed, youths share their epitaphs and query one another about the reasons for choosing particular goals.

Any self-study should provoke a discussion of inconsistencies in adolescents' plans for the future. Professionals and young people can identify competing and mutually exclusive goals. Regardless of whether they change their objectives, adolescents can anticipate troublesome areas that sooner or later will cry for attention. One high school senior wanted to be a jazz saxophonist and a professional ski instructor. The young man had applied to college, and he and his girlfriend planned to marry after high school. The youth knew his dreams might not materialize simultaneously. But only after objectively plotting the days ahead did he fully fathom the bind he would be in. Not without anguish, he revised his goals and avoided worse unpleasantness later.

A final touch of realism in career planning happens when adolescents assess their ability to delay external gratification (Mischel and Mischel, 1976; Mischel and Patterson, 1976). Once they generate a range of job choices, youths project time frames for entering careers and for reaping first yields. These time frames take into account the years and foregone opportunities before a tangible payoff occurs. Young people determine if they can make the needed investment, forestall immediate reinforcement, and whether the rewards are worth the effort. Vicki's career objective is to learn the plumbing trade and to open her own shop. Before being licensed, she has to serve a 5-year apprenticeship during which she will earn less than she could in another field. In addition to the costs of her preparation, Vicki must obtain a loan to establish her business and to buy a van. Only gradually will she build a clientele sufficient to repay her debts and to underwrite a desirable standard of living. The young woman is undaunted because she appreciates the independence and income of self-employed plumbers. Vicki believes she has a history of passing up immediate rewards in favor of larger gains. And she prospectively tests her will power by recording the length of time she can study while the rest of her family watches television, and by opening a bank account and seeing how much she can save.

In sum, choosing a career is learnable and enjoyable when done within the life skills approach. Fundamental strategies translate into procedures for young people to select remunerative and personal objectives that neither overextend them nor force them into nonsatisfying life styles. The approach maximizes youths' participation in deciding their careers and discounts the roles of chance, luck, and uncontrollable outside factors. Knowing their options and weighing the costs and advantages of career choices equips adolescents to reduce future unknowns. Adolescents thereby take charge of their destinies, and they happily greet adult responsibilities.

JOB HUNTING

Counseling adolescents in the skills needed to locate and obtain employment is a related component that can be separate from or part of career decision making.

The importance of job training is magnified by statistics that show youth unemployment at an all time high. Due to changes in the population pyramid and increasing youth participation in the labor force, over 3 million 16- to 24-year-olds are without jobs and are available and looking for work (United States Department of Labor, 1980). Unemployment rates (unemployed workers as a percentage of all those employed and unemployed) range from 9.8 for high school graduates to 22.9 for school dropouts (United States Department of Labor, 1981b). Women and minority adolescents suffer most. Eighteen percent of female teenage students who seek work are unemployed; their counterparts who quit school are unemployed at a rate of 24.6%. Black adolescent students have an out-of-work rate of 44.8%. Forty-four percent of black adolescents who leave school—often to take a job—are unemployed (United States Department of Labor, 1981b). As a benchmark, 5.6% of all Americans were unable to locate work during the period these numbers were reported (United States Department of Labor, 1980).

By every indication, young people will have unprecedented difficulty getting future jobs. In the short run, economic barometers point to extreme joblessness for every age group in the United States (United States Department of Labor, 1981a). Because young laborers are hardest hit in bad times (Dayton, 1978), the ranks of unemployed adolescents will swell before diminishing. In addition, with more sustained consequences, unskilled and semiskilled positions for which young people qualify are becoming anomalies. While president, Jimmy Carter observed, "The traditional picture of the American workplace as the foundry, the factory, the automobile assembly line, will no longer be accurate in the 80s. Our post-industrial economy is service-oriented, white collar and technical. Blue collar jobs will give way to white collar jobs, and more skilled workers will be needed. Without assistance, most of our best youths will be unable to compete" (Dodd, 1981, p. 362). In other words, characteristics that make youths attractive to employers—physical strength, agility, flexibility—are no longer in demand. Tough economic straits are pitting young persons against older, more qualified workers for fewer unskilled positions. Barred from the labor market, adolescents are denied access to the experience they need for skilled nonindustrial jobs. Another vehicle for earning job credentials, postsecondary education, is difficult for youth and their parents to finance during inflationary times. The capacity to locate a job may be the factor that lets adolescents survive the next decade.

Aside from career track advantages, adjunctive benefits accrue to youth who are adequately prepared for job hunting. Adolescents who know how to find work can garner part-time positions and summer employment during high school and college (McGee, 1981). Learning to sell oneself is crucial when requesting promotions and raises and when switching positions. Moreover, employment counseling seems to counteract juvenile delinquency (Mills and

Walter, 1977). A plausible explanation for the relationship between unemployment and crime is that antisocial adolescents feel that legitimate routes to personal fulfillment are closed (Filipczak et al., 1979). The ability to obtain work tells young people that deviancy is not the sole avenue to material benefits and recognition. Once employed, former delinquent adolescents adhere to societal rules, avoid trouble, and become good workers (Shore, 1977). The social consequences of teenage pregnancy also are amenable to employment training. Schinke et al., (1980) detail how young parents-to-be who can get jobs are able to master the multiple struggles they face, change their fates, and create better lives for their babies. The realization that they have adaptive abilities apparently enhances their self-image, interpersonal relationships, and independence.

Studies show that ethnic-minority youngsters inordinately profit from employment skills counseling (Heimberg et al., 1979; Schinke et al., 1978). We have already noted compelling figures on unemployment and job dissatisfaction among black and Hispanic teenagers. In all likelihood, disparities in joblessness between majority and minority groups will widen as the economic picture becomes bleaker (United States Department of Labor, 1981a). Slim gains from equal employment legislation are already being offset by a lethargic national growth that ironically gives officials license to ignore affirmative action regulations (Dodd, 1981). Both minority and nonminority young people in the job market suffer discrimination because of their unconventional dress and comportment, and their lack of transportation to visit industrial parks and suburban manufacturing firms where young laborers are traditionally needed. As well as their inexperience in how to apply for employment and their poor understanding of the hiring process, adolescents are prone to misinterpret initial rejection as meaning they are unemployable (United States Department of Labor, 1979). The weight of evidence indicates a need for counseling which encompasses the assessment and training of adolescents' job-hunting skills.

Assessment

Although professionals can assume that young people have a paucity of job-seeking skills, they can launch effective programs based upon the assessment of adolescent deficits and surfeits (Atlas, 1978). From assessment, professionals can learn how geography, age, sex, and ethnicity affect adolescents' employment facility; they can also derive information on their peculiar needs and strengths, in order to focus the counseling program accordingly (McClure, 1978). Open-ended and experiential assessment procedures whet youths' interest in employment training and pinpoint areas for supplemental measurement. For instance, professionals might ask their clients to pretend that in the next 5 days they have to get a job that pays $50.00 a week. They must specify how they would go about the task, and all aspects of the job itself have to be in the realm of reality. Oral or written responses can be judged in regard to how young persons found an opening, whether they fit the job description, if they considered competition, whether they would have been among the top candidates, and if they were able to work within the employer's constraints.

Given such broad assessment, professionals can narrow pretraining data collection through closed-ended procedures. The Assertive Job-Hunting Survey (Becker, 1980; Becker et al., 1979) asks people to rate the probability that they will do such things as: "If I heard someone talking about an interesting job opening, I'd be reluctant to ask for more information unless I knew the person." "I downplay my qualifications so that an employer won't think I'm more qualified than I really am." "If a secretary told me that a potential employer was too busy to see me, I would stop trying to contact that employer." "Getting the job I want is largely a matter of luck." "With the job market as tight as it is, I had better take whatever job I can get." Sandifer and Hollandsworth (1978) assess employment ability with questions people face when job interviewing—for example, "Are you reliable?" "Do you get along well with other people?" "What has been your most rewarding experience?" A *vade mecum* of assessment instruments and counseling guidelines in the *Job Club Counselor's Manual* by Azrin and Besalel (1980). The authors publish 46 forms that include background sheets on the job hunter, logs of employment-seeking activities, lists of telephone contacts, sample resumes, model letters of recommendation, flow charts for job interviews, and schemata that quantify decisions about relocating and changing positions.

Job-Seeking Tasks   An assessment procedure from Mathews et al. (1980) measures a sequence of job-seeking tasks that include how to obtain job leads, write and call for interviews, interview for employment, accept suggestions and criticism from employers, constructively criticize others, tell supervisors about problems, compliment co-workers, and accept compliments. Job seekers simulate the tasks and are rated for evidence of competent performance. As an illustration, here are steps for soliciting employment leads from relatives and acquaintances: 1) Make a conversational opener; 2) State the need for a job; 3) Specify the type of job sought; 4) Comment on personal experience; 5) Ask for suggestions about possible openings; 6) Express appreciation for help. A year after the initial report on this instrument, Mathews et al. (1980) demonstrate that it is able to predict both the persons who will become successfully employed and those who will remain unemployed. Other preemployment instruments assess young people's capacity for vocational and technical duties (Irvin et al., 1981). When employment in fields such as word processing, dentistry, and electronics requires both mental and motoric acumen, youths are well advised to get objective feedback on both kinds of abilities before going too far in the career and job search process.

Mock Applications   Additional data on employment readiness issue from mock job applications. Prototype forms should contain what employers can legally ask—for example, the applicant's name, address, citizenship, general health, education, work experience, military status, past employers, and character references. Applications must assiduously exclude questions that cannot be put to job seekers—for example, requests for information about their sex, bodily characteristics of height, weight, and nonvisible handicaps, marital status, family composition, living arrangement, and irrelevant criminal and financial matters (Bolles, 1980). Actual forms used with permission of area employers lend realism and encourage adolescents to take the assessment process seriously. Employment applications should be filled out as if young persons were visiting the community business or company (McGee, 1981). Youths might complete the forms in a public area because few employers afford applicants the amenities of a desk, table, and private space. Applicants ought not be given substantive assistance when responding to items on the forms.

Both adolescents and professionals go over the finished applications. Young people note different interpretations of the same item and compare one another's answers. Professionals score applications for completeness (percentage of items answered), neatness (percentage of responses written within the space provided), legibility (percentage of words and numbers easily read by someone unfamiliar with the applicant), and internal consistency (percentage of responses that match up with related items). Written applications can also be scored by collaborators, persons who commonly screen entry-level candidates for real-life jobs. Because these collaborators are prima facie valid, they will judge adolescents by their own subjective standards. Collaborators quantify their judgments by indicating the probability that they would tender a job if the written application were the sole source of information (definitely would hire = 100; definitely would not hire = 0).

Scoring   To find willing collaborators, professionals search their agencies, institutions, or schools for colleagues charged with hiring responsibilities No matter how small, every employer has some mechanism for processing job applicants (Greenberger and Steinberg, 1981). In addition, section heads in public agencies and civil service offices are credible people to score employment applications due to the large number of young people who seek government jobs (United States Department of Labor, 1980). The private sector should not be overlooked when searching for outside collaborators. One commentator foretells business participation in youth employment counseling.

> As the birthrate declines, the level of skills required in the workplace continues to rise; meanwhile, job programs fail to effectively reach the "hardcore" unemployed youths. . . . In this light, youth unemployment becomes a much more important issue to personnel managers and private industry. Not only does the private sector have the capability to train and place unemployed youths, but also

the obligation. . . . "Business has come to recognize in structural unemployment a threat to the business system itself," says Reginald Jones of General Electric. "As the committed defenders of the private enterprise system, we in business leadership must step up to this challenge if we want the system to survive" (Dodd, 1981, p. 362).

Persons from government and industry who can assist in assessment are business owners, middle managers, and supervisors. In many instances, outside collaborators will not be from personnel departments because these units rarely have decision-making power in regard to hiring (Keenan, 1976). According to some predictions, "personnel departments, at least as hirers, are either on the way out or on the way to dramatic restructuring" (Bolles, 1980, p. 159). Those who score mock job applications or any assessment measures should be aware that these instruments are solely for the purpose of data gathering. If possible, outsiders should be kept ignorant of youths' identities. Young people deserve to be informed about all those who will see their data, and anyone who does so must be sworn to secrecy (Schinke, 1981b).

Job Interviews   A companion assessment procedure is the face-to-face interview. Like the written application, the interview is presented as an entrance requirement for filling any job opening. Young people call for an appointment, report to a designated office, and apply for a specific position. An archetypal situation might center on a new fast-food restaurant that has openings for a grill person, counter people to take and fill orders, a cook's assistant, and clean-up help for a variety of shifts and days. Someone unknown to the applicant orchestrates the interview and delivers a series of probes: "Have you done this kind of work before?" "Can we count on you?" "Will you be on time?" "Can you be called on short notice?" "How do you work under pressure?" "Will you keep busy when it's quiet?" "What can you offer us that someone else cannot?" "What will your co-workers think of you?" "How do you accept supervision and criticism?" "What is your biggest weakness?" "Can you supervise others?" "What kind of wages do you expect?"

Assessment interviews are scored in several ways. Professionals unobtrusively observe the exchanges and score interviewees on the relevance, adequacy, and positiveness of their responses, their speech fluency, tone, and volume, and their posture, fidgeting, and gestures (Imada and Hakel, 1977). Interviewers score applicants' eye contact, facial characteristics, enthusiasm, sincerity, and overall competitiveness (Hollandsworth et al., 1977). When done, young people reflect on the interview and rate their clarity, confidence, organization, anxiety, comfort, honesty, and whether they will be offered a job (Wheeler, 1977). Videotape is ideal for scoring employment interviews. The camera can be positioned behind and to one side of the interviewer so that it captures applicants without stultifying interaction. As long as the camera remains static, young people acclimate to it and rarely see it as an intrusion (Kent et al., 1979; Schinke et al., 1978).

Tape recordings serve a variety of purposes. Youth play back the tapes and say why they acted as they did. "I lied about being out of school because I figured you couldn't work in a restaurant unless you were 18." "When she asked me when I could begin, I thought she meant what time. That's why I said 'eight.' After she said 'The eighth of what month?', I really got freaked; that's what started me squirming and mumbling." Videotaped interviews suggest the locus of training (Tessler and Sushelsky, 1978). Professionals can look at the tapes and ascertain whether adolescents need to increase their ability to be more specific. For example, "From December 1982 to August 1983, I delivered the *Post-Intelligencer* to 75 people every day and to about 110 people on Sunday" is specific compared to "I used to be a paper carrier." Interviews can be examined for negative $(-)$, neutral (0), and positive $(+)$ statements: "I hate to work in the morning" $(-)$; "I guess I could work the early shift" (0); "I work best after noon" $(+)$. The appropriateness of their responses can be measured by pairing youths' answers to each question asked. "Will anything prevent you from getting to work on time?" "Well, once I got a ticket for speeding" and "Tell me about your interests" "Umm, I haven't made up my mind about my interests." are inappropriate responses; whereas "What five words describe you best?" "Gee, I'm friendly, honest, easy to get along with, polite, and energetic." and "Why did you leave your last job?" "Well, that quarter I was taking calculus and trig and had to study a lot" exemplify appropriate responses.

Recorded interviews can also be used to evaluate the efficacy of employment skills counseling. Young people are taped before and after counseling, with both sets of tapes retrospectively scored. The portability of videotape means interviews can be scored by persons who are blind to which interviews occurred before and after counseling. As in the assessment of written applications, colleagues and employers may use taped interviews to validate gains from counseling. Professionals from the organization hosting the project might score interviews respective to youths' nonverbal and verbal behavior. Employers from government and business can watch videotapes and indicate those interviewees who present themselves in the best light and who would be hired on the basis of videotape data alone. Third-party viewings have adjunctive benefits for adolescents. Once they learn that the interviews will be seen by people who actually hire employees, young job seekers more earnestly participate in assessment and training. Feedback on posttraining skills adds confidence to their real-life interviews when young people enter the job market. Naturally, youths must be told that they will not be hired or passed over because of their tapes, which are for assessment purposes only. In addition, collaborators should understand the conditions under which interviews are done and appreciate the need for confidentiality (Wilson, 1978).

Training

Professionals who provide counseling in job-hunting skills for adolescents should first inform them about how people get jobs in this country. For example, a national survey of over 10 million people shows that 13% of job seekers are hired after taking civil service examinations, and that federal and state employment offices net positions for 14% of their clients (United States Bureau of Census, 1980). Twenty-two percent of Americans who rely on friends, relatives, and teachers thereby locate employment; a similar percentage get jobs through school placement bureaus, and 24% do likewise through private agencies. Less than one in four people find employment by searching classified ads. Another study (Bolles, 1980) discovered fewer than 0.07% of those who mail out resumes garner jobs this way. Yet a third investigation (Crystal and Bolles, 1974) found that 86% of unemployed persons find work after career choices counseling and job-hunting skills.

Applying for jobs requires young people to present themselves in writing and in person. Assessment findings provide professionals with the facts on youths' need for improvement in both areas. A method for teaching adolescents to complete employment applications involves forms being transferred onto clear overlays. Transparencies are projected on a screen or wall, and, in response to the professional's queries, young people call out the requisite information. All items are discussed because applicants who are stumped, shy, or embarrassed may guess at what to put down or leave puzzling questions blank (Reed, 1977). The authors have read more than one form with the applicant's name as a response for every item beginning with "Name"—"Name of High School," "Name of College," "Name of Former Employer," "Name of Military Branch," "Name of Personal Reference," "Name of Person Who Should Be Contacted in an Emergency," and so forth. While one youth or the professional marks the transparency, each adolescent completes an individual application. Youths exchange forms and check one another's responses.

In spite of handwriting idiosyncrasies, young people can learn to legibly fill in employment applications by trying various writing instruments and seeing which leave a neat image. Sharp point mechanical pencils are handy due to an array of lead thicknesses and hardnesses and the capacity to erase mistakes. Once they hit upon an instrument they like, adolescents carry it along when visiting prospective employers. They have a familiar tool that gives a predictably tidy impression, are not forced to use whatever is thrust at them, and are never caught without a pen or pencil. Youths practice printing their responses and staying within the space provided until they and their peers are satisfied with the content and penmanship of their responses. Young persons so trained complete employment applications with the philosophy that their candidacy rests on the written document (Bostwick, 1980).

Adolescents likewise learn to interview in vivo as if this were the single avenue to employment. Youths are warned that initial impressions often decide the job interview. Stanat and Reardon (1977) say the majority of employers form a snap, lasting opinion in the first minutes of an interview, sometimes before it is officially underway. Other research (Tucker and Rowe, 1977) claims employers need but 10 minutes with an applicant to reach their decision. We can attest that thousands of semiskilled positions are offered and denied after brief exchanges in which interviewer and interviewee remain standing. Not long ago, a personnel officer at an industrial complex told us that most applicants' fates are decided between the waiting room and the time the interview starts. When adolescents expect the interview to begin the moment they enter the employment setting, they can arrange their dress and demeanor to make a favorable impression from the onset.

Arguments are raised over the ethics of tampering with youths' natural style in the employment interview (Babcock and Yeager, 1973). Preparing young people for this interview could be dishonest because applicants present themselves in an uncharacteristic manner. Well-trained adolescents may mask weaknesses that the interview aims to uncover. Overly coached applicants might be inhibited during interviews, and preparing interviewees for the encounter could polarize employers into an adversary role (Galassi and Galassi, 1978). In defense of job interview training, there are compelling data that Dunnette and Bass's (1963) observation of two decades ago has withstood the test of time: "The personnel interview continues to be the most widely used method for selecting employees despite the fact that it is a costly, inefficient, and usually invalid procedure" (p. 117). Just a few years back, Bolles (1980) penned this accurate homily: "He or she who gets hired is not necessarily the one who can do that job best; but the one who *knows the most about how to get hired* (p. 179, italics in original).

Behavioral Components   Job interview training takes into account the physical and behavioral presence of a desirable employee (Bostwick, 1981; Dipboye and Wiley, 1978). Physical attributes include washed and combed hair, freshly brushed teeth, and clean clothes befitting the occasion. Even if jeans and a T-shirt are appropriate for the job, adolescents are told to dress as nice or nicer than their prospective boss. Applicants in the know curb their smoking, nail biting, and gum chewing, are punctual, polite, and formal, and in no fashion get chummy with the interviewer. Young people learn to wait for an invitation to be seated, let the interviewer lead the conversation, and do not give superfluous information.

Training also encompasses both nonverbal and verbal components (Hollandsworth et al., 1979). A key nonverbal behavior is the handshake. Because this convention launches the interview and is a novelty for adolescents, both young women and young men learn the timing and grip of a firm handshake. More complex behaviors crop up as youths field questions during the interview. For instance, listening to questions requires adolescents to look at the interviewer, move closer if standing or lean forward if sitting, nod appropriately, listen without interrupting, momentarily break eye contact, and reflect on a response. To answer questions, interviewees have to regain eye contact, use positive words, first-person pronouns, and subtle arm and hand gestures, be succinct and to the point, and pause for indications that they addressed the interviewer's question. Adolescents are taught to summarize their strong points and to solicit information from employers. Inclusion of these behaviors makes young persons more competitive and increases their confidence in an otherwise intimidating situation (Korda, 1977).

Job interview training readies young people for negatively valenced and illegal questions. Handicapped persons as an example could counter innuendoes about their limited mobility by recalling specific strengths that far exceed any weaknesses. Queries in obvious violation of the law are trickier. Adolescents may gratuitously assume employers are not current with ever-changing regulations and answer illegal questions. Certainly, applicants have the right to call questions out of order and to report employers to the Equal Employment Opportunity Commission (Bolles, 1980). A middle ground is for applicants to respond and to add that the question seems irrelevant. Although the latter two tactics may cost them the job, youths might wonder if they want to work for someone so concerned about their private lives.

Information   Competencies for the job interview are developed through life skills strategies of using relevant information, problem solving, self-instruction, coping, communicating, and using support systems. Relevant information includes the facts about job hunting that were detailed above in the introduction to this section. Adolescents are also informed of their rights in employment interviews. Adapted from McGovern (1976), the interviewee's rights are:

Right to assume that one will be listened to.
Right to communicate important information about oneself.
Right to seek as much necessary information about the job in order to make a good decision.
Right to answer questions in one's own manner and style.
Right to expect truthfulness and accurate information from the interviewer.
Right to be treated fairly, without discrimination due to sex, race, age, or previous experience.
Right to express a healthy self-confidence and feel good about one's accomplishments.
Right to make mistakes (pp. 256–257).

Problem Solving   Problem solving allows young people to weigh their options and to arrive at balanced decisions about applying for employment.

Mick, for example, wanted to apply for a job parking cars at a fancy restaurant. Yet Mick knew the restaurant manager had turned down two fellows with long hair like his. Knowing that short hair alone would not land him the position compounded Mick's woes. Coveting a prestigious, lucrative job, yet despairing to sell out and no longer look hip, the youth was assisted by the problem-solving paradigm. Mick defined the issues, identified who and what could resolve his internecine values, generated a range of solutions, predicted the payoffs of each one, and chose and planned to implement the most feasible solution. The youth decided to get a haircut and to apply for the car parker job as well as for openings at other places predisposed to men with short hair— restaurants, haberdasheries, and grocery stores, for instance. Mick reasoned that later, depending on where he was hired, he could grow his hair a bit longer after proving to be a valued employee.

Self-Instruction   With self-instruction, young persons calm and coach themselves before and throughout nerve-racking interviews. While waiting to meet employers, adolescents relax and repeat to themselves what they will do in the interview. "Wow, have I got the jitters. I'd better relax. I'll take big breaths and loosen up my arms and legs. Ah, that's more like it. Now, what will I do when I go in and see Ms. Sweeney about being an assistant bookkeeper at her drug store? Well, one thing's for sure, Ms. Sweeney is not going to torture me; just ask me a few questions that I can answer. Remember: Stand up straight; Firm hand shake; Don't fool with my glasses. . . ." In the interview young persons use self-instructions to analyze difficult questions and to formulate their responses. "Yup, just like me and the counselor predicted, it didn't take Ms. Sweeney long to get around to my G.P.A. Well, that's OK. After I tell her the college-prep and accounting courses I took this year, she'll understand why 2.83 is nothing to sneeze at."

Coping   Coping lowers the stress from employment interviews. Tom is visibly anxious preceding his interview with the produce manager at Safeway. His friend Alex offers him a lift, suggesting the two of them share a bong of Alex's newest dope to "get your head right." Mindful of his dropped eyelids, flushed face, and babbled speech when stoned, Tom refuses the invitation. Instead he takes the bus, gets off a block early, stops at a newsstand, and flips through the motorcycle magazines before the interview. Coping also gives young people the wherewithal to anticipate and affably meet discouragement in the job search. Galassi and Galassi (1978) speak to the issue: "Regardless of preparation, most applicants will experience rejection at some point. A counseling program should build in the expectation that rejection is not uncommon in a job search and should help applicants develop skills for coping with it. Without such provisions, applicants are likely to experience what Zehring (1975) called rejection shock: emotional and physical symptoms, depression,

lack of motivation, low self-esteem, and alienation'' (p. 191). Labor Department data verify that young job seekers are easily disillusioned by the lack of
quick success (United States Department of Labor, 1980).

Coping with rejection begins as soon as the application process is over,
regardless of how it went. Young folks congratulate themselves for getting
through the ordeal. They treat themselves to a hot fudge sundae, a new piece of
clothing, an afternoon at the movies, or whatever they enjoy. In advance they
arrange to tell friends, teachers, or parents about job interviews within an hour
or two of their completion. Rejection is taken in stride. Applicants review what
they learned since the last interview and how they can use the knowledge in the
next one. Assuming they are employable and have not committed a fundamental faux pas, rejection from one position increases the chances of youths
being offered another—that is, as their chief competitors are hired, young
people ascend in relative ranking. Conditions will persist where racial, sexual,
or age discrimination work against adolescents. But coping by attributing
rejection to demographic factors does more harm than good. Young people who
suffered past discrimination may self-defeatingly give up hope and cease job
hunting (Atlas, 1978; Herrera, 1978). The results of such inactivity were
described in the doleful observations that opened this chapter. An earlier article
concludes that youths' blame and bitterness after failed quests for employment
have a ''negative impact on individuals, who begin to lose confidence in
themselves and faith in the nation's economic and social system. Such scars
may be long lasting and difficult to heal'' (Dayton, 1978, p. 3).

Communication   Counseling and communication skills enable adolescents to successfully interact with the adult authority figures they will
encounter when applying for and holding down jobs. Employed peers who
replay their job application experiences can aid in effective communication.
Future applicants get credible data on what lies ahead, and they observe
interactional styles that paid off. Role models are revered and closely studied
when they approximate clients' age, race, and background (Kirkland and
Thelen, 1977). If feasible, peer models will be the same sex as the client group.
Models are prepotent when they enjoy slightly higher social or academic
standing than the target youths (Rosenthal and Bandura, 1978). A large
measure of the models' status stems from their employment, gotten in part
through job-hunting skills that they will demonstrate. Demonstrations can run
from narrative descriptions of the application process to live scenes in which
models set the stage, assign key roles, and direct the action. In every instance,
models and professional underscore behavioral variables, not dispositional
traits or unique qualifications that won the job. Greater emphasis is therefore
accorded to Marianne's conduct in the interview than to her future boss's
business dealings with her father, although the latter may have tipped the scales
in her favor.

Modeled demonstrations are followed by mock interviews with employers. At first, pairs of adolescents enact the interviewer-interviewee dyad. Later interactions draw in unfamiliar adults as job interviewers. With both kinds of interviewers young people communicate by means of the nonverbal and verbal behaviors that were specified above. Professionals explicate and model the behaviors, then youths try out each one. Adolescents ease into communication practices with prepared scripts. The interviewer asks a series of questions, the applicant paraphrases scripted responses, and the professional crouches on the sidelines, offering feedback, reinforcement, and suggestions. As they grow skilled and secure in these interactions, youths take on unscripted situations. Practices are best when adolescents are already qualified for the prospective opening. According to the age group and region, relevant job titles include newspaper carrier, dishwasher, retail salesperson, farm hand, construction worker, gardener, stock clerk, apprentice, tradesperson, and unskilled laborer in food services and manufacturing. Young people ad lib their roles within a set of general instructions as the lines below illustrate.

Leader: "Merle, you be Ms. Wong, the supervisor at the mill where Stephen wants to work. Remember what Stephen said about the kind of jobs that are done there. Stephen, you be yourself 6 months from now when you've graduated and are ready for work. Ms. Wong will sit behind this table like it's her desk; I'll sit here beside you and whisper how you're doing. Go ahead, Ms. Wong."

Ms. Wong: "Well, Stephen, what brings you to the Fort Vancouver Plywood Company?"

Stephen: "I'd like a job here."

Ms. Wong: "I see that by your application. I mean, why do you want to work for us? Why not Mount St. Helens or one of the other mills?"

Stephen: "Well, they're all pretty good, I guess, but you're the best. People who work for you really like it here. And Fort Vancouver Plywood goes all over the world; everybody knows that."

Leader (sub voce):   "Great! That was a tricky question and you handled it well."

Ms. Wong: "What are your qualifications for the lumber business?"

Stephen: "Last summer I was a warehouseman at Schmidt's Lumber Yard. I learned to punch and patch plywood. I can run electric and gas mules. I even have an expensive pair of calks."

Leader (sub voce):   "Nice summary."

Ms. Wong: "I see. Well, we're a lot bigger than Schmidt's, and we work around the clock. Are you dependable?"

Stephen: "Yes."

Leader (sub voce):   "Be more specific."

Stephen: "Umm, yes, people call me dependable."

Leader (sub voce):   "Nope, still not good enough. Give it another shot. This time, personalize your answer and be specific."

Stephen: "Yes, I am a dependable person. Last summer I usually clocked in before 7:00. I stayed after 4:00 most of the time. The supervisor also told my uncle that I worked hard. This year at school I only missed 3 days and that was when I had the flu."

Leader (sub voce):   "Now you're talking!"

Ms. Wong: "My, you're almost too good to be true. I don't suppose you have any faults."

Stephen: "Yes, I do, and I've got lots to learn. For one thing, I'm kind of a perfectionist. But I am proud of my work. I want whatever I do to be right. So I keep at something until it's done like I want it."

Leader (sub voce):   "Another tricky one and you answered it masterfully."

Practices run for 10–15 minutes or until the dialogue bogs down. Young people receive detailed feedback from trainers and peers and repractice as necessary. Videotapes of these communication practices give youths a glimpse of the way they come across to employers. In addition, knowledge that they can retrospectively watch and critique themselves seems to release adolescents from the rigid, defensive postures that are typical during employment interviews (Clowers and Fraser, 1977).

Supports   Support systems of individual cognitions, interpersonal relationships, and environmental trappings remove some of the chill from plunging into the labor force. Thoughts and perceptions concerning the world of work are facilitative cognitive supports for adolescents. Rather than perceiving it as an ineluctable evil, young people anticipate employment as providing opportunities to be valued, to meet people, manage time, and learn about self-strengths and priorities (Ferner, 1980; LeBoeuf, 1979). In the early days of job seeking, they welcome the chance to sample a variety of positions before making a commitment to any one career. Once employed, they regard negative criticism as feedback on how well they measure up to societal standards while on the job. Perhaps the career track or their particular niche are disharmonious with their life goals. Steinberg et al. (1981) contend, "One of the most important lessons—if not the single *most* important lesson—a young person may learn from working is how to interact more effectively with others. Put otherwise, experience in work roles may contribute to the development of general social cognitive abilities and interpersonal competence in ways in which the family, peer group, and school do not" (p. 142, italics in original).

Interpersonal supports are provided by a circle of persons who appreciate the plight of the job hunter. Family members and significant adults listen to adolescents' tribulations, suggest tips and contacts, and soothe battered egos as young people learn that they are less sought after than they hoped. Unsuccessful applicants can obtain peer support by getting together and exchanging troubles, hints, and leads. Even though professional assistance has not been forthcoming, young adults who have extra difficulty landing jobs can be engaged in group counseling. Such groups permit young people to ferret out the causes of multiple rejections so that they and others can remediate their deficiencies before succumbing to a sense of failure.

Environmental supports encourage young people to explore a range of jobs and worksites. Access to employment openings is important—for example, fresh job listings in the papers and postings at school, community colleges, neighborhood centers, and public and private employment agencies. Transportation is necessary to visit employers and, once hired, to get to work on time. Job specialization means a priori investment in the tools of one's trade. For instance, journey-level drafting positions demand expensive drawing instruments. Books and manuals have to be purchased for any technical field. Employee pilferage from factories results in employers requiring workers to obtain personal sets of small and portable equipment. Some construction firms now ask workers to own pickup trucks. Interviewing with prospective employers generally necessitates new clothes. Most young people must drastically upgrade their wardrobes before embarking on a career. Other supports occur when youths rearrange their life styles to suit increased responsibilities. A changed schedule of sleeping, eating, and leisure time often accompany the employment debut.

SUMMARY

Despite the homely assumption that work is onerous—best avoided, minimized, or barely tolerated—adolescents who get life skills counseling view career and job as rich opportunities. Career choices are not relegated to chance or to the whims of others. Adolescents decide which job titles fit their abilities and goals, and they validate their decisions before stepping on a career ladder. Competing in the job market is nonthreatening and fun when young people are prepared to apply for employment. Life skills counseling is a synergetic approach for adolescents requiring this preparation. Young folks armed with the prerequisites go into careers and jobs knowing what rewards and pressures to expect. These youth are happier, more stable and successful, and less disappointed than young people who are left without assistance to the existing, chthonic system for entering the world of work.

Chapter 8

Building Social Responsibility

Socrates said that adaptive individuals are "those who manage well circumstances which they encounter daily, and who possess a judgment which is accurate in meeting occasions as they arise and rarely miss the expedient course of action" (Goldfried and D'Zurilla, 1969, p. 155). The ensuing 2300 years have not changed interpretations of societal adaptation as a 1973 definition attests: "Mastering of the social environment or social competence is defined as the ability of the person to participate effectively in developing a better social, psychological, and moral life" (Roosa, 1973, p. 1). Five years later, Zigler and Trickett (1978) make a similar assertion: "Social competence must reflect the success of the human being in meeting societal expectancies. . . . [and] the self-actualization or personal development of the human being" (p. 795). In regard to high schoolers, a 1980 study concluded as follows: "Adaptation is seen to have two major components, competence and satisfaction. The competence component reflects the individual's instrumental performance or degree of ability, skill, or mastery in specific areas. The satisfaction component is determined by the sense of efficacy, gratification, or pleasure which is associated with current performance" (Edwards and Kelly, 1980, pp. 203–204). Other research from the same year leads to a similar conclusion: "Social competence. . . . [is] conceptualized as social adaptive ability . . . . which is positive in quality and effective in achieving social goals" (Wright, 1980, p. 18).

Genial definitions together with the harmonious lives of many adolescents make societal adaptation seem deceptively easy. Consider a day in the life of Josie M.: The 15-year-old went to school, sat quietly at her desk, smiled at the teacher, raised her hand before speaking, attended basketball practice, played hard, bought a cookie on the way home, and spent the evening studying and watching television with her family. Her day may seem unremarkable. Yet in each of her accomplishments, Josie exercised planning, self-control, adherence to implicit rules, and compliance with intermittently enforced codes. Her adaptation at school, home, and in the community drew upon a repository of original and vicarious learning, educated guesses, conviction, and restraint. Josie and most of her agemates manifest faith in a just world and the belief that wavering from the straight and narrow path begets evil consequences.

To fathom why young people go astray, consider what would happen if Josie tested her faith by skipping school, or by going and cutting up in class, not playing basketball, stealing a cookie, and so forth. Not only might the youth experience no pain, she could realize the benefits of reading a novel, window shopping, relaxing in the park, getting a free snack, going to a movie, and enjoying an evening with friends. Virtue is not always rewarding. On the contrary, adolescents soon learn that sin is more fun and that the alleged effects of deviant behavior may never materialize. Deviance can be entirely overlooked. A teenager's parents might hopefully associate social isolation with renewed interest in school work (Asher et al., 1977). Such problems as neglected studies, drug experimentations, and criminal acts, are facilely hidden with little imagination (Inciardi, 1980). Once discovered, deviances in adolescence may be inconsistently met with weak palliations. One of the authors happily remembers a week's worth of diurnal parties during a 5-day school suspension for playing hooky.

PROFESSIONAL ATTENTION

Adolescent maladaptation concerns professionals when an adult referrer—parent, teacher, health-care provider, police officer—asks for assistance. Less typically do young people themselves request outside aid (National Institute of Mental Health, 1979). Without being privy to objective background information and etiological data, professionals toil with subjective and varying problem definitions (Hartmann et al., 1979; Keefe et al., 1978). For example, Ms. Maxwell complains about Jim's classroom inattention. The young man's parents blame his school disinterest on drugs and a bad circle of friends. Jim finds fault with unstimulating classes and doting parents, and discloses plans to quit school and find work. In addition, even though inaccurate referrals can occur in any field (Day, 1979b; Nelson and Hayes, 1979), the assessment of young persons' societal adaptation is especially plagued by nonstandard problem definitions (Gottman, 1977; Haynes and Wilson, 1979).

Vague terms and a dearth of assessment typologies additionally hamper clinical services with the target group and area (Foster and Ritchey, 1979; Kirschenbaum, 1979). Compounding these flaws, there are unfair status offenses that define (for adults) societal maladaptation in adolescence. Curfew violation, incorrigibility, delinquency, truancy, and underage smoking and drinking lack analogies for adults and are illegal only when the perpetrators are minors (Boisvert and Wells, 1980). As a whole, these multiple factors in referral and assessment are perhaps the reasons behind the many past efforts to help adolescents adapt that have turned out poorly (Braukmann and Fixsen, 1975; Bry, 1978; Cowen, 1977; Filipczak et al., 1979; Jesness, 1975; McAlister et al., 1979; O'Rourke, 1980; Payton, 1981; Room, 1981).

ANALYSIS

The life skills approach is grounded on an analysis of the thoughts, interactions, meanings, and norms that synergistically shape adolescents' societal adaptation. Cognitive messages are influential because adaptive, good behavior is not inherently reinforcing, whereas maladaptive, bad behavior is (Kendall et al., 1977; Leon, 1979)—for example, clearing the dinner table and loading the dishwasher versus sneaking out of the house and getting stoned. Interactions with both positive and negative peer models and the resulting tangible and interpersonal rewards also promote important cues for adaptation (Biddle et al., 1980; Young, 1981). Seeing a friend deftly slip a new pair of jeans under her old slacks and walk out of a store, for instance, Sheryl filches an expensive top. Afterward, oblivious of the tainted origin, Sheryl's classmates and teachers compliment her for sporting vogue clothes.

Cultural forces emerge in the social setting of young people's adaptation. Adolescents puzzle over the coexistence of hard work, dumb luck, honesty, chicanery, righteous ethics, and unscrupulous tactics that frequently delineates the careers of successful Americans and provides grist on U.S. leaders for the daily press (Feinstein et al., 1980; Offer et al., 1979). Youths' ethnic-minority affiliation is an analytic ingredient that warrants extra care. To be culturally syntonic, life skills counseling with black, Hispanic, Indian, Asian, and all other nonmajority youth should be geared to each group's unique prerogatives (Center for Multicultural Awareness, 1981; Dana, 1981; Resnik, 1980; Youngman and Sadongei, 1979).

The vague developmental period of adolescence, as a transition between childhood and adulthood, permits young persons to explore deviancies otherwise frowned upon (Combs and Slaby, 1977; Green, 1980). Young people publicly parade smoking, drinking, cursing, rudeness and disrespect as signs of social maturation (Topper, 1981). Another characteristic of the age is the adolescent susceptibility to mimick folk heroes (Clayton, 1979; Plant, 1980; Tudor et al., 1980). Musicians, television and movie idols and crooks glamorized in the media who flagrantly display deviant habits give admiring adolescents license to perform similar asocial acts (Andrews and Conley, 1977; Fisher and Magnus, 1981). By the same token, narcissism associated with the teen years renders young people hypersensitive to comments on their behavior, and makes them all too apt to mislabel both purposeful and inadvertent feedback (Coleman, 1979; Manaster, 1977).

Notably absent in this analysis is any reference to organically determined patterns of adaptation. Despite relationships between the societal struggles of individuals, and such factors as demography, family history, personality, and childhood trauma (Baum et al., 1981; Shafer et al., 1978), no single known feature pushes young persons toward or away from antisocial behavior (Baizerman et al., 1974; Korte, 1980; Schwartz, 1978). Rather, people adapt to society just as they acquire any skill: through principles of learning (Bandura, 1977; Dollard and Miller, 1950; Fixsen et al., 1973; Skinner, 1953). Correlates of deviancy are only useful to suggest at-risk populations and critical age periods (Gilchrist et al., 1979; Goldfried, 1979). Thus, data showing that 84% of 9- to 11-year-old children who steal are adjudicated to be delinquents at age 16 imply that referral and treatment must occur before mischievous pilfering becomes felonious theft (Moore et al., 1979).

Fundamental to the present analysis is the assumption that societal adaptation goes beyond merely reacting to trouble (Kendall and Finch, 1976). More importantly, young persons are equipped to thrive at school, home, work, and elsewhere. These two statements suggest that social problems in adolescence arise from discrepancies between the adaptive skills youths' need and those they have. This point of view calls to mind Rogers's (1975) concept of psychotherapy as an attempt to reduce "incongruence . . . . between the actual experience of the organism and the self picture of the individual insofar as it represents that experience" (p. 96). Differing from Rogerian and related modes of treatment that reactively serve clients "in a state of incongruence, being vulnerable or anxious" (Rogers, 1957, p. 96), however, the life skills approach prospectively trains young people to adapt in society.

LIFE SKILLS TRAINING

Teaching adolescents to competently handle diverse social situations is a formidable challenge. As McFall (1982) warns, "Competence is not an observable general attribute that a person has more or less of; nor is it something that accounts for the adequacy of the person's performance across tasks. . . . In fact, without engaging in a great deal of additional study, knowledge about a person's performance on one task tells us little about that person's likely performance on any other task" (p. 13). McFall's second statement is the key to life skills counseling. By learning conceptual strategies and by using them in everyday contexts, young people are prepared for a variety of social tasks. Chapters 2 through 7 have applied life skills counseling to adolescents' interpersonal storms with family and friends, personal trials with sex, psychological stress, health problems, and employment. The following application illustrates the approach with youths at-risk for school failure, encounters with the law, difficulties with both formal and informal institutions, and an unusually bumpy voyage through a world that tolerates precious little antisocial behavior.

METHODS

Forty-seven male adolescents in residential treatment received life skills counseling. These young men were referred for treatment because of hyperactivity, truancy, incorrigibility, delinquency, learning disabilities, and emotional disturbance. They were slated for re-entry into their homes and regular classrooms as soon as they accomplished their individual treatment goals. For the sake of evaluation, the young men were randomly placed in one of four categories or treatment conditions.

Cognitive and Behavioral Counseling   Two groups of six adolescents were counseled in eight, 90-minute sessions. A pair of child care workers surveyed stressful and achievement-related situations that earlier had been solicited from youths, their parents, and treatment center staff. Situations included temptations to shoplift and to vandalize public property, opportunities to cheat, responding to criticism, answering teachers, accepting praise, submitting to insults, fighting, being polite, volunteering to do chores, and asking to take part in extracurricular activities. Group members discussed the costs of acting impulsively, the benefits of self-control, and the ways in which they might behave if they found themselves in situations.

Leaders introduced problem solving by showing adolescents that issues of societal adaptation can be anticipated, met head-on, and satisfactorily resolved. Youths learned a sequence for making responsible choices (Meichenbaum and Asarnow, 1979): "Stop and think"; "Play turtle—pull into your shell for a minute"; "Think up lots of ideas for getting out of the problem"; "Go over your ideas and pick the best one—something that won't hurt anyone or get you in trouble." With cartoons, demonstrations, and role play, adolescents related the sequence to their own circumstances.

Young people in the cognitive and behavioral counseling category also acquired ways of thinking to aid in problem solving. Matthew learned self-instructions for getting on the soccer team as he practiced what he might think to overcome his fear of speaking with the coach. "Well, I know Coach Kelly likes guys to practice very night. So I'll go to the field after school, find the coach, and tell him if I was on the team I could play every night because I live near school. Then I'll ask him if I can try out for B Team. Even if he says 'no,' he'll know who I am and maybe he'll ask me to be on the team if somebody quits." At first Matthew spoke his thoughts aloud, then whispered them, and finally repeated them to himself. Throughout, leaders and group members were a sounding board and feedback source for Matthew's overt and covert practices.

Learning to cope had special meaning for these young men because they (like most socially disordered adolescents) had limited techniques to fend off pressure (Mahoney, 1979; Wodarski, 1981a; Wodarski et al., 1979). To replace lashing out or turning inward when frustrated, the youths learned ways to harmlessly relieve stress. Leaders demonstrated and adolescents practiced coping thoughts such as the following: "OK, I guess Sid is just going to keep on bugging me. He really knows how to get my goat. I'd love to punch him. But I'll pretend I couldn't care less. If I ignore him long enough, pretty soon he'll let me be.'' Group members acquired coping thoughts as they saw leaders respond to frustration, and then rehearsed the modeled responses. For instance, Brian was in the habit of slamming his desk top and hurling his books when he was tense or angry in Ms. Scott's class. While group members offered praise and suggestions, Brian rehearsed asking Ms. Scott's permission and getting up from his desk and sharpening his pencil or gazing at the aquarium to calm himself and to regain control.

Nonverbal and verbal communication skills were introduced by two videotaped segments of an adolescent and adult interacting. One segment depicted a communication style common for antisocial youth—slumped posture, no eye contact, low voice volume, mumbled words, flat affect, hands clenched, arms rigid (Cox et al., 1976; Fielder et al., 1979; Matson et al., 1980). The second segment showed communication associated with socially adept young people—erect stance, eyes on listener, clearly audible voice, fluency, live intonation, gestural animation (Barone and Rinehart, 1978; Michelson and Wood, 1980; Van Hasselt et al., 1979). Youths and leaders discussed the videotape, and leaders summarized the discussion by suggesting that positive nonverbal and verbal communication profits interactions with friends, family, teachers, and strangers.

After modeling good communication for one another, the youths broke into triads to practice communicating. One youth was a protagonist, another an antagonist, the third a feedback giver; leaders coached and reinforced protagonist youths. Whenever the young men practiced communication and any counseling strategy, they provided feedback by commenting on positive aspects of the protagonist's behavior, noting ways he could improve, and summing up their comments in constructive terms. Laudatory remarks, hints for improvement, and other kinds of helpful feedback relieved protagonist adolescents' fears of being criticized. In addition, feedback givers had explicit assignments of carefully attending to protagonists and of watching for positive, facilitative responses. The young men were expressly forbidden from sniping or otherwise derogating their peers. They could only point out improvements if they stated how the correction could be effected. Feedback giver Pat thus reflects on Norton's ability in the protagonist role: ''Nort, I liked it when you looked straight at Mr. Lange and told him you busted down his fence. It was really neat how you said you could fix the fence and paint it to boot because you didn't have your summer job any more. Next time, maybe you could not fool so much with your hands. How about holding them together like this? Anyway, you did real good that time. Keep looking at Mr. Lange and saying what you did.''

The young men eased into communication practices with prepared vignettes as shown in Figure 7. Group leaders initially took forceful roles, coaching protagonists, modeling reinforcement, and offering suggestions. Later, the leaders were passive observers except to praise the young men for

Role play this scene in your subgroup. Use good posture, looks, and words like the ones you saw modeled. Give feedback after each practice. Remember to be positive and helpful. Say at least two things the practicing person did right. Tell him how he can do better next time. Review all the good things he did. Switch roles so everyone practices three times.

You and your friends are hanging out at the Seven-Eleven. Ted wants you to go with him while he "borrows" the family care. You don't want to because neither of you has a license and you might get caught. Ted talks first, then you respond.

Ted: "Hey, let's you and me cut out to my place. My folks are gone, and I know where they hid the key to the Bonneville. We can take the old buggy for a spin."
You:

Ted: "What are you saying?"
You:

Ted: "C'mon, I'll even let you drive."
You:

Ted: "What's the matter with you?"
You:

Ted: "Quit stalling. Let's get moving."
You:

Ted: "Are we together or not?"
You:

Ted; "Some friend you are!"

Figure 7.   Structured vignette for communication practice.

enacting their respective roles and to intercede if they went off task or lapsed into negative modes of feedback. Once they had become confident and competent in the prepared vignettes, the adolescents could launch their practice of communication skills for their own idiosyncratic purposes and goals. Both leaders and group members came up with responsive nonverbal and verbal components, and the young people planned and wrote scripts for future interactions. Again in triads, group members practiced communicating while both adolescents and leaders assisted the protagonists through coaching, reinforcement, feedback, and suggestions.

The construction of cognitive, interpersonal, and environmental systems of support augmented the counseling for young men in this category. Cognitive systems of information, problem solving, self-instruction, and coping were buttressed with informal relationships within each small group. Leaders took advantage of the peer group by pairing adolescents as mutual helpers or buddies. Buddies worked together in experiential exercises and contacted each other between group meetings. Natural friendships came about when youths casually interacted before and after group sessions and during breaks. Environmental supports were structured as the young men mapped and implemented changes in their physical milieus at home, school, and other nontreatment settings. For instance, Hank found the bus ride home for the weekend particularly troublesome. He arranged for his father to pick him up and accordingly avoided chances to fight with other boys who also had hair-trigger tempers on Friday afternoons.

Cognitive Counseling Alone   To juxtapose and contrast cognitive and behavioral strategies, two six-person groups received counseling in using information, problem solving, self-instruction, coping thoughts, and using cognitive support systems in eight 90-minute sessions. However, the two child care worker leaders omitted coping acts, nonverbal and verbal communication, and interpersonal and environmental systems of support. Cognitive curricula and teaching methods were identical to those outlined above.

Information Only   A third category included 12 young men who received information only. Two child care workers met with separate groups of six adolescents for eight 90-minute sessions in which the leaders presented and the youths discussed the information described for the first two categories.

No Counseling   A control condition was provided by 11 adolescents who received no counseling at all.

Measurement

At the end of counseling, the young men in all categories took four tests. These tests were administered by three colleagues from an outside agency who were ignorant of study objectives and conditions.

Locus of Control   The Nowicki-Strickland Locus of Control Scale for Children (Nowicki and Strickland, 1973) ascertained whether the youths thought they themselves or luck, fate, or the whims of others controlled their lives. The choice of this instrument was based on research data which indicated that cognitive counseling strategies skew young persons' perceptions of control (Lefcourt, 1976; McClure et al., 1978).

Perspective Taking   The adolescents' ability to deal with problems in a constructive way was measured by the Perspective Taking Test (Shure and Spivack, 1970). The young men were asked to provide several approaches to handling tricky situations such as the following: "During math, another boy grabs your workbook and starts copying from it. What's the problem? What are some good ways of solving the problem? What other solutions do you see?'' The responses were audiotaped, transcribed, and independently blind-scored by two assistants. Checked with the Pearson product-moment correlation coefficient (r), the assistants' scoring reliability was 0.986.

Means-End Thinking   The Means-End Thinking Test (Shure and Spivack, 1972) quantified adolescents' linking of intermediate steps to goal achievement. The young men were told only the beginning and conclusion of stressful situations and then asked to fill in the gap. For example: "You're playing your friend's stereo and accidently scratch his favorite record. Later, your friend is not mad and lets you play his stereo again. What happened in the meantime?'' The audiotaped and transcribed responses were independently blind-scored by two assistants. Scoring reliability (r) was 0.914.

Interpersonal Performance   A videotaped test required the adolescents to interact with an agemate and with an adult in situations that called for apologizing for tactless behavior, sharing a prized possession with a peer, initiating contact with a newcomer at school, responding to an angry parent, asking a teacher for assistance with school work, and returning stolen property to a shopkeeper. The videotaped interactions were timed, indexed with anonymous codes (Schinke and Smith, 1979), and rated according to criteria for social comportment (Matson et al., 1980; Michelson and Wood, 1980; Van Hasselt et al., 1979). Two assistants who were naive of study conditions and hypotheses separately rated all tapes. Interrater reliability (r) was 0.924.

Consumer Satisfaction   Adolescents in the first three categories judged counseling substance and form with a consumer satisfaction questionnaire (Kazdin, 1977a; Kazdin et al., 1981; Wolf, 1978). At the close of every session, the young men anonymously filled in checklists, indicating what they did and did not like, failed to understand, and wished to change. They also indicated if and how they applied life skills counseling, and rated the subjective worth of the strategies used.

In Vivo Behavior   Socially validating data (Rusch et al., 1980; Whittaker, 1979; Willner et al., 1977) were gathered from treatment center staff. Several weeks after counseling, six staff members who were unaware of which youth had been assigned to what category independently rated each young man with the Devereux Elementary School Behavior Rating Scale (Spivack and Swift, 1967). Selection of the Devereux was based on correlations between ratings of childhood behavior and subsequent adult functioning (Bolstad and Johnson, 1971; Janes et al., 1979). Reliability (r) among the six staff raters reached a mean of 0.897.

Results and Discussion

Analyses of these measures verified the positive results from societal adaptation counseling. According to the consumer satisfaction data, the bulk of the young men enjoyed counseling, understood most material, and wanted no major changes in counseling process and content. Adolescents in the cognitive and behavioral condition often and advantageously applied counseling to their daily lives; fewer cognitively counseled youths had done so; and young people in information only groups gave no instances of applying their counseling.

Locus of control results were not statistically different across the four categories. Nonetheless, adolescents in cognitive and behavioral groups had the best scores, young men who got cognitive counseling had the next best scores, and less positive scores were reported by youths in information only and no counseling categories. As shown in Table 1, condition effects are evident for Perspective Taking Tests, with young persons in the cognitive and behavioral category most able to objectively look at problems ($p<0.05$), Means-End Thinking Tests failed to statistically distinguish one category from another, but mean scores were higher for youths in the first two categories than for those in the latter two. Although nonsignificant, the videotaped data favored the young men who acquired the full complement of counseling strategies, as shown in their eye contact, body posture, affect, assertive statements, and overall effectiveness.

The Devereux scores yielded significantly discriminating staff ratings of adolescents for scales of disturbance ($p<0.05$). Impatience ($p<0.05$), disrespect ($p<0.05$), blame ($p<0.05$), reliance ($p<0.01$), withdrawal ($p<0.05$), and responsiveness ($p<0.05$). In the main, the scales revealed greater adaptation by the young men in cognitive and behavioral counseling and cognitive counseling categories than for those receiving information only, who in turn received better ratings than the young people who received no counseling. Nine of 11 Devereux scales ranked the young men who received the first two kinds of counseling as most adaptive. The power of the in vivo ratings as predictors of adult adaptation was confirmed by the Devereux findings (Bolstad and Johnson, 1977; Janes et al., 1979).

The data from this field evaluation bear out the superiority of information, problem solving, self-instruction, coping thoughts and acts, nonverbal and verbal communication, and cognitive, interpersonal, and environmental systems of support to increase societal adaptation among high-risk adolescents. Consistent with findings from similar investigations (Dickie and Gerber, 1980; Glenwick and Barocas, 1979; Higgins and Thies, 1981; Little and Kendall, 1979; Marsh et al., 1980), the present results imply that life skills counseling aids young people who express early patterns of antisocial disturbance. The consumer satisfaction responses endorse the attraction and value of group counseling. Life skills counseling did not disrupt and seemed to enhance the treatment center's missions of education, treatment, and habilitation.

TABLE 1.   Means for tests of Perspective Taking and Means-End Thinking and for Devereux Behavior Scales

Measure	Condition			
	Cognitive and behavioral counseling	Cognitive counseling only	Information only	No counseling
Perspective taking	2.75	2.18	1.55	.65
Means-end thinking	6.25	6.46	4.55	4.91
Devereux scales[a]				
Disturbance	12.58	14.00	14.18	16.91
Impatience	12.75	13.36	15.91	17.64
Disrespect	11.00	12.18	12.55	14.73
Blame	13.83	13.46	15.18	18.09
Anxiety	13.67	13.55	13.91	15.73
Reliance	16.67	17.73	21.45	23.18
Comprehension	12.92	12.09	10.64	12.00
Withdrawal	10.17	12.46	15.00	14.46
Responsiveness	11.25	10.36	12.91	13.73
Creativity	12.00	10.91	11.18	12.18
Closeness	14.92	13.18	13.36	15.09

[a]Low scores are positive on all Devereux scales except Comprehension, Creativity, and Closeness.

SUMMARY

Adapting in society can test anyone's mettle. Young people in particular are likely to cross those fuzzy lines that separate social from asocial acts. Both unwritten and legally sanctioned rules stipulate adolescent offenses that have no parallel for adults. Youths are expected to pick up imperceptible cues for social intercourse on their own while being titillated by the fruits of deviancy. However, life skills counseling can smooth the path toward happy, healthy adaptation.

Adolescents who experience life skills counseling strategies avoid trouble and flourish within familial, school, legal, and community approbations. Empirical research documents the viability, impact, cost-effectiveness, and utility of the counseling approach. Work with adolescents referred because of antisocial acts confirms the benefits of cognitive and behavioral strategies in a small group format. Youths who learned how to augment their knowledge and thoughts and improve their interactions through these strategies had more felicitous attitudes and problem-solving abilities than young people who received less counseling. Compared to them, the adolescents who were taught a range of life skills strategies had better interchanges with peers and adults. Treatment center staff saw cognitively and behaviorally counseled young persons as more able to manage conflicts of school and play than lesser trained young people. Equally important, adolescents felt that the counseling was fun and worthwhile. In view of these results, life skills counseling is a responsive approach for professionals to use in helping adolescents adapt in society.

Chapter 9

Implementation and Evaluation

Throughout this volume are instances of life skills counseling in a variety of contexts. Chapter 3 presents ways to measure adolescents' interpersonal abilities with parents, siblings, and peers. The fourth chapter demonstrates that the delicate area of sex can be addressed and evaluated without controversy or breech of ethics. Chapter 5 adapts counseling to stress management. The sixth chapter offers suggestions for teaching health promotion and for developing effective programs to prevent youths' future bad habits. Chapter 7 includes detailed methods to assess young persons' employment readiness before and after responsive life skills counseling. The preceding chapter discusses counseling aimed at promoting adaptive social behavior.

Because the examples in these chapters occurred in practice settings, each counseling program can be appropriate for similar client groups, problems, and clinical conditions. Colleagues working in the same circumstances can replicate the methods and profit from the forms, flow charts, and vignettes included in program descriptions. Professionals in different situations, however, cannot automatically present the material to their clients in identical ways. Moreover, practitioners may want to innovate and try out new counseling approaches. With this end in mind, the present chapter offers guidelines for the conduct and analysis of life skills programs in any milieu, with attention given first to needs assessment, pilot testing, and process analysis of curricula development, delivery of counseling, and acquisition of counseling before moving on to a discussion of outcome evaluation, which covers aims definition, measurement, data collection and interpretation, and dissemination. A final section notes caveats to launching and evaluating life skills programs in community settings.

NEEDS ASSESSMENT

Life skills programs work best when based on an appraisal of services and resources provided by the host organization (Schinke and Schilling, 1980). Professionals start needs assessment by objectively looking at how well their agency, school, or institution meets its missions. Every public and private organization has an expressed mission, be it education, habilitation, health care, or recreation. Just as important, sometimes more so, are the adjunctive missions of being a teenage daycare center, an institution to delay youths' entry into the labor market, a place to go in lieu of roaming the streets, and so on (Fine, 1980). Both kinds of missions are scrutinized to see if the organization is responsive to young persons, their families, and the community. For instance, a church program may ostensibly be an after-school meeting place for junior high and middle-school students. But low student participation suggests that the program fails to compete with secular hangouts, or that its latent goal of religious socialization turns off young people. Those in charge could survey the program's participants, nonparticipants, and originators regarding its direction and future (Kirkpatrick, 1977).

Those responsible for needs assessment should consider the evolution of organizational missions. Thus, public schools are no longer concerned with just the three R's. Cuts in social service and health-care programs burden schools with functions that traditionally fell on outsiders. Social workers, nurses, and physicians in some schools in St. Paul, Minnesota, for example, give senior high students information and counseling on human sexuality, contraception, and parenting, and provide them with pregnancy diagnosis and services in regard to venereal disease, birth control, prenatal care, nutrition, and oral hygiene (Edwards et al., 1980). During a typical academic year, 75% of the students in two such schools received one or more of these nonpedagogical services. Future budget reductions will result in other solvent institutions assimilating the missions of less fortunate ones (Peters and Sibbison, 1980; Washington et al., 1979).

Shifting social norms uncover additional areas for life skills counseling. The increase in teenage coitus and pregnancy (Zelnik and Kantner, 1980) and the fact that nearly all young mothers keep their babies (Zelnik and Kantner, 1978) signal the importance of counseling for single parenthood. A climbing divorce rate (National Center for Health Statistics, 1982b) supports this focus. Counseling areas are added by new sex-role definitions, innovative living arrangements, and emergent facts on adolescent substance abuse. For instance, researchers claim that geographic relocation, environmental pressure, and an external locus of control cause young persons to take drugs (Maisto and Caddy, 1981; McCoy and Watkins, 1980; Spoth, 1980). Needs assessment data further issue from studies on personal and social stress that suggest primary prevention curricula (McAlister, 1981; Mikhail, 1981). Counseling here might lead to the prevention of adolescents' physical illnesses, phobias, anxieties, reliance on tobacco, alcohol, and tranquilizers, overeating, poor nutrition, lack of exercise, and poor money and time management (Kutash and Schlesinger, 1980; Light, 1981; Sklar and Anisman, 1981). In short, the areas for life skills counseling are boundless.

Resources

Once preliminary assessment has determined that a life skills program is needed, practitioners are ready to seek and commit the expertise and resources to carry out counseling. Professional staff are primordial resources (Dickinson and Bremseth, 1979). Are professionals facile with the life skills approach? Digesting the present volume is one way to begin to acquire this facility. Life skills counselors should at least be competent in the content area. Before starting a program to help teenage mothers cope with parenthood, we screened potential counselors for their coping and problem-solving abilities with regard to handling conflicting demands of job and home, responding to hassles from in-laws and parents, and countering feelings of inadequacy and failure. Prospective counselors should guarantee the time and organizational backing necessary for successfully implementing a life skills program. These commitments are concretely documented by written agreements with administrators and supervisors (Zober, 1980). As well as counseling time per se, professionals must allot time for preparation and debriefing. Colleagues who are friendly to the life skills approach and who may lend a hand are valuable resources. Co-leadership is an ideal arrangement for professionals to help one another learn the interventionist approach.

The physical resources that are determined by needs assessment include both the basics of successful programs and the extras that make counseling fun. Among the former, there is the space needed for life skills counseling. Are rooms and offices adequate in size, lighting, and layout? How about their accessibility to the target population? Can clients be promised privacy in terms of low visibility, sound proofing, and low probability of intrusion? Choice of counseling site should take into account the clients' perspective. Thus, youths' perceptions of school classrooms may be colored by their prior schooling experiences. Content areas may be skewed according to the nature of the counseling site—for example, substance abuse prevention at a drug treatment agency draws different participants than a program at a neighborhood recreation center. Any meeting place ought to be attractive. Because adolescents associate the immediate environment with the counseling they expect, professionals should make sure chairs and tables are properly arranged and that the room communicates comfort and confidentiality.

Needs assessment of the counseling site environment should take into consideration the availability of video- and audiotape equipment. Such equipment aids life skills counseling in a number of ways. The action-oriented approach yields lively interactions and rehearsals that can be recorded and played back. Audio-visual media are unparalleled in giving adolescents a glimpse of how others perceive them. The novelty of videorecording is a drawing card for young people to attend counseling sessions. Even so, the existence of videotape equipment is not equivalent to its correct use. Before the inaugural counseling session, professionals must familarize themselves with the techniques as well as the ethics of using video recordings (Kent et al., 1979; Schinke, 1981b; Schinke and Smith, 1979). If video equipment is not available, audiotape recorders can let adolescents experience one other channel of feedback. Audiotaping, however, also requires practice before its clinical application (Gentry, 1978; Mercer and Loeschi, 1979).

Not the least of needs assessment concerns is the budget for life skills counseling. Fundamental to start and finish a coherent program, adequate funds indicate an organization's ability to follow through on its pledge to counselors and clients (Weiner, 1980). Professionals have to be remunerated for planning, implementing, and evaluating the program. They should either get compensatory time or overtime pay for each counseling phase. Good intentions aside, counselors cannot run a program without compensation. Volunteers—be they professionals or lay persons—are unlikely counselors; they ought not be counted on for critical duties (Pecora and Gingerich, 1981). Adolescents may need monetary incentives, especially if counseling competes with employment or extramural activities. Youth who derive quick returns for their participation are generally punctual and committed (Braukmann and Fixsen, 1975; Hersen, 1981).

Youthful pecuniary wants may be satisfied via several mechanisms. At various times the authors have compensated youths after counseling sessions, paid them for assessment and evaluation, and contributed their pooled earnings to a school or community drama club, band, or drum and bugle corps. The budget should provide the wherewithal to reimburse counseling participants for transportation costs. Nice but not crucial are dollars for treats during life skills sessions. Depending upon the time of day, juice, soft drinks, fruit, cookies, popcorn, tacos, hamburgers, and pizzas induce ambivalent adolescents to join life skills counseling and to conscientiously attend meetings. Budget estimates should include film and media rental, honoraria for guest speakers, and field trip expenses.

In sum, needs assessment generates facts for deciding the locus and extent of life skills counseling. Lest professionals be put off by needs assessment and so decide to dispense with it and get on with counseling, they are forewarned that a life skills program launched without background data might be nonproductive or irrelevant, and fail from the outset.

PILOT PROJECTS AND PROCESS ANALYSIS

Once they have obtained needs assessment data that remove prior unknowns, suggest content areas, and indicate program resources, professionals are ready to test the feasibility of life skills counseling through clinical work with adolescents. At this point, counselors continue to eliminate any impediments to a successful final program by conducting a pilot project (Fawcett et al., 1981). As approximations of the ultimate program, pilot projects are limited in scope, magnitude, and goals. A pilot test of life skills counseling involves just a few adolescents, truncates the number of counseling sessions, and simply seeks to determine whether counseling can be implemented and how it is received. In this fashion, pilot projects are opportunities to analyze the process of life skills counseling.

Pilot projects and process analyses have long been country cousins to the grand implementation of social programs (Rothman, 1980). As Bevan (1976) observed, ''When the Pentagon develops a new weapons system, the research and development process involves an elaborate sequence of testing and comparing alternative technologies, retaining finally only the one that comes off best in competitive testing. In contrast, when our government confronts a major societal problem in the civilian sector, its solution is usually intuitive and immediate and, often to our ultimate sorrow, implemented on a full scale'' (p. 490). Only recently has process analysis gotten its due. Judd and Kenny (1981) specify its function. ''When a treatment is judged effective, regardless of the procedure used to estimate its effects, it is usually informative to examine the *mediating process* that produces those effects. Such a process analysis is an attempt to specify the causal chain responsible for the observed treatment effects. With a process analysis one asks not *whether* a treatment produced the desired effects, but rather *how it did so*'' (p. 603, italics in original).

Calling it ''social research and development (R & D),'' Whittaker and Pecora (1981) put process analysis in the context of child welfare. ''Social research and development is a systematic process for bridging the gap between research and application. . . . With respect to child and youth services, social R & D would facilitate the translation and conversion of theoretical abstractions and empirical research data into practical and effective methods'' (p. 309). Thomas (1978) relates the methodology to social work. ''Developmental research may be the most appropriate model of research in social work because it consists of methods directed explicitly toward the analysis, development, and evaluation of the technical means by which social work objectives are achieved—namely, its interventional technology'' (p. 605). The aspects of life skills counseling that require analysis before large-scale community programs can be implemented include curricula development, delivery of training, and acquisition of training.

Curricula Development

Neither life skills counseling nor any other therapeutic mode is universally applicable. Professionals must tailor the model to their own points of view and to their own particular adolescent clients. Accordingly, process analysis enables each counselor to systematically recognize and assess the theoretical and sociocultural factors that affect each unique life skills program. Theory is germane because professionals' perceptions of and expectations about human behavior affect their work with adolescents. For example, the social learning concepts advanced in this book take the view that adolescents acquire good and bad habits through a synergism of thoughts, acts, and surroundings. Instead of conflicting with this view, other psychosocial theories complement the cognitive, behavioral, and environmental change strategies detailed in preceding chapters.

The sociocultural factors examined in process analysis include the life histories and future prospects of adolescent clients. Data are gathered on the client's age, sex, race, family, previous human services treatment, history, and past institutionalization. These data tell professionals how to mold a life skills curriculum for their clients' problems. A program planned by the authors to prevent drug abuse among Native American adolescents is an example that will take into account Indian traditions, values, family relationships, and other sociocultural variables that should be considered in an adaptation of life skills counseling for this particular group (Schinke, 1981d). The social contexts of future placement enter into curricula development as professionals design counseling that is specific to the places where young people will live and use their learning. Information on the schools, homes, jobs, and communities of adolescent clients is important because different kinds of societal cues influence youths' thoughts and behavior in different ways (Harris, 1979; Sarason and Sarason, 1981). For example, residential treatment demands skills seldom required of noninstitutionalized young persons (Whittaker, 1979).

Process data on curricula development ought to be recorded in some kind of retrievable form. Chronological journals help professionals note theoretical support for their emphasis and the demographic and contextual variables that influenced the choice of counseling content and methods. Journal entries are most accurate if logged when facts and decisions are fresh. Later on, professionals can read the journal to recall why a life skills curriculum turned out the way it did. They and those who come after them may thereby avoid repeating past mistakes in subsequent counseling programs.

Delivery of Training

A glaring omission from the bulk of clinical program analyses is documentation of the techniques of intervention. Time and again professionals are in the dark about the day-to-day operations of treatment or counseling (Hersen, 1981; Kazdin, 1980; Wilson, 1981). Mahoney (1978) discusses the weakness in evaluations of psychological treatments. "One of the most common (and frustrating) shortcomings of an experimental article is the failure to clearly specify the independent variable(s)" (p. 664). When life skills programs are vague about their actual operations, colleagues who attempt to replicate counseling are afforded meager guidance. Counselors themselves are often unsure of what they did and why it worked. Process analysis systematically fills this gap. A small investment in data collection gives professionals and their protegés instant facts on the who, how, what, and when of life skills counseling.

One way of garnering these data is for professionals to catalogue each step of curricula delivery in the aforementioned journals. Timely journal entries specify the counselors, clients, guest speakers, observers, and procedures of every life skills session. A method to structure the collection of data without sacrificing flexibility involves the use of an easy checklist. Completed after the session and suited for both individual and group counseling, the checklist in Figure 8 jogs counselors' recollections of the most recent session and aids their preparation for the next one. This and similar brief forms detail whether counselors presented the material consistently. Professionals willing to share their checklists with colleagues can strengthen each other's programs and advance the science of life skills counseling. However the data are used, counselors must guard journals, checklists, and all client information as confidential (Nye, 198; Wilson, 1978).

Acquisition of Skills

Just as teaching does not necessitate learning, delivery of counseling does not mean adolescents automatically acquire life skills. Young people may understand the material, and seem to enjoy counseling, yet privately loathe the program. Adolescents in the closed settings of schools, residential centers, penal institutions, and psychiatric wards have ample cause to feign involvement. Not unlike incarcerated prisoners, these captive individuals may humor the authorities with the illusion that they are benefitting from the rehabilitative program and thus be discharged on schedule (Solkoff, 1981). Another reason for scrutinizing adolescents' receipt of the life skills counseling stems from legal approbations on psychological treatments with a behavior modification bent (Budd and Baer, 1976; Cantwell and Carlson, 1978; Martin, 1975; Ross, 1980). Ethical concerns with counseling minors complicate this aspect of process analysis (Bermant et al., 1978; Bower and de Gasparis, 1978; Diener and Crandall, 1978; DuVal, 1979; Stolz and Associates, 1978). Kazdin et al. (1981) discuss the ethics of treating underage clients: "Concerns about treatment acceptability are frequently raised in child treatment, and for obvious reasons. Children, by virtue of their age and legal status, are often viewed as (and perhaps frequently are) incapable of understanding or making decisions about their own treatment. They rarely have access to detailed information about alternative procedures and are not apprised of or do not appreciate the opportunities they may have to refuse or terminate treatment'' (p. 901).

Professionals may choose several ways to verify adolescents' acquisition of life skills counseling. Journals and checklists mentioned above note counselors' perceptions of clients. In addition, young people can disclose their thoughts about counseling on anonymous feedback sheets. Shown in Figure 9,

Date _____   Counselor _____

Session No. _____   Guests _____

Location _____   _____

Time _____   Observer _____

1. Complete this information for each youth present.

Name	Homework finished	Level of participation	Homework assigned	Comments

2. What worked well this session?

3. What did not work well?

4. Summarize the guest speaker's presentation. Include youths' responses. Will you invite the guest again? Why?

5. Describe supplementary materials, films, or aids. How were these received? Will you use them again?

6. Specify departures from your curriculum and reasons for making the changes.

7. If material was omitted, how can it be covered at the next session?

8. What will make training better next time?

9. What problems came up?

10. How much professional time was devoted to preparation _____, delivery _____, and debriefing _____? Total time _____.

11. What were the dollar expenditures for transportation _____, snacks _____, payment to youths _____, and guests _____, films and equipment rental _____, and miscellaneous items _____? Total $ _____.

Figure 8.   Checklist for recording process analysis information.

Date _____   NO NAME

1. What did you like about today's session?

2. What didn't you like?

3. If we had a guest speaker, what do you think about what she or he said?

4. Did you do your homework? Yes _____ No _____
    If yes, was it worthwhile?

    If no, why didn't you do it?

5. Will you come to the next session? Yes _____ No _____
    Why or why not?

6. What would you like to do differently the next time we meet?

7. Circle the numbers that show how much you learned and how much you like today's session.

    I didn't learn   I learned
    anything   1   2   3   4   5   6   7   8   9   10   a lot.

    Training was   Training was
    awful!   1   2   3   4   5   6   7   8   9   10   great!

8. Any other comments?

Figure 9.   Feedback sheet for adolescent clients.

feedback sheets enable adolescents to frankly comment on each session and to suggest improvements. At a program's close, professionals might request that clients judge the overall worth of the curriculum on a larger version of the feedback sheet. Youths can rank the relative efficacy of life skills strategies and anonymously tell if and how they applied counseling. Should young people fear that their responses will be identified, professionals can designate a third party to collect and collate feedback sheets, compile a blind summary statement, and destroy the original forms. Observational data on life skills sessions reveal adolescents' acceptance of counseling. With consent from everyone involved, observers may sit in on sessions and rate the quality, quantity, and intensity of youths' participation. Observers might employ conventional and open-ended rating forms to assess manifestations of cohesiveness and interest, measure the frequency, length, direction, nature, and valence of client-counselor interchanges, and mark counseling session interactions as on and off task (Rose, 1981; Schinke and Schilling, 1980; Schinke and Wong, 1977).

Outside data on the acquisition of counseling come from significant actors in adolescents' everyday worlds. Professionals find such sources by asking adolescents to name trustworthy persons who can be contacted about their participation in the life skills program (Whittaker, 1979; Whittaker and Small, 1977; Wodarski and Ammons, 1981). Once they have granted permission, these people are polled for their opinions about the extent to which youths were committed to the life skills program, the value of counseling, and the program's effect on both adolescents and on them. Counseling programs housed in agencies and schools can be checked with clinical and educational staff. Questions put to teachers, child care workers, therapists, ward attendants, custodians, and administrators should seek a fair appraisal of the counseling process. Was the life skills program a boon or an intrusion? Were clients removed from more important activities to attend counseling sessions? Did adolescents and program staff look forward to sessions? How did young people refer to counseling outside of counseling sessions? Were clients any different after life skills counseling? Assuming it does no harm, should the program be implemented again? If so, why? Answers to such questions, together with other impressionistic and objective data, facilitate balanced conclusions about life skills curricula, delivery, and acquisition.

OUTCOME EVALUATION

Process analysis and outcome evaluation may be simultaneous. Nonetheless, each is sufficiently complex to warrant separate phases (Epstein and Tripodi, 1977; Toseland, 1981; Wodarski, 1981b). Whereas the former analyzes life skills counseling's operations, the latter evaluates its payoffs. The components of outcome evaluation are aims definition, measurement, data collection and interpretation, and dissemination.

Aims Definition

The first task of outcome evaluation is to set explicit aims for each life skills program. Outcome aims ought to be positive, specific, and prescribed by time and situation. Positive aims are best because life skills strategies are meant to aid in constructing new ways of thinking and behaving (Furman and Drabman, 1981; Goldiamond, 1974; Sulzer-Azaroff and Mayer, 1977). Thus, the problems of delinquency, drug abuse, aggression, and most personal and social disorders can be more easily addressed by building up youths' positive, incompatible repertoires of behavior instead of merely eliminating their negative responses (Curran, 1979b; Levine and Pearson, 1979; McCullough et al., 1977; Schinke, in press-c). Rather than just aiming to stop on-campus pot smoking, for example, professionals might boost high schoolers' ability to join team sports, school clubs, special interest groups, and community recreations. The specificity requirement of outcome aims is met through quantifiable indices. Aims are specific if someone with a written definition that includes specific criteria can differentiate between youths who achieved the aims and those who did not. For instance, "becoming a well-rounded student" is vague and hard to see; however, "participating in extra-curricular events and earning a 2.75 GPA" is both precise and quantifiable.

Prescribed times and situations indicate when and where aims are achieved. A time for young people to make career choices might be "before the last quarter of the junior year." Situations for preventing pregnancy are: "while a high school student," "before the age of 18," "while financially dependent and living at home," and "when not wanting a baby." Sample aims that combine the three requirements include: "Within one month of the program and during the school year, Hal will attend 80% of his classes," "Kate and her father will converse for 15 minutes a day on a mutually agreeable topic beginning the week of March 12, 1984," "By the end of counseling, Gina will have applied for a summer job."

Measurement

Clear aims are amenable to assessment by a variety of outcome measures. Theoretically, psychosocial measures are valid and reliable indicators of change. But adolescents' idiographic problems and researchers' nomothetic measures separate theory and practice (Nelson and Hayes, 1979). To close the gap, professionals have scrutinized human service outcomes with myriad instruments and data-gathering procedures (Beere, 1979; Buros, 1978; Hudson, 1982). Information on treatment effects is usually teased from respondents' scores by means of elaborate statistical analyses (Goldfried and Kent, 1972; Goldfried and Sprafkin, 1976; Hersen, 1976). Such measurement neglects many of the effects of counseling (Barlow, 1977; Bloom and Fischer, 1982; Cone and Hawkins, 1977a; Day, 1979b; Haynes, 1978; Haynes and Wilson, 1979; Hersen and Bellack, 1976a; Hudson, 1982; Keefe et al., 1978; Mash and Terdal, 1976).

Clinicians in the last few years have promoted a fuller and more precise view of behavior change by measuring multiple facets of an intervention outcome (Agras et al., 1979; Bellack, 1979a, b; Bellack and Hersen, 1978; Ciminero, 1977; Cone, 1979; Cone and Hawkins, 1977b; Curran, 1979; Curran and Mariotto, 1980; Eisler, 1976; Hersen and Bellack, 1978; Kazdin, 1979a, 1980). Multifaceted measures attempt to assemble the client's traits, actions, and responses into a composite image. Thus, an outcome of the aim to increase Rona's confidence with members of the opposite sex may be expressed as she reports how well she can talk to boys of the same age. Her anxiety can be observed by noting Rona's eye contact, fluency, gestures, and mannerisms when she approaches a male classmate. The client's confidence could be autonomically evidenced through electronic measurement of her galvanic skin response and heart rate during interactions with young men. A second example of multifaceted measurement is the smoking prevention program described in Chapter 6. There, outcomes were measured as adolescents reported their knowledge of tobacco hazards, attitudes toward smoking, and intentions to take up the tobacco habit. Youths were observed while role playing in tobacco-use vignettes, refusing cigarettes, and extolling the virtues of nonsmoking, and they gave saliva samples that were analyzed for the tobacco by-product thiocyanate.

Resource limitations can compromise the multiple measurement of life skills programs (Hersen et al., 1978; Twentyman et al., 1979; Van Hasselt et al., 1979). Professionals should get at least one piece of empirical data for every adolescent client. Toward this goal, thousands of paper and pencil instruments purport to measure everything from acrophobia and happiness to xenophobia and loneliness (Chun et al., 1975; Johnston, 1976; Karmel and Karmel, 1978; Levis and Plunkett, 1979; Nelson, 1980; Savin-Williams and Jaquish, 1981; Strober, 1979). Given the time and wherewithal, professionals should collect observational data in the natural environment. Various codes and in vivo measures exist and are not hard to use (Elder et al., 1979; Foster and Cone, 1980; Patterson and Cobb, 1971; Strain and Ezzell, 1978). Trickier but worth the trouble are physiological measures of muscle tension, pulse rate, blood pressure, perspiration, stomach contractions, body and skin temperature, and breathing (Blanchard and Epstein, 1977, 1978; Kallman and Feuerstein, 1977; Lang, 1977).

A key outcome measure is the cost of counseling (Masters et al., 1978). Costs in terms of time, money, and foregone opportunities can be recorded in journals or on forms like the Counseling Checklist (Figure 8). However they do it, professionals should record these costs for all phases of a life skills program. A program being run by Janet B. can provide an illustration of cost measurement. After she, Eleanor, and Theo met for 1½ hours to plan group counseling, Janet led an hour-long session with 12 adolescents at a community mental health center. Janet looked over her notes to debrief for 30 minutes after the session, including 15 minutes to consult with Eleanor. Professional time for the session was $[(90 \text{ min} \times 3) + (60 \text{ min} \times 1) + (15 \text{ min} \times 1) + (15 \text{ min} \times 2)] = 375 \text{ min} = 6¼$ hours. Time commitments are translated into dollars by multiplying the professionals' hours by their salaries (Shepard and Thompson, 1979). Using a guide like item 11 in Figure 8, counselors can itemize their financial outlays. Summing time and money allocations and dividing by the number of youth counseled gives the per person cost. In the above example, Janet's 8-week life skills program cost $768, or an average of $64 for each participant. The third dimension of cost measurement is the opportunity loss that professionals and young people experience during life skills counseling

(Yates, 1979). For instance, Janet may have passed by more remunerative individual cases while conducting her group program. Youthful participants might have given up extra hours at their jobs to attend counseling sessions. Although less precise than time and money expenses, estimates of foregone opportunities put in perspective the resources committed to a life skills program.

Data Collection and Interpretation

Outcome measures are optimally administered according to a research model. At the very least, adolescents should be assessed when the counseling session is over. Professionals can score the measures and contrast their clients' responses with normative data (Bachman et al., 1981; Bachman et al., 1978; Heffermann and Turman, 1981; Johnston et al., 1978; Manaster, 1977; Rogers, 1977). Although this method may result in showing gains that are attributable to life skills counseling, an improved procedure is to administer the measures both before and after the program and compare the responses. Counselors then have a basis for judging and revising the program. Single-case and control-group research models are even better. In single-case models professionals measure outcomes throughout the course of counseling by continually collecting and comparing their findings (Jayaratne and Levy, 1979; Kazdin, 1978; Kratoch-will, 1978; Polster et al., 1981; Schinke, 1979, 1981a–c). By juxtaposing the data that were collected at each time period, one can determine if the program reached its aims. In control-group models, professionals engage some youths in counseling while intentionally not counseling others (Cook et al., 1977; Kazdin, 1980; Sommer and Sommer, 1980). By contrasting the outcomes for both counselors and control group, professionals can see if the curriculum was more potent than maturational and other extraneous factors.

Measurement data gathered according to these research models can be graphed, statistically analyzed, subjectively weighed, and interpreted for cost-effectiveness. Graphs depict the level and trends of outcome data before, during, and after counseling (Elashoff and Thoresen, 1978; Glass et al., 1975). Figure 10 represents such an interpretation of a life skills program to remediate a teenager's drug abuse. The graph shows that counseling built up the client's social supports, increased his time practicing for school band, and lowered his use of drugs. In addition, there are statistical analyses in which hand calculators and noncomplex formulae are used to determine if pre- to posttreatment differences result from counseling or from chance (Bentler et al., 1976; Brunig and Kintz, 1977; Goodman, 1978; Tukey, 1977). Through subjective inter-pretations, one can ascertain if clients progressed according to their own standards and those of family, friends, and professionals (Kazdin, 1977a; Kazdin and Wilson, 1978; Wolf, 1978). Life skills counseling for a group of overweight adolescents, for example, becomes statistically significant as the

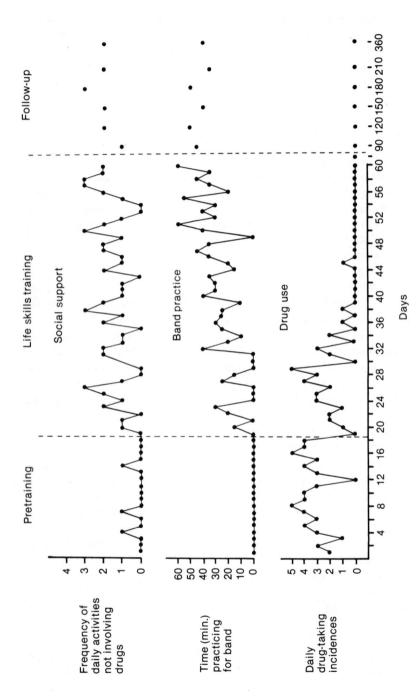

Figure 10.   Graphic analysis of life skills counseling with a drug-abusing teenager.

group mean goes down by 12 pounds during the first few weeks of counseling. Because two group members failed to lose any weight, the program is not terminated until every youth drops at least 7 pounds.

Cost analyses look at life skills counseling's known expenditures and its realized and expected payoffs. A program to prevent unwanted pregnancy recently cost $96 for each adolescent counseled. With government expenditures of $20,710 in medical care and welfare payments for every teenage mother, the cost-benefit ratio is 96:20710, or about 1:216, per adult pregnancy averted due to life skills counseling ("Black and white, unwed all over," 1981; Card, 1981; Hofferth and Moore, 1979). Programs to promote youths' emotional and social health can be similarly studied for their economic advantages (Costello and Hodde, 1981; Hu et al., 1981; Meyer et al., 1980). Life skills counseling certainly should not be pronounced effective just because it saves money. But in times of shrinking public and private funds no human services program will long survive unless its outcomes are reported in black ink (Goldston, 1979; Room, 1981; Rosenbaum, 1981).

Dissemination

The final task of outcome evaluation is to disseminate information on why life skills counseling was planned, how it was done, who was counseled, and what resulted from the program (Reid and Smith, 1981). To be sure, practitioners do not commonly share the fruits of their labors (Schinke, 1983a). Academics still dominate collegial communications through both oral and written media, despite Briar and Miller's (1971) exhortation a decade ago: "New theory and new techniques are of no value if such developments perish with their creators. The accumulation of knowledge is not a private effort, and a professional ethic demands that such accretions become part of the public domain" (p. 82). Eight years later, Robert A. Day observed, "A scientific experiment, no matter how spectacular the results, is not completed until the results are *published*. In fact, the cornerstone of the philosophy of science is based on the fundamental assumption that original research *must* be published; only thus can new scientific knowledge be authenticated and then added to the existing data base that we call science" (Day, 1979a, p. iv., italics in original). The present writers concur. Life skills counseling is science and ought to be regarded as such, right up to conference presentations and scholarly publications.

Professional communication cannot be cavalier, but must be planned and accorded sufficient time for the production of careful papers. Client anonymity and confidentiality are paramount. One style book provides a familiar homily for writing conservative reports: "Do not infer trends from data that fail by a small margin to meet the usual levels of significance. Such results are best interpreted as caused by chance and are best reported as such. Treat the results section like an income tax return. Take what's coming to you, but no more" (American Psychological Association, 1974, p. 19). Professionals should own up to the weak spots and limitations in their programs. Suggestions for colleagues who may initiate similar counseling programs are appropriate for rounding out life skills program descriptions. Although sharing their methods and data exposes professionals to public view, fear of scrutiny should not dissuade a full disclosure of either successful or disappointing results. Honest communication expresses accountability, adds scientific knowledge, and lets colleagues and consumers examine life skills programs and products.

CAVEATS

The approach we advocate is not a panacea for the ills of human services interventions. The vicissitudes of client practice will contraindicate life skills counseling for some milieus, and the approach's behavioral trappings may mar its reception in other circles. Unavoidable organizational hitches can doom a life skills program. Moreover, certain situations advise against needs assessment, process analysis, and outcome evaluation. Ethics, too, may constrain the blanket use and acceptance of life skills counseling. Accordingly, in the following paragraphs we will wrestle with these caveats to the life skills approach.

Milieu Limitations

Many of the myriad practice settings in which adolescents are served may not lend themselves to life skills counseling. Although residential treatment centers, most schools, and community mental health agencies are appropriate settings for life skills programs, places like crisis intervention agencies, drop-in centers, and overnight detention facilities are less logical sites for counseling. Others such as family planning agencies, probation offices, health care clinics, drug treatment centers, and neighborhood houses may be open to the approach, depending upon whether there is a population of adolescent clients who regularly attend the clinical or educational program, an organizational mission of psychosocial treatment or counseling, or an institutional staff willing to entertain new ideas.

Behavioral Methods

Borrowings from education and developmental psychology aside, life skills counseling is laced with social learning concepts. Goals that are intended to help adolescents alter their thoughts and acts suggest images of behavior modification. This term's tarnished reputation in turn may chill the welcome given a life skills program by both professionals and the general public (Buckholdt and Gubrium, 1980; Hilts, 1974; Rabichow, 1980; Watson, 1979). Half of what the media prints about behavioral interventions is inaccurate (Turkat and Feuerstein, 1978), and invidious comparisons are more the exception than the rule (Turkat and Forehand, 1980; Turkat et al., 1979). Even though frontal attacks on behavioral methods are waning, years will pass before psychosurgery, brainwashing, solitary confinement, torture, curare and emetic drugs, and other odious practices cease being called "behavior modification" (Burgess, 1963; Redd and Andersen, 1981; Risley, 1975).

The scholarly literature bears out the low status of behaviorally based interventions. Research with college students found that a film of "behavior modification" elicited more negative judgments than the same film labeled "humanistic education" (Woolfolk et al., 1977). A replication study (Woolfolk and Woolfolk, 1979) in which students were told that behavioral techniques were highly effective and should not be confused with simple conditioning resulted in a classroom demonstration being rated less favorably when couched as "behavior modification" than when presented as "humanistic education." Propaedeutic remarks "that behavior modification was really nonmechanistic, good educational practice, and that conditioning-based descriptions were really inaccurate and metaphorical" softened the harsh judgments of undergraduate students but adversely struck graduate students. The authors concluded as follows: "Possibly the statement that behavior modification is not what it has been depicted by its critics was not believed by the less naive graduate students. These students all had prior coursework in learning theory and the standard academic explanations of behavior modification. Attempting to 'soft-sell' behavior modification to relatively sophisticated groups with preexisting attitudes toward behavioral approaches may well backfire" (Woolfolk and Woolfolk, 1979, p. 577). The negative connotations of behavioral terminology spill over into business and industry. A sample of industrial psychology and organizational management trainees, for instance, saw operant techniques as evincing greater support, interest, flexibility, decision making, facilitation, efficacy, and leadership if viewed as "humanistic" than if thought of as "organizational behavior modification" (Barling and Wainstein, 1979).

In fact, behavior modification's blemishes go deeper than superficial semantics. After controlling the effects of label and content, Kazdin and Cole (1981) proved that methods "which emphasized the control and manipulation of the child's behavior via the teacher's attention, material rewards, and privileges" are pejoratively rated when contrasted with methods "which emphasized the development and expression of children's feelings and awareness." The researchers sum up: "It might be a misplaced emphasis to focus on the label of the procedures with the tacit implication that all we need to do is to relabel what we do. This is not only an oversimplification of our woes but may also be deceptive by suggesting the presentation of the proverbial old medicine in a new bottle" (Kazdin and Cole, 1981, p. 66). All told, these data caution life skills counselors to stress their cognitive and interpersonal methods and to steer clear of value-laden words. By unashamedly asserting that adolescents can shape their own lives, professionals can meet and resolve ideological opposition (Schinke, 1981c). Vitriolic and unrelenting criticism nevertheless should indicate to professionals that the time may not be right for life skills training.

Organizational Variables

A host organization's norms and regulations are cogent influences on life skills programs. Before initiating a program, prospective counselors have to assess the prevailing climate in the school, agency, or institution targeted for counseling. But the most thorough needs assessment cannot anticipate every glitch in program implementation (Reppucci, 1977). Only after counseling becomes a reality do some problems loom insurmountable. A case example is a program that failed to replace the work-for-pay system in a residential school with a token economy (Kazdin, 1977b).

> Institutional constraints have been largely responsible for our inability to change the work-for-pay program. At the top level of administration, the commissioner of the state department responsible for the training school was agreeable to our plan in theory, but he pointed out that, in practice, any changes in the allocation of work-for-pay money would require approval by the state legislature—a task outside the realm of political possibility. At the middle level of administration, the head of the business office seemed interested, but insisted that the business office could not become involved in exchanging points for money. At the bottom level, various staff who normally supervised youngsters in the work-for-pay program pointed out that they were responsible for doing work the right way and that teaching skills at the same time would impair their effectiveness and might even be dangerous. Thus, at every level there were institutional constraints that blocked any changes in the work-for-pay program. Although we eventually managed to make adjustments that prevented the work-for-pay program from competing economically with the token economy system on campus, it has not become the therapeutic and educational tool it could have been because of these institutional constraints (Reppucci and Saunders, 1974, p. 651).

Research Impositions

The reasons for needs assessment, process analysis, and outcome evaluation are not so compelling as to foist these activities on organizations and clients. As noted, certain milieus preclude any part of life skills counseling. Colleagues, even those friendly to the approach, may not hold up to its demands. It should be obvious by now that all phases of a program rise and fall at the whim of people besides counselors. Co-workers, parents, and adjunctive third parties may be disinclined to plod through needs assessment and pilot testing. Tharp and Wetzel (1969) recall their experience with preintervention data collection. "The establishment and recording of baseline rates for behaviors occurring in the natural environment proved difficult, at least as a standard procedure. There was much pressure from the environment to intervene rather than take baseline recordings. School personnel and parents would not easily tolerate observations over long periods of time if the behavior was a disturbance to them" (p.

151). Knowing that their power pales when compared to that exerted by outsiders, professionals learn to be understanding and grateful when requesting favors.

Adolescent clients may be unsuitable for a rational progression of assessment, training, and evaluation. Youths with histories of psychoses, serious delinquency, crimes against the person, suicide risk, corporal violence, anorexia nervosa, opiate addition, alcoholism, or life-threatening and destructive behavior cannot await leisurely assessment. Intervention must be immediate. Even less noxious problems such as verbal aggression, truancy, incorrigibility, chronic smoking, drinking, drug taking, and overeating warrant quick remediation. Needy adolescent clients deserve powerful techniques from the outset. Slow-acting intervention could dash youths' hopes of changing their behavior, and cause them to quit life skills counseling and shy away from finding further aid.

Process analyses could become solely the counselors' bailiwick, outcome evaluations may need to be scaled down, and professionals must have the foresight to relinquish measures that burden adolescents or mediators. In addition, research models can prove unwieldy, particularly if they require counseling to be delayed, denied or withdrawn. Many single-case models ask for more data than adolescents and collaborators design to give in routine clinical programs. Control-group research models are troublesome when professionals try to recruit young people for untreated or contrast groups. Finally, process analysis and outcome evaluation are hindered by those adolescents who do not consent to research, and those who go along with the plan but sabotage it by resisting data collection or by reporting mendacious information. Naturally, professionals' desire for client compliance does not give them license to coerce or deceive anyone about assessment, training, and evaluation (Shelton and Levy, 1981). Furthermore, research procedures must not preempt client services nor jeopardize relationships with the sponsoring organization (Rinn and Vernon, 1975; Stuart et al., 1979).

Ethics

A last set of caveats has to do with the ethical values of life skills counseling. Here, the approach shares weaknesses endemic to all psychotherapies, as unflinchingly outlined by Bergin (1980b): "An applied field, psychotherapy is directed toward practical goals that are selected in vague terms. It is even necessary when establishing criteria for measuring therapeutic change to decide, on a value basis, what changes are desirable. This necessarily requires a philosophy of human nature that guides the selection of measurements and the setting of priorities regarding change" (p. 97). Another paper by Bergin (1980a) urges professionals to throw value judgments into the public limelight. "Although there is a widespread aversion to (a) taking overt value positions and (b) justifying them, both of these must be done for the sake of clarity and honesty. It will not do for therapists to hide their prejudices behind a screen of scientific jargon. Not only do ethical clarity and honesty demand a change, but consumerism is also pressing all of us to be explicit about what we are inviting clients into, why, and with what consequences'' (Bergin, 1980a, pp. 11–12).

Even so, professionals face hard choices about the clients and foci of life skills programs. These choices arise when parents and colleagues question whether adolescents need to be taught socially responsible behavior. Lots of grown-ups expect young folks to innately be compliant, quiet, caring, punctual, amicable. In order words, adolescents should not have to be taught to act normally (O'Leary et al., 1972). Ethics also becomes an issue if adolescents do not fully fathom what life skills counseling entails, or if they have no opportunity to choose their outcome aims. In the first category are clients so impaired by age, mental capacity, or physical disability that they cannot discuss and refuse counseling (Schinke, 1981a; Schinke and Olson, 1982). The second category includes incarcerated youths, psychotic adolescents, and young people referred for culture-bound problems of hyperkinesis, acting out, homosexuality, and depression (Bieber, 1976; Davison, 1976; Halleck, 1976; Hudson, 1982; O'Leary, 1980; Stuart, 1970; Teasdale, 1979; Tennov, 1975).

SUMMARY

Implementing and evaluating life skills counseling goes beyond a professional commitment to helping adolescents solve their problems. Professionals have to exercise discipline when planning and conducting applied programs. Whether life skills counseling is necessary and, if so, what form it takes are determined through needs assessment. During this phase, professionals gather reliable information on how well the host organization addresses its stated and unstated missions. Preliminary assessment also looks at resources for life skills programs. These include potential counselors, physical amenities, funding, and equipment. Before beginning a comprehensive program, professionals test their plans for feasibility. As miniature versions of a final life skills program, pilot projects provide an opportunity for process analysis of curricula development, counseling delivery, and counseling receipt.

Tested and revised life skills counseling is ready for outcome evaluation. Professionals and young persons initially define aims for each counseling participant. These outcome aims are positively stated in specific terms in the context of time and situation. Measurement instruments tap youths' knowledge, attitudes, feelings, performance, and physiology. Measures administered in both single-case and control-group research models definitely reveal the extent of personality and behavior change. The interpretation of outcome data involves graphs, statistics, subjective estimates, and cost-benefit equations to denote the efficiency and efficacy of counseling. At the close of each program, professionals assist colleagues and the lay public by disseminating their experiences. Oral presentations and written reports convey the trials and rewards of life skills counseling.

However, there are cautions for those who intemperately apply life skills counseling. Schools, agencies, institutions, and communities where youth congregate may not choose to sponsor life skills programs. The terms and methods of behavior modification render counseling susceptible to being disparaged and undercut. Organizational variables may discourage counseling programs that impinge on youths' everyday routines, interactions, and duties. Needs assessment, process analysis, and outcome evaluation are ill-advised in some instances. Ethical considerations may complicate the development and implementation of life skills programs. This chapter has mapped life skills counseling's promises and pitfalls. Following the outlined path will bring professionals closer to their goal of teaching adolescents life skills.

References

Agras, W. S., Kazdin, A. E., and Wilson, G. T. 1979. Behavior Therapy: Toward an Applied Clinical Science. Freeman, San Francisco.

Albert, N., and Beck, A. T. 1975. Incidence of depression in early adolescence: A preliminary study. J. Youth Adolescence 4:301–307.

Alberti, R. E., and Emmons, M. L. 1970. Your Perfect Right. Impact, San Luis Obispo, CA.

Alexander, J. F., and Parsons, B. U. 1973. Short-term behavioral intervention with delinquent families: Impact on family process and recidivism. J. Abnorm. Psychol. 81:219–225.

Allport, F. H. 1924. Social Psychology. Houghton Mifflin, New York.

American Humane Association. 1978. National Analysis of Official Child Neglect and Abuse Reporting: An Executive Summary. American Humane Association, Englewood, CO.

American Psychological Association. 1974. Standards for Educational and Psychological Tests. Rev. ed. American Psychological Association, Washington, DC.

Amonker, R. G. 1980. What do teens know about the facts of life? J. School Health 50:497–502.

Anastasiow, N. J., Everett, M., O'Shaughnessy, T. E., et. al., 1978. Improving teenage attitudes toward children, child handicaps, and hospital settings: A child development curriculum for potential parents. Am. J. Orthopsych. 48:663–672.

Andrews, G., Tennant, C., Hewson, D., and Schonell, M. 1978. The relation of social factors to physical and psychiatric illness. Am. J. Epidemiol. 108:27–35.

Andrews, J., and Conley, J. 1977. Beer, pot, and shoplifting: Teenage abuses. Am. Ann. Deaf 122:557–562.

Andrus, C. H. 1964. Smoking by high school students: Failure of a campaign to persuade adolescents not to smoke. Calif. Med. 101:246–247.

Argyris, C. 1965. Explorations in interpersonal competence—I. J. Appl. Behav. Sci. 1:58–83.

Argyris, C. 1968. Conditions for competence acquisition and therapy. J. Appl. Behav. Sci. 4:147–177.

Aries, P. 1962. Centuries of Childhood. Vintage Books, New York.

Asher, S. R., Oden, S. L., and Gottman, J. M. 1977. Children's friendships in school settings. In: L. G. Katz (ed.), Current Topics in Early Childhood Education, Vol. 1. L. Erlbaum Associates, Hillsdale, NJ.

Atlas, J. W. 1978. Career planning needs of unemployed minority persons. J. Employment Counsel. 15:171–179.

Azrin, N. H., and Besalel, V. A. 1980. Job Club Counselor's Manual: A Behavioral Approach to Vocational Counseling. University Park Press, Baltimore.

Babcock, R. J., and Yeager, J. C. 1973. Coaching for the job interview. J. College Placement 33:61–64.

Bachman, J. G., Johnston, L. D., and O'Malley, P. M. 1981. Smoking, drinking, and drug use among American high school students: Correlates and trends, 1975–1979. Am. J. Public Health 71(1):59–68.

Bachman, J. G., O'Malley, P. M., and Johnston, L. D. 1978. Youth in Transition. Vol.

II: Adolescence to Adulthood—Change and Stability in the Lives of Young Men. Institute for Social Research, Ann Arbor, MI.

Baizerman, M. 1979. Preventive health programs for and with adolescents and youth. In: W. T. Hall and C. L. Young (eds.), Health and Social Needs of the Adolescent: Professional Responsibilities. Proceedings of a conference sponsored by the University of Pittsburgh Graduate School of Public Health. March, Pittsburgh, PA.

Baizerman, M., Sheehan, C., Ellison, D. L., and Schlesinger, E. R. 1974. A critique of the literature concerning pregnant adolescents, 1960–1970. J. Youth Adolescence 3:61–74.

Baldwin, W. H. 1980. Adolescent pregnancy and childbearing—Growing concerns for Americans. Popul. Bull. 31:1–37.

Baldwin, W. H. 1981a. Adolescent childbearing today and tomorrow (Updated statement prepared for U.S. Senate Human Resources Committee June 14, 1978). In: Adolescent Pregnancy and Childbearing—Rates, Trends and Research Findings from the CPR, NICHD. Center for Population Research, NICHD, DHEW, Bethesda, MD.

Baldwin, W. H. 1981b. Adolescent pregnancy and childbearing—An overview. Sem. Perinatol. 5:1–8.

Baldwin, W. H., and Cain, V. S. 1980. The children of teenage parents. Family Plan. Perspect. 12:34–43.

Bandura, A. 1969. Principles of Behavior Modification. Holt, Rinehart, & Winston, New York.

Bandura, A. 1977. Social Learning Theory. Prentice-Hall, Inc. Englewood Cliffs, NJ.

Bandura, A., and Schunk, D. H. 1981. Cultivating competence, self-efficacy, and intrinsic interest through proximal self-motivation. J. Personality Soc. Psychol. 41:586–598.

Bandura, A., and Simon, K. M. 1977. The role of proximal intentions in self-regulation of refractory behavior. Cognitive Ther. Res. 1:177–194.

Bandura, A., and Walters, R. M. 1959. Adolescent Aggression. Ronald, New York.

Barling, J., and Wainstein, T. 1979. Attitudes, labeling bias, and behavior modification in work organizations. Behav. Ther. 10:129–136.

Barlow, D. H. 1977. Behavioral assessment in clinical settings: Developing issues. In: J. D. Cone and R. P. Hawkins (eds.), Behavioral Assessment: New Directions in Clinical Psychology. Brunner/Mazel, New York.

Barnes, G. 1979. Solvent abuse: A review. Int. J. Addictions 14:1–26.

Barone, D. F., and Rinehart, J. M. 1978. Assertive training vs. group counseling for junior-high youth. Paper presented at the meeting of the Association for Advancement of Behavior Therapy, November, Chicago.

Barth, R. P., and Schinke, S. P. Handling difficult situations among pregnant and parenting adolescents. J. Soc. Serv. Res. In press.

Barth, R. P., Schinke, S. P., and Maxwell, J. S. Coping strategies of counselors and school-age mothers. J. Counsel. Psychol. In press.

Baum, A., Singer, J. E., and Baum, C. S. 1981. Stress and the environment. J. Soc. Issues 37:4–35.

Baumrind, D. 1981. Clarification concerning birthrate among teenagers. Am. Psychol. 36:528–530.

Beachy, G. M., Petersen, D. M., and Pearson, F. S. 1979. Adolescent drug use and delinquency: A research note. J. Psychedelic Drugs 11:313–316.

Beck, M., Hager, M., and Koberg, K. 1982. Telltale birth control. Newsweek April 5:33.

Becker, H. A. 1980. The Assertive Job-Hunting Survey. Meas. Eval. Guidance 13:43–48.

Becker, H. A., Brown, S. A., LaFitte, P. C., et al., 1979. Assertive Job-Hunting

Survey. Career Choice Information Center, University of Texas at Austin, Austin, TX.

Beere, C. A. 1979. Women and Women's Issues: A Handbook of Tests and Measures. Jossey-Bass, San Francisco.

Bell, L. G., and Bell, D. C. 1982. Family climate and the role of the female adolescent: Determinants of adolescent functioning. Family Relations 31:519–527.

Bellack, A. S. 1979a. A critical appraisal of strategies for assessing social skill. Behav. Assess. 1:157–176.

Bellack, A. S. 1979b. Behavioral assessment of social skills. In: A. S. Bellack and M. Hersen (eds.), Research and Practice in Social Skills Training. Plenum Publishing, New York.

Bellack, A. S., and Hersen, M. 1978. Assessment and single-case research. In: M. Hersen and A. S. Bellack (eds.), Behavior Therapy in the Psychiatric Setting. Williams & Wilkins, Baltimore.

Bellack, A. S., and Hersen, M. (eds.). 1979. Research and Practice in Social Skills Training. Plenum Publishing, New York.

Bellack, A. S., Hersen, M., and Lamparski, D. 1979. Role play tests for assessing social skills: Are they valid? Are they useful? J. Consult. Clin. Psychol. 47:335–342.

Belmont, L., Stein, Z., and Zybert, P. 1978. Child spacing and birth order: Effect on intellectual ability in two-child families. Science 202:995–996.

Benson, H. 1976. The Relaxation Response. Avon Books, New York.

Bentler, P. M., Lettieri, D. J., and Austin, G. A. 1976. Data Analysis Strategies and Designs for Substance Abuse Research. National Institute on Drug Abuse, Rockville, MD.

Berenson, G. S., McMahan, C. A., Voors, A. W., and Associates. 1980. Cardiovascular Risk Factors in Children—The Early Natural History of Atherosclerosis and Essential Hypertension. Oxford University Press, New York.

Bergin, A. E. 1980a. Behavior therapy and ethical relativism: Time for clarity. J. Consult. Clin. Psychol. 48:11–13.

Bergin, A. E. 1980b. Psychotherapy and religious values. J. Consult. Clin. Psychol. 48:95–105.

Bergland, B. W., and Lundquist, G. W. 1975. The vocational exploration group and minority youth: An experimental outcome study. J. Vocational Behav. 7:289–296.

Berlin, S. B. 1981. Women and self-criticism. In: S. P. Schinke (ed.), Behavioral Methods in Social Welfare. Aldine Publishing, Hawthorne, NY.

Bermant, G., Kelman, H. C., and Warwick, D. P. (eds.). 1978. The Ethics of Social Intervention. Hemisphere, New York.

Berndt, T. J. 1978. Developmental changes in conformity to peers and parents. Paper presented at the Annual Meeting of the American Psychological Association, August, Toronto.

Bernstein, D. A., and Borkovec, T. D. 1973. Progressive Relaxation Training: A Manual for the Helping Professions. Research Press, Champaign, IL.

Berzonsky, M. D. 1981. Adolescent Development. Macmillan Publishing, New York.

Bevan, W. 1976. The sound of the wind that's blowing. Am. Psychol. 31:481–491.

Biddle, B. J., Bank, B. J., and Marlin, M. J. 1980. Social determinants of adolescent drinking: What they think, what they do, and what I think and do. J. Stud. Alcohol 41:215–241.

Bieber, I. 1976. A discussion of ''Homosexuality: The Ethical Challenge.'' J. Consult. Clin. Psychol. 44:163–166.

Bienvenu, M. 1969. Measurement of parent-adolescent communication. Family Coord. 18:117–121.

Black and white, unwed all over. 1981. Time 118(19):67.

Blanchard, E. B., and Epstein, L. H. 1977. The clinical usefulness of biofeedback. In: M. Hersen, R. M. Eisler, and P. M. Miller (eds.), Progress in Behavior Modification, Vol. 4. Academic Press, New York.

Blanchard, E. B., and Epstein, L. H. 1978. A Biofeedback Primer. Addison-Wesley Publishing Co., Reading, MA.

Blechman, E. A. 1975. Family Contract, A Game for Adolescents To Play with Parents or Teachers. (Available from E. A. Blechman, 62 Yankee Peddler Path, P.O. Box 389, Madison, CT 06443).

Blechman, E. A. 1978. Solutions, A Game for School-age Children To Play with Parents or Teachers. (Available from E. A. Blechman, 62 Yankee Peddler Path, P.O. Box 389, Madison, CT 06443).

Blechman, E. A. 1980. Family problem-solving training. Am. J. Family Ther. 8:3–22.

Blechman, E. A. 1981. Competence, depression, and behavior modification with women. In: M. Herson, R. M. Eisler, and P. M. Miller (eds.), Progress in Behavior Modification, Vol. 12. Academic Press, New York.

Blechman, E. A., Kotanchik, N. L., and Taylor, C. J. 1981. Families and schools together: Early behavioral intervention with high-risk students. Behav. Ther. 12:308–319.

Blechman, E. A., Taylor, C. J., and Schrader, S. M. 1981. Family problem solving vs. home notes as early intervention with high-risk children. J. Consult. Clin. Psychol. 49:919–926.

Bloch, D. 1974. Sex education practices of mothers. J. Sex Educ. Ther. 7:7–12.

Block, R. W., and Block, S. A. 1980. Outreach education: A possible prevention of teenage pregnancy. Adolescence 15:658–660.

Bloom, M., and Fischer, J. 1982. Evaluating Practice: Guidelines for the Accountable Professional. Prentice-Hall, Englewood Cliffs, NJ.

Blythe, B. J., Gilchrist, L. D., and Schinke, S. P. 1981. Pregnancy-prevention groups for adolescents. Soc. Work 26:503–504.

Boisvert, M. J., and Wells, R. 1980. Toward a rational policy on status offenders. Soc. Work 25:230–234.

Bolles, R. N. 1978. The Three Boxes of Life and How To Get Out of Them. Ten Speed Press, Berkeley, CA.

Bolles, R. N. 1980. What Color is Your Parachute? Ten Speed Press, Berkeley, CA.

Bolstad, O. D., and Johnson, S. M. 1977. The relationship between teachers' assessment of students and the students' actual behavior in the classroom. Child Devel. 48:570–578.

Bongaards, J. 1980. Does malnutrition effect fecundity? A summary of evidence. Science 208:564–569.

Borker, S. R., Loughlin, J., and Rudolph, C. S. 1979. The long-term effects of adolescent childrearing: A retrospective analysis. J. Soc. Serv. Res. 2:341–355.

Bornstein, M. R., Bellack, A. S., and Hersen, M. 1977. Social-skills training for unassertive children: A multiple-baseline analysis. J. Appl. Behav. Anal. 10:183–195.

Bornstein, M., Bellack, A. S., and Hersen, M. 1980. Social skills training for highly aggressive children. Behav. Modif. 4:173–186.

Bostwick, B. E. 1980. Resume Writing: A Comprehensive How-To-Do-It Guide. 2nd Ed. John Wiley & Sons, Somerset, NJ.

Bostwick, B. E. 1981. 111 Proven Techniques and Strategies for Getting the Job Interview. John Wiley & Sons, Somerset, NJ.

Bower, R. T., and de Gasparis, P. 1978. Ethics in Social Research. Prager Publishers, New York.

Bradshaw, P. W. 1973. The problem of cigarette smoking and its control. Int. J. Addictions 8:353–371.

Branden, N. 1983. If You Could Hear What I Cannot Say: Learning To Communicate with the Ones You Love. Bantam Books, New York.

Braukmann, C. J., and Fixsen, D. L. 1979. Behavior modification with delinquents. In: M. Hersen, R. M. Eisler, and P. M. Miller (eds.), Progress in Behavior Modification, Vol. 1. Academic Press, New York.

Braukmann, C. J., Wolf, M. M., Maloney, D. M., et al. 1975. An analysis of a selection interview training package for predelinquents at Achievement Place. Crim. Justice Behav. 1:30–42.

Briar, S., and Miller, H. 1971. Problems and Issues in Social Casework. Columbia University Press, New York.

Bronfenbrenner, U. 1970. Two Worlds of Childhood: U.S. and U.S.S.R. New Russell Sage Foundation, New York.

Brown, B. B. 1982. The extent and effects of peer pressure among high school students: A retrospective analysis. J. Youth Adolescence 11:121–133.

Brown, L. (ed.) 1981. Sex Education in the Eighties: The Challenge of Healthy Sexual Evolution. Plenum Publishing, New York.

Brown, M. E. 1979. Teenage prostitution. Adolescence 14:665–680.

Brunig, J. L., and Kintz, B. C. 1977. Computational Handbook of Statistics. 2nd Ed. Scott, Foresman & Co., Glenview, IL.

Brunson, B. I., and Matthews, K. A. 1981. The Type A coronary-prone behavior pattern and reactions to uncontrollable stress: An analysis of performance strategies, affect, and attributions during failure. J. Personality Soc. Psychol. 40:906–918.

Bry, H. H. 1978. Research design in drug abuse prevention: Review and recommendations. Int. J. Addictions 13:1157–1168.

Buckholdt, D. R., and Gubrium, J. F. 1980. The underlife of behavior modification. Am. J. Orthopsych. 50:279–290.

Budd, K. S., and Baer, D. M. 1976. Behavior modification and the law: Implications of recent judicial decisions. J. Psych. Law 4:171–244.

Buehler, R. E., Patterson, G. R., and Furniss, J. M. 1966. The reinforcement of behavior in institutional settings. Behav. Res. Ther. 4:157–167.

Bureau of the Census, United States Department of Commerce. 1978. Statistical abstract of the United States: 1978. U.S. Government Printing Office, Washington, DC.

Bureau of Labor Statistics, U.S. Department of Labor. 1980b. Profile of the Teenage Worker: Bulletin 2039. U.S. Government Printing Office, Washington, DC.

Burgess, A. 1963. A Clockwork Orange. W. W. Norton, New York.

Burnham, D. 1982. Induced terminations of pregnancy: Reporting states, 1979. NCHS Monthly Vital Stat. Rep. 7:1–36.

Buros, O. K. (ed.). 1978. The Eighth Mental Measurements Yearbook, Vols. 1 and 2. Gryphon, Highland, Park, NJ.

Butler, L., and Meichenbaum, D. 1981. The assessment of interpersonal problem-solving skills. In: P. C. Kendall and S. D. Hollon (eds.), Assessment Strategies for Cognitive-behavioral Interventions. Academic Press, New York.

Cacioppo, J. T., Glass, C. R., and Merluzzi, T. V. 1979. Self-statements and self-evaluations: A cognitive-response analysis of social anxiety. Cognit. Ther. Res. 3:249–262.

Caghan, S. B. 1975. The adolescent process and the problem of nutrition. Am. J. Nursing 75:1728–1731.

Califano, J. A. 1978. Keynote Address: Conference on Adolescent Behavior and Health, Summary. National Academy of Sciences, Washington, DC.

Cammaert, L. P., and Larsen, C. C. 1979. A Woman's Choice: A Guide to Decision Making. Research Press, Champaign, IL.

Campbell, B. K., and Barnlund, D. C. 1977. Communication patterns and problems of pregnancy. Am. J. Orthopsych. 47:134–139.

Cantwell, D. P., and Carlson, G. A. 1978. Stimulants. In: J. S. Werry (ed.), Pediatric Psychopharmacology: The Use of Behavior Modifying Drugs in Children. Brunner/Mazel, New York.

Card, J. J. 1981. Long-term consequences for children of teenage parents. Demography 18:137–157.

Center for Disease Control, United States Department of Health, Education, and Welfare. 1977. VD Statistical Letter, May, 1977. U.S. Government Printing Office, Washington, DC.

Center for Multicultural Awareness. 1981. A Guide to Multicultural Drug Abuse Prevention: Evaluation, Vol. 6. Department of Health and Human Services, Rockville, MD.

Chamie, M., Eisman, S., Forrest, J. D., et al. 1982. Factors affecting adolescents' use of family planning clinics. Family Plan. Perspect. 14:126–139.

Change in DHHS Leadership. 1983. Washington Memo January 19. (The Alan Guttmacher Institute, Washington, DC).

Cherry, V. P. 1980. Teen pregnancy: Prevention strategies. Focus Women 1:153–162.

Chesler, J. 1980. Twenty-seven strategies for teaching contraception to adolescents. J. School Health 50:18–21.

Chiauzzi, E., Heimberg, R. G., and Doty, D. 1982. Task analysis of assertive behavior revisited: The role of situational variables with female college students. Behav. Counsel. Q. 2:42–50.

Chilman, C. S. 1979. Teenage pregnancy: A research review. Soc. Work 24:492–498.

Chng, C. L. 1980 Adolescent homosexual behavior and the health educator. J. School Health 50:517–521.

Chun, K. T., Cobb, S., and French, Jr., J. R. P. 1975. Measures for Psychological Assessment: A Guide to 3,000 Original Sources and Their Applications. University of Michigan Institute for Social Research, Survey Research Center, Ann Arbor.

Ciminero, A. R. 1977. Behavioral assessment: An overview. In: A. R. Ciminero, K. S. Calhoun, and H. E. Adams (eds.), Handbook of Behavioral Assessment. Wiley, New York.

Ciminero, A. R., Calhoun, K. S., and Adams, H. E. (eds.). 1977. Handbook of Behavioral Assessment. Wiley, New York.

Clapp, D. F., and Raab, R. S. 1978. Follow-up of unmarried adolescent mothers. Soc. Work 23:149–153.

Clayton, R. C. 1979. The family and federal drug abuse policies—programs: Toward making the invisible family visible. J. Marriage Family 41:637–647.

Clemson, E. 1981. Disadvantaged youth: A study of sex differences in occupational stereotypes and vocational aspirations. Youth Society 13:39–56.

Clowers, M. R., and Fraser, R. T. 1977. Employment interview literature: A perspective for the counselor. Vocational Guidance Quarterly 26:13–26.

Coates, T. J., Jeffery, R. W., and Slinkard, L. A. 1981. Heart healthy eating and exercise: Introducing and maintaining changes in health behaviors. Am. J. Public Health 71:15–23.

Cobb, S. 1976. Social support as a moderator of life stresses. Psychomat. Med. 38:300–319.

Coelho, G. V. 1980. Environmental stress and adolescent coping behavior: Key ecological factors in college student adaptation. In: I. G. Sarason and C. D. Spielberger (eds.), Stress and Anxiety, Vol 7. Hemisphere, Washington, DC.

Cohen, F., and Lazarus, R. S. 1979. Coping with the stresses of illness. In: G. C. Stone, F. Cohen, N. Adler, and Associates, Health Psychology—A Handbook. Jossey-Bass, San Francisco.

Cohen, S. J. 1982. Helping parents to become the "potent force" in combating and preventing the drug problem. J. Drug Educ. 12:341–344.

Cohen-Sandler, R., Berman, A. L., and King, R. A. 1982. Life stress and symptomatology: Determinants of suicidal behavior in children. J. Am. Acad. Child Psych. 21:178–186.

Coleman, J. C. 1979. Who leads who astray? Causes of anti-social behavior in adolescents. J. Adolescence 2:179–185.

Combs, M. L., and Slaby, D. A. 1977. Social-skills training with children. In: B. B. Lahey and A. E. Kazdin (eds.), Advances in Clinical Child Psychology, Vol. 1. Plenum Publishing, New York.

Cone, J. D. 1979. Confounded comparisons in triple response mode assessment research. Behav. Assess. 1:85–95.

Cone, J. D., and Hawkins, R. P. (eds.). 1977a. Behavioral Assessment: New Directions in Clinical Psychology. Brunner/Mazel, New York.

Cone, J. D., and Hawkins, R. P. 1977b. Current status and future directions in behavioral assessment. In: J. D. Cone and R. P. Hawkins (eds.), Behavioral Assessment: New Directions in Clinical Psychology. Brunner/Mazel, New York.

Connor, J. M., Dann, L. N., and Twentyman, C. T. 1982. A self-report measure of assertiveness in young adolescents. J. Clin. Psychol. 38:101–106.

Cook, T. D., Cook, F. L., and Mark, M. M. 1977. Randomization and quasi-experimental designs in evaluation research. In: L. Rutman (ed.), Evaluation Research Methods: A Basic Guide. Sage, Beverly Hills, CA.

Coombs, R., Fry, L., and Lewis, P. 1976. Socialization in Drug Abuse. Shankman, Cambridge, MA.

Cordrey, S. U. 1979. Nutritional needs during adolescence. In: W. T. Hall and C. L. Young (eds.), Health and Social Needs of the Adolescent: Professional Responsibilities. Proceedings of a conference sponsored by the University of Pittsburgh Graduate School of Public Health. March, Pittsburgh, PA.

Costello, R. M., and Hodde, J. E. 1981. Costs of comprehensive alcoholism care for 100 patients over 4 years. J. Stud. Alcohol 42:87–93.

Cowen, E. L. 1977. Baby-steps toward primary prevention. Am. J. Commun. Psychol. 5:1–22.

Cowen, E. L., Pederson, A., Babigian, H., et al. 1973. Long-term follow-up of early detected vulnerable children. J. Consult. Clin. Psychol. 41:438–446.

Cox, R. D., Gunn, W. B., and Cox, M. J. 1976. A film assessment and comparison of the social skillfulness of behavior problem and non-problem male children. Paper presented at the meeting of the Association for Advancement of Behavior Therapy, December, New York.

Coyne, J. C., Aldwin, C., and Lazarus, R. S. 1981. Depression and coping in stressful episodes. J. Abnorm. Psychol. 90:439–447.

Crosbie, P. V., and Bitte, D. 1982. Taking chances: A test of Luker's theory of contraceptive risk-taking. Studies Family Plan. 13:67–78.

Crystal, J. C., and Bolles, R. N. 1974. Where Do I Go from Here with My Life? Ten Speed Press, Berkeley, CA.

Curran, J. P. 1979a. Pandora's box reopened? The assessment of social skills. J. Behav. Assess. 1:55–71.

Curran, J. P. 1979b. Social skills: Methodological issues and future directions. In: A. S.

Bellack and M. Hersen (eds.), Research and Practice in Social Skills Training. Plenum Publishing, New York.

Curran, J. P., and Mariotto, M. J. 1980. A conceptual structure for the assessment of social skills. In: M. Hersen, R. M. Eisler, and P. M. Miller (eds.), Progress in Behavior Modification, Vol. 10. Academic Press, New York.

Cvetkovich, G., and Grote, B. 1979a. Psychosocial maturity, ego identity and fertility-related behavior. Paper presented at the American Psychological Association meeting, September, New York.

Cvetkovich, G., and Grote, B. 1979b. Male teenagers—Sexual debut, psychosocial development and contraceptive use. Paper presented at the American Psychological Association meeting, September, New York.

Cvetkovich, G., and Grote, B. 1980. Psychosocial development and the social problems of teenage illegitimacy. In: C. S. Chilman (ed.), Adolescent Pregnancy and Childbearing: Findings from Research, NIH Publication No. 81–2077. U.S. Government Printing Office, Washington, DC.

Cvetkovich, G., and Grote, B. 1981. Psychosocial maturity and teenage contraceptive use: An investigation of decision-making and communication skills. Popul. Envir. 4:211–226.

Cvetkovich, G., Grote, B., Bjorseth, A., and Sarkissian, J. 1975. On the psychology of adolescents' use of contraceptives. J. Sex Res. 11:256–270.

Cvetkovich, G., Grote, B., Lieberman, E. S., and Miller, W. 1978. Sex role development and teenage fertility-related behavior. Adolescence 8:231–236.

Dana, R. H. (ed.). 1981. Human Services for Cultural Minorities. University Park Press, Baltimore.

Davis, M. H. 1983. Measuring individual differences in empathy: Evidence for a multidimensional approach. J. Personality Soc. Psychol. 44:113–126.

Davison, G. C. 1976. Homosexuality: The ethical challenge. J. Consult. Clin. Psychol. 44:157–162.

Day, R. A. 1979a. How to Write and Publish a Scientific Paper. ISI Press, Philadelphia.

Day, W. R. 1979b. Multimethod Clinical Assessment. Gardner Press, New York.

Dayton, C. W. 1978. The dimensions of youth employment. J. Employment Counsel. 4:3–27.

Dayton, C. W. 1981. The young person's job search: Insights from a study. J. Counsel. Psychol. 28:321–333.

DeAmicis, L. A., Klorman, R., Hess, D. W., and McAnarney, E. R. 1981. A comparison of unwed pregnant teenagers and nulligravid sexually active adolescents seeking contraception. Adolescence 16:11–20.

Dembo, M. H., and Lundell, B. 1979. Factors affecting adolescent contraception practices: Implications for sex education. Adolescence 14:657–664.

DiCaprio, N. S. 1980. Adjustment: Fulfilling Human Potentials. Prentice-Hall, Inc., Englewood Cliffs, NJ.

Dickie, J. R., and Gerber, S. C. 1980. Training in social competence: The effect on mothers, fathers, and infants. Child Devel. 51:1248–1251.

Dickinson, N., and Bremseth, M. 1979. Assessing the Training Needs of Child Welfare Workers: A Self-Help Manual for Trainers of Child Welfare Staff. University of Tennessee, Knoxville.

Diener, E., and Crandall, R. 1978. Ethics in Social and Behavioral Research. University of Chicago Press, Chicago.

Dillard, K. D., and Pol, L. G. 1982. The individual economic costs of teenage childbearing. Family Relations 31:249–259.

Dipboye, R. L., and Wiley, J. W. 1978. Reactions of male raters to interviewee self-presentation style and sex: Extensions of previous research. J. Vocational Behav. 13:192–203.

Dodd, J. 1981. The youth unemployment dilemma. Personnel J. 60:362–366.

Dollard, J., and Miller, N. E. 1950. Personality and Psychotherapy. McGraw-Hill, New York.

Douvan, E., and Adelson, J. 1966. The Adolescent Experience. Wiley, New York.

Dryfoos, J. G. 1982. Contraceptive use, pregnancy intentions and pregnancy outcomes among U.S. women. Family Plan. Perspect. 14:81–94.

Dryfoos, J. G., and Heisler, T. 1978. Contraceptive services for adolescents: An overview. Family Plan. Perspect. 10:223–233.

DuVal, Jr., B. S. 1979. The human subjects protection committee: An experiment in decentralized Federal regulation. Am. Bar Found. Res. J. 3:571–688.

Dunnette, M. D., and Bass, B. M. 1963. Behavioral scientists and personnel management. Industrial Relations 2:115–130.

Dworkin, R. J., and Poindexter, A. N. 1980. Pregnant low-income teenagers: A social structural model of the determinants of abortion-seeking behavior. Youth Society 11:295–309.

D'Zurilla, T. J., and Goldfried, M. R. 1971. Problem-solving and behavior modification. J. Abnorm. Psychol. 78:107–126.

D'Zurilla, T. J., and Nezu, A. 1982. Social problem solving in adults. In: P. C. Kendall (ed.), Advances in Cognitive-Behavioral Research and Therapy, Vol. 1. Academic Press, New York.

Earls, F., and Siegel, B. 1980. Precocious fathers. Am. J. Orthopsych. 50:469–480.

Ebaugh, H. R. F., and Haney, C. A. 1980. Shifts in abortion attitudes: 1972–1978. J. Marriage Family 42:491–499.

Eckard, E. 1982. Contraceptive use patterns, prior source, and pregnancy history of female family planning patients: United States, 1980. In: Advance Data From Vital and Health Statistics. No. 82 (DHHS Pub. No. (PHS) 82–1250). National Center for Health Statistics, June 16, Hyattsville, MD.

Edwards, D. W., and Kelly, J. G. 1980. Coping and adaptation: A longitudinal study. Am. J. Commun. Psychol. 8:203–215.

Edwards, L. E., Steinman, M. E., Arnold, K. A., and Hakanson, E. Y. 1980. Adolescent pregnancy prevention services in high school clinics. Family Plan. Perspect. 12:6–14.

Egger, D., Makovsky, E., and Merrill, C. 1980. Why Weight: An Adolescent Weight Control Program. University of Colorado Health Sciences Center, Denver, CO.

Eisler, R. M. 1976. The behavioral assessment of social skills. In: M. Hersen and A. S. Bellack (eds.), Behavioral Assessment: A Practical Handbook. Pergamon Press, New York.

Elashoff, J. D., and Thoresen, C. E. 1978. Choosing a statistical method for analysis of an intensive experiment. In: T. Kratochwill (ed.), Single Subject Research: Strategies for Evaluating Change. Academic Press, New York.

Elder, Jr., G. H. 1975. Adolescence in the life cycle: An introduction. In: S. E. Dragastin and G. H. Elder (eds.), Adolescence in the Life Cycle. Wiley, New York.

Elder, J. P., Edelstein, B. A., and Narwick, M. M. 1979. Adolescent psychiatric patients: Modifying aggressive behavior with social skills training. Behav. Modification 3:161–178.

Elkind, D. 1967. Egocentrism in adolescence. Child Development 38:1025–1034.

Elkind, D. 1968. Adolescent cognitive development. In: J. F. Adams (ed.), Understanding Adolescence. Allyn & Bacon, Boston.

Elkind, D. 1981. The Hurried Child, Growing Up Too Fast, Too Soon. Addison-Wesley, Reading, MA.

Elkind, D. and Bowen, R. 1979. Imaginary audience behavior in children and adolescents. Devel. Psycho. 15:38–44.

Elliott, G. R., and Eisdorfer, C. (eds.). 1982. Stress and Human Health: Analysis and Implications of Research. Springer, New York.

Ellis, A., and Harper, R. A. 1975. A New Guide to Rational Living. Prentice-Hall, Englewood Cliffs, NJ.

Ensminger, M. E., Brown, C. H., and Kellam, S. G. 1982. Sex differences in antecedents of substance use among adolescents. J. Soc. Issues 38:25–42.

Epstein, I., and Tripodi, T. 1977. Research Techniques for Program Planning, Monitoring, and Evaluation. Columbia University Press, New York.

Erikson, E. H. 1968. Identity: Youth and Crisis. W. W. Norton, New York.

Evans, R. I. 1976. Smoking in children: Developing a social psychological strategy of deterrence. J. Prevent. Med. 5:122–127.

Evans, R. I. 1979. Smoking in children and adolescents: Psychosocial determinants and prevention strategies. In: Smoking and Health: A Report of the Surgeon General. U.S. Department of Health, Education and Welfare, Washington, DC.

Evans, R. I., Rozelle, R. M., Mittelmark, M. B., et al. 1978. Deterring the onset of smoking in children: Knowledge of immediate physiological effects and coping with peer pressure, media pressure, and parent modeling J. Appl. Soc. Psychol. 8:126–135.

Everly, Jr., G. S., Rosenfeld, R., and Associates. 1981. The Nature and Treatment of the Stress Response: A Practical Guide for Clinicians. Plenum Publishing, New York.

Family planning funds hit. 1981. Seattle Post-Intell. April 1:A4.

Farmer, H. S. 1983. Career and homemaking plans for high school youth. J. Counsel. Psychol. 30:40–45.

Farquhar, J. W. 1978. The American Way of Life Need Not Be Hazardous to Your Health. W. W. Norton, New York.

Fawcett, S. B., Seekins, T., and Braukmann, C. J. 1981. Developing and transferring behavioral technologies for children and youth. Chil. Youth Serv. Rev. 3:319–342.

Feindler, E. L., and Fremouw, W. J. 1983. Stress inoculation training for adolescent anger problems. In: D. Meichenbaum and M. E. Jaremko (eds.), Stress Reduction and Prevention. Plenum Publishing, New York.

Feinstein, S. C., Giovacchini, P. L., Looney, J. G., et al. (eds.). 1980. Adolescent Psychiatry: Developmental and Clinical Studies. University of Chicago Press, Chicago.

Feldman, H. W., Agar, M. H., and Beschner, G. M. 1979. Angel Dust. Lexington Books, Lexington, MA.

Ferner, J. D. 1980. Successful Time Management. John Wiley & Sons, New York.

Fielder, P. E., Orenstein, H., Chiles, J., et al. 1979. Effects of assertive training on hospitalized adolescents and young adults. Adolescence 14:524–528.

Filipczak, J., Archer, M. B., Neale, M. S., and Winett, R. A. 1979. Issues in multivariate assessment of a large-scale behavioral program. J. Appl. Behav. Anal. 12:593–613.

Fine, J. 1980. Planning and Assessing Agency Training. U.S. Department of Health, Education, and Welfare, Washington, DC.

Finkelstein, J. W. Finkelstein, J. A., Christie, M., et al. 1982. Teenage pregnancy and parenthood: Outcomes for mother and child. J. Adolescent Health Care 3:1–7.

Finn, P. 1979. Teenage drunkenness: Warning signal, transient boisterousness, or symptom of social change? Adolescence 14(56):819–834.

Finn, P., and O'Gorman, P. A. 1981. Teaching About Alcohol: Concepts, Methods, and Classroom Activities. Allyn & Bacon, Boston.

Fishbein, M. 1977. Consumer beliefs and behavior with respect to cigarette smoking: A critical analysis of the public literature. Unpublished report, Federal Trade Commission, Washington, DC.

Fishburne, P. M., Abelson, H. I., and Cisin, I. 1979. National Survey on Drug Abuse: Main Findings, 1979. National Institute on Drug Abuse, Rockville, MD.

Fisher, D. A., and Magnus, P. 1981. "Out of the mouths of babes . . ." The opinions of 10 and 11 year old children regarding the advertising of cigarettes. Commun. Health Stud. 5:22–26.

Fixsen, D. L., Wolf, M. M., and Phillips, E. L. 1973. Achievement Place: A teaching family model of community-based group homes for youth in trouble. In: L. A. Hammerlynck, L. C. Handy, and E. J. Mash (eds.), Behavior Change: Methodology, Concepts, and Practice. Research Press, Champaign, IL.

Flay, B. R., d'Avernas, J. R., Best, J. A., et al. 1981. Cigarette smoking: Why young people do it and ways of preventing it. In: P. Firestone and P. McGrath (eds.), Pediatric Behavioral Medicine. Springer Verlag, New York.

Flowers, J. V., and Booraem, C. D. 1980. Simulation and role playing methods. In: F. H. Kanfer and A. P. Goldstein (eds.), Helping People Change: A Textbook of Methods. 2nd Ed. Pergamon Press, New York.

Folkman, S., and Lazarus, R. S. 1980. An analysis of coping in a middle-aged community sample. J. Health Soc. Behav. 21:219–239.

Forrest, J. D., Sullivan, E., and Tietze, C. 1979. Abortion in the United States, 1977–1978. Family Plan. Perspect. 11:329–341.

Foster, J. 1981. Family planning visits by teenagers: United States, 1978. Vital Health Stat. 13:1–24.

Foster, S. C., and Ritchey, W. L. 1979. Issues in the assessment of social competence in children. J. Appl. Behav. Anal. 12:625–638.

Foster, S. L., and Cone, J. D. 1980. Current issues in direct observation. Behav. Assess. 2:313–338.

Fox, G. L. 1980. The mother-adolescent daughter relationship as socialization structure: A research review. Family Relations 29:21–28.

Fox, G. L., and Inazu, J. K. 1982. The influence of mother's marital history on the mother-daughter relationship in black and white households. J. Marriage Family 44:143–152.

Francome, C. 1980. Abortion policy in Britain and the United States. Soc. Work 25:5–9.

Freedman, B., Rosenthal, L., Donahoe, Jr., C. P., et al. 1978. A social-behavioral analysis of skill deficits in delinquent and nondelinquent adolescent boys. J. Consult Clin. Psychol. 46:1448–1462.

French, W. A. 1981. National Research Report on Shoplifting, 1980–1981. National Coalition to Prevent Shoplifting, Atlanta.

Freud, A. 1958. Adolescence. In: R. S. Eissler, A. Freud, H. Hartmann, and M. Kris (eds.), The Psychoanalytic Study of the Child, Vol. 13. International Universities Press, New York.

Friedman, M., and Rosenman, R. H. 1974. Type A Behavior and Your Heart. Fawcett Crest, New York.

Frieze, I. H., Parsons, J. E., Johnson, P. B., et al. 1978. Women and Sex Roles, A Social Psychological Perspective. W.W. Norton, New York.

Furman, W., and Drabman, R. S. 1981. Methodological issues in child behavior therapy. In: M. Hersen, R. M. Eisler, and P. M. Miller (eds.), Progress in Behavior

Modification, Vol. II. Academic Press, New York.

Gad, M. T., and Johnson, J. H. 1980. Correlates of adolescent life stress as related to race, SES, and levels of perceived social support. J. Clin. Child Psychol. 9:13–16.

Galassi, J. P., and Galassi, M. D. 1978. Preparing individuals for job interviews: Suggestions from more than 60 years of research. Personnel Guidance J. 57:188–192.

Gallup, G. 1978. Epidemic of teenage pregnancies: Growing numbers of Americans favor discussion of sex in classrooms. Gallup Poll. January 23.

Gambrill, E., and Richey, C. 1975. An assertion inventory for use in assessment and research. Behav. Ther. 6:550–561.

Gambrill, E., and Richey, C. 1976. It's Up to You: Developing Assertive Social Skills. Les Femmes, Millbrae, CA.

Gardner, D. C., Beatty, G. J., and Bigelow, E. A. 1981. Locus of control and career maturity: A pilot evaluation of a life-planning and career development program for high school students. Adolescence 16:587–592.

Gelman, D., Weathers, D., Whitman, L., et al. 1980. The games teen-agers play. Newsweek September 1:48–53.

Gentry, M. E. 1978. Tape recording group sessions: A practical research strategy. Soc. Work Groups 1:95–101.

Gerrard, M. 1982. Sex, sex guilt, and contraceptive use. J. Personality Soc. Psychol. 42:153–158.

Gibbs, J. T. 1981. Depression and suicidal behavior among delinquent females. J. Youth Adolescence 10:159–167.

Gilchrist, L. D. 1981a. Group procedures for helping adolescents cope with sex. Behav. Group Ther. 3:3–8.

Gilchrist, L. D. 1981b. Group interpersonal-skills training with adolescents. In: S. P. Schinke (ed.), Behavioral Methods in Social Welfare. Aldine Publishing, Hawthorne, NY.

Gilchrist, L. D., and Schinke, S. P. Coping with contraception: Cognitive and behavioral methods with adolescents. Cognit. Ther. Res. In press.

Gilchrist, L. D., and Schinke, S. P. 1983a. Counseling with adolescents about their sexuality. In: C. S. Chilman (ed.), Adolescent Sexuality In a Changing American Society. Wiley, New York.

Gilchrist, L. D., and Schinke, S. P. 1983b. Teenage pregnancy and public policy. Soc. Serv. Rev. 57:307–322.

Gilchrist, L. D., Schinke, S. P., and Blythe, B. J. 1979. Primary prevention services for children and youth. Children Youth Serv. Rev. 1:379–391.

Gilchrist, L. D., Schinke, S. P., Blythe, B. J., and Renggli, A. J. Prevention and health promotion services for adolescents: The validation of a model. In: J. R. Anderson (ed.), Social Work in Health Care: Fission or Fusion? University of Washington, Seattle. In press.

Gingerich, W. J., Kleczewski, M., and Kirk, S. A. 1982. Name-calling in social work. Soc. Serv. Rev. 56:366–374.

Ginsberg, B. G. 1979. Parent-adolescent relationship development program. In: B. G. Guerney, Jr., (ed.), Relationship Enhancement. Jossey-Bass, San Francisco.

Gladwin, T. 1967. Social competence and clinical practice. Psychiatry 30:30–43.

Glass, C. R., and Arnkoff, D. B. 1982. Think cognitively: Selected issues in cognitive assessment and therapy. In: P. C. Kendall (ed.), Advances in Cognitive-Behavioral Research and Therapy, Vol. 1. Academic Press, New York.

Glass, C. R., Merluzzi, T. V., Biever, J. L., and Larsen, K. H. 1982. Cognitive assessment of social anxiety: Development and validation of a self-statement questionnaire. Cognit. Ther. Res. 6:37–55.

Glass, D. C. 1977. Behavior Patterns, Stress, and Coronary Disease. Erlbaum, Hillsdale, NJ.

Glass, G. V., Willson, V. L., and Gottman, J. M. 1975. Design and Analysis of Time-series Experiments. Colorado Associated University Press, Boulder, CO.

Glenwick, D. S., and Barocas, R. 1979. Training impulsive children in verbal self-control by use of natural change agents. J. Special Educ. 13:387–398.

Glenwick, D. S., Croft, R. G. F., Barocas, R., and Black, H. K. 1979. Reflection-impulsivity in predelinquent preadolescents in a residential facility. Crim. Justice Behav. 6:34–40.

Goldfarb, J. L., Mumford, D. M., Schum, D. A., et al. 1977. An attempt to detect "pregnancy susceptibility" in indigent adolescent girls. J. Youth Adolescence 6:127–143.

Goldfried, M. R. 1979. Behavioral assessment: Where do we go from here? Behav. Assess. 1:19–22.

Goldfried, M. R., and Davison, G. 1976. Clinical Behavior Therapy. Holt, Rinehart, & Winston, New York.

Goldfried, M. R., and D'Zurilla, T.J. 1969. A behavioral-analytic model for assessing competence. In: C. D. Spielberger (ed.), Current Topics in Clinical and Community Psychology, Vol. 1. Academic Press, New York.

Goldfried, M. R., and Goldfried, A. P. 1980. Cognitive change methods. In: F. H. Kanfer and A. P. Goldstein (eds.), Helping People Change. 2nd Ed. Pergamon Press, New York.

Goldfried, M. R., and Kent, R. N. 1972. Traditional versus behavioral assessment: A comparison of methodological and theoretical assumptions. Psychol. Bull. 77:409–420.

Goldfried, M. R., and Sprafkin, J. N. 1976. Behavioral personality assessment. In: J. T. Spence, R. C. Carson, and J. W. Thibaut (eds.), Behavioral Approaches to Therapy. General Learning Press, Morristown, NJ.

Goldiamond, I. 1974. Toward a constructional approach to social problems. Behaviorism 2:1–84.

Goldsmith, S., Gabrielson, M., and Gabrielson, I. 1972. Teenagers, sex and contraception. Family Plan. Perspect. 4:32–38.

Goldstein, A. P., Sprafkin, R. P., Gershaw, N. J., and Klein, P. 1980. Skill-Streaming the Adolescent: A Structured Learning Approach to Teaching Prosocial Skills. Research Press, Champaign, IL.

Goldston, S. E. 1979. Primary prevention programming from the federal perspective: A progress report. J. Clin. Psychol. 3:80–83.

Goodman, L. A. 1978. Analyzing Qualitative/Categorical Data: Log-Linear Models and Latent-Structure Analysis. Abt Books, Cambridge, MA.

Goodstadt, M. S. 1980. Drug education—A turn on or a turn off? J. Drug Educ. 10:89–99.

Gordon, S. 1981. Preteens are not latent, adolescence is not a disease. In: L. Brown (ed.), Sex Education in the Eighties: The Challenge of Healthy Sexual Evolution. Plenum Publishing, New York.

Gore, S. 1978. The effect of social support in moderating the health consequences of unemployment. J. Health Soc. Behav. 19:157–165.

Gormally, J. 1982. Evaluation of assertiveness: Effects of gender, rater involvement, and level of assertiveness. Behav. Ther. 13:219–225.

Gormally, J., and Rardin, D. 1981. Weight loss and maintenance and changes in diet and exercise for behavioral counseling and nutrition education. J. Counsel. Psychol. 28:295–304.

Gottleib, B. H., and Todd, D. M. 1979. Characterizing and promoting social support in natural settings. In: R. F. Munoz, L. R. Snowden, and J. G. Kelly (eds.), Social and Psychological Research in Community Settings. Jossey-Bass, San Francisco.

Gottman, J. M. 1977. Toward a definition of social isolation in children. Child Devel. 48:513–517.

Grady, K. E., Brannon, R., and Pleck, J. H. 1979. The Male Sex Role: A Selected and Annotated Bibliography. National Institute of Mental Health, Rockville, MD.

Green, D. E. 1980. Teenage smoking behavior. In: F. R. Scarpitti and S. K. Datesman (eds.), Drugs and the Youth Culture. Sage, Beverly Hills, CA.

Green, L. W. 1981. Lessons from the past, plans for the future. Health Educ. Q. 8:105–117.

Greenberger, E., and Steinberg, L. D. 1981. The workplace as a context for the socialization of youth. J. Youth Adolescence 10:185–210.

Greenberger, E., Steinberg, L., and Vaux, A. 1981. Adolescents who work: Health and behavioral consequences of job stress. Devel. Psychol. 17:691–703.

Greydanus, D. E. 1982. Adolescent sexuality: An overview and perspective for the 1980s. Pediatr. Ann. 11:714–726.

Guerney, Jr., B., Coufal, J., and Vogelsong, E. 1981. Relationship enhancement versus a traditional approach to therapeutic/preventative/enrichment parent-adolescent programs. J. Consult. Clin. Psychol. 49:927–939.

Gumerman, S., Jacknik, M., and Sipko, R. 1980. Sex education in a rural high school. J. School Health 50:478–480.

Gunter, N. C., and LaBarba, R. C. 1980. The consequences of adolescent childbearing on postnatal development. Int. J. Behav. Devel. 3:191–214.

The Alan Guttmacher Institute. 1978. Contraceptive Services for Adolescents: United States, Each State and County, 1975. The Alan Guttmacher Institute, New York.

The Alan Guttmacher Institute. 1979. Abortion: Need, Services and Policies, 50 State Profiles. The Alan Guttmacher Institute, New York.

The Alan Guttmacher Institute. 1980. Family planning services and population research. Planned Parenthood-World Popul. Spec. Rep. May.

The Alan Guttmacher Institute. 1981. Teenage Pregnancy: The Problem that Hasn't Gone Away. The Alan Guttmacher Institute, New York.

Hacker, S. S. 1981. It isn't sex education unless. . . . J. School Health 51:207–210.

Haldane, B., Haldane, J., and Martin, L. 1976. Job Power Now! The Young People's Job Finding Guide. Acropolis, Washington, DC.

Halleck, S. L. 1976. Another response to "Homosexuality: The ethical challenge." J. Consult. Clin. Psychol. 44:167–170.

Hamburg, B. A. 1974. Early adolescence: A specific and stressful stage of the life cycle. In: G. V. Coelho, D. A. Hamburg, and J. E. Adams (eds.), Coping and Adaptation. Basic Books, New York.

Hamburg, D. A., Elliott, G. R., and Parron, D. L. 1982. Health and Behavior: Frontiers of Research in the Biobehavioral Sciences. National Academy Press, Washington, DC.

Hardy, J. B. 1982. Adolescents as parents: Possible long-range implications. In: T. J. Coates, A. C. Petersen, and C. Perry (eds.), Promoting Adolescent Health: A Dialog on Research and Practice. Academic Press, New York.

Harragan, B. L. 1977. Games Mother Never Taught You: Corporate Gamesmanship for Women. Warner Books, New York.

Harris, A. 1979. An empirical test of the situation specificity/consistency of aggressive behavior. Child Behav. Ther. 1:257–270.

Harris, M. B., Sutton, M., Kaufman, E. M., and Carmichael, C. W. 1980. Correlates of success and retention in a multifaceted, long-term behavior modification program for obese adolescent girls. Addictive Behav. 5:25–34.

Hartmann, D. P., Roper, B. L., and Bradford, D. C. 1979. Some relationships between behavioral and traditional assessment. J. Behav. Assess. 1:3–21.

Hawkins, Jr., R. O., 1982. Adolescent alcohol abuse: A review. Devel. Behav. Pediatr. 3:83–87.

Haynes, L. A., and Avery, A. W. 1979. Training adolescents in self-disclosure and empathy skills. J. Counsel. Psychol. 26:526–530.

Haynes, S. N. 1978. Principles of Behavioral Assessment. Gardner Press, New York.

Haynes, S. N., and Horn, W. F. 1982. Reactivity in behavioral observation: A review. Behav. Assess. 4:369–385.

Haynes, S. N., and Wilson, C. C. 1979. Behavioral Assessment: Recent Advances in Methods, Concepts, and Applications. Jossey-Bass, San Francisco.

Hazel, J. S., Schumaker, J. B., Sherman, J. A., & Sheldon-Wildgen, J. 1981. ASSET, A Social Skills Program for Adolescents. Research Press, Champaign, IL.

Heffernan, J., and Turman, B. 1981. Searching the literature. In: R. M. Grinnell, Jr., (ed.), Social Work Research and Evaluation. F. E. Peacock, Itasca, Il.

Heimberg, R., Cunningham, J., and Heimberg, J. S. 1979. Facilitating employment of disadvantaged youth by job-interview-skills-training. Paper presented at the meeting of the Association for Advancement of Behavior Therapy, December, San Francisco.

Hendricks, L. E. 1980. Unwed adolescent fathers: Problems they face and their sources of social support. Adolescence 15:861–869.

Henshaw, S. K., and Martire, G. 1982. Abortion and the public opinion polls: 1. Morality and legality, 2. Women who have had abortions. Family Plan. Perspect. 14:53–62.

Herrenkohl, E. C., and Herrenkohl, R. C. 1979. A comparison of abused children and their nonabused siblings. J. Am. Acad. Child Psych. 18:260–269.

Herrera, J. A. 1978. The occupational status of the Latino in the United States. J. Employment Counsel. 15:157–163.

Hersen, M. 1976. Historical perspectives in behavioral assessment. In: M. Hersen and A. S. Bellack, (eds.), Behavioral Assessment: A Practical Handbook. Pergamon Press, Elmsford, NY.

Hersen, M. 1981. Complex problems require complex solutions. Behav. Ther. 12:15–29.

Hersen, M., and Bellack, A. S. (eds.). 1976a. Behavioral Assessment: A Practical Handbook. Pergamon Press, Elmsford, NY.

Hersen, M., and Bellack, A. S. 1976b. Social skills training for chronic psychiatric patients: Rationale, research findings, and future directions. Comp. Psych. 17:559–580.

Hersen, M., and Bellack, A. S. (eds.). 1978. Behavior Therapy in the Psychiatric Setting. Williams & Wilkins, Baltimore.

Hersen, M., Bellack, A. S., and Turner, S. M. 1978. Assessment of assertiveness in female psychiatric patients: Motor and autonomic measures. 9:11–16.

Higgins, J. P., and Thies, A. P. 1981. Problem solving and social position among emotionally disturbed boys. Am. J. Orthopsych. 51:356–358.

Hilts, P. J. 1974. Behavior Modification. Harper, & Row, New York.

Hofferth, S. L., and Moore, K. A. 1979. Early childbearing and later economic well-being. Am. Sociol. Rev. 44:784–815.

Hofmann, A. D. 1982. Biological and Psychological Correlates of Contraception in Adolescence: A Review. Report submitted to the Maternal and Child Health Division of the World Health Organization, March 18, Geneva.

Holinger, P. C. 1979. Violent deaths among the young: Recent trends in suicide, homicide, and accidents. Am. J. Psych. 136:1144–1147.

Holinger, P. C., and Offer, D. 1982. Prediction of adolescent suicide: A population model. Am. J. Psych. 139:302–307.

Hollandsworth, J. G., Dressel, M. E., and Stevens, J. 1977. Use of behavioral versus traditional procedures for increasing job interview skills. J. Counsel. Psychol. 24:503–510.

Hollandsworth, Jr., J. G., Kazelskis, R., Stevens, J., and Dressel, M. E. 1979. Relative contributions of verbal, articulative, and nonverbal communication to employment decisions in the job interview setting. Personnel Psychol. 32:359–367.

Hollmann, T. D. 1972. Employment interviewer errors in processing positive and negative information. J. Appl. Psychol. 56:130–34.

Horn, D. 1976. A model for the study of personal choice health behaviour. Int. J. Health Educ. 19:89–98.

Hoyman, H. S. 1967. Sex and American college girls today. J. School Health 37:28–32.

Hoyt, L. L. 1981. Effects of marijuana on fetal development. J. Alcohol Drug Educ. 20:30–36.

Hu, T. W., McDonald, N. S., and Swisher, J. 1981. The application of cost-effectiveness analysis to the evaluation of drug abuse prevention programs: An illustration. J. Drug Issues 11:125–138.

Huba, G. J., Wingard, J. A., and Bentler, P. M. 1981. A comparison of two latent variable causal models of adolescent drug use. J. Personality Soc. Psychol. 40:180–193.

Hudson, W. W. 1982. The Clinical Measurement Package: A Field Manual. The Dorsey Press, Homewood IL.

Hurd, P. D., Johnson, C. A., Pechacek, T., et al. 1980. Prevention of cigarette smoking in seventh grade students. J. Behav. Med. 3:15–28.

Imada, A. S., and Hakel, M. D. 1977. Influence of nonverbal communication and rater proximity on impressions and decisions in simulated employment interviews. J. Appl. Psychol. 62:295–300.

Inazu, J. K., and Fox, G. L. 1980. Maternal influence on the sexual behavior of teen-age daughters. J. Family Issues, 1: 81–102.

Inciardi, J. A. 1980. Youth, drugs, and street crime. In: F. R. Scarpitti and S. K. Datesman (eds.), Drugs and the Youth Culture. Sage, Beverly Hills, CA.

Ingersoll, G. M. 1981. Adolescents in School and Society. D. C. Heath, Lexington, MA.

Inhelder, B., and Piaget, J. 1958. The Growth of Logical Thinking from Childhood to Adolescence. Basic Books, New York.

Irvin, L. K., Gerstein, R., Taylor, V. E., et al. 1981. Vocational skill assessment of severely mentally retarded adults. Am. J. Ment. Defic. 85:631–638.

Jackson, M. F., and Marzillier, J. S. 1982. The Youth Club Project: A community-based intervention for shy adolescents. Behav. Psychother. 10:87–100.

Jacobs, J. 1971. Adolescent Suicide. Wiley, New York.

Jacobson, E. 1938. Progressive Relaxation. University of Chicago Press, Chicago.

Jacobson, E. 1978. You Must Relax. McGraw-Hill, New York.

Jalali, B., Jalali, M., Crocetti, G., and Turner, F. 1981. Adolescents and drug use: Toward a more comprehensive approach. Am. J. Orthopsych. 5: 120–130.

Janes, C. L., Hesselbrock, V. M., Myers, D. G., and Penniman, J. H. 1979. Problem boys in young adulthood: Teachers' ratings and twelve-year follow-up. J. Youth Adolescence 8:453–472.

Jaremko, M. E. 1983. Stress inoculation training for social anxiety, with emphasis on dating anxiety. In: D. Meichenbaum and M. E. Jaremko, (eds.), Stress Reduction and Prevention. Plenum Publishing, New York.

Jason, L. A. 1979. Preventive community interventions: Reducing school children's smoking and decreasing smoke exposure. Prof. Psychol. 10:744–751.

Jayaratne, S., and Levy, R. L. 1979. Empirical Clinical Practice. Columbia University Press, New York.

Jekel, J. F., Tyler, N. C., and Klerman, L. V. 1979. Continued childbearing among women who were pregnant as adolescents. J. Popul. 2:328–337.

Jesness, C. F. 1975. The impact of behavior modification and transactional analysis on institution social climate. J. Res. Crime Delinquency 12:79–91.

Jessor, R. 1982. Problem behavior and developmental transition in adolescence. J. School Health 52:295–300.

Jessor, R., and Jessor, S. L. 1977. Problem Behavior and Psychosocial Development, A Longitudinal Study of Youth. Academic Press, Inc., New York.

Jessor, R., Chase, J. A., and Donovan, J. E. 1980. Psychosocial correlates of marijuana use and problem drinking in a national sample of adolescents. Am. J. Public Health 70:604–613.

Johnson, S. M., and Bolstad, D. D. 1973. Methodological issues in naturalistic observation: Some problems and solutions in field research. In: L. A. Hamerlynck, L. C. Handy, and E. J. Mash (eds.), Behavior Change: Methodology, Concepts, and Practice. Research Press, Champaign, IL.

Johnston, L. D., Bachman, J. G., and O'Malley, P. M. 1978. Highlights from Drug Use among American High School Students 1975–1977. U.S. Government Printing Office, Washington, DC.

Johnston, L. D., Bachman, J. G., and O'Malley, P.M. (eds.). 1980. Monitoring the Future: Questionnaire Responses from the Nation's High School Seniors, 1979. Institute for Social Research, University of Michigan, Ann Arbor, MI.

Johnston, O. G. 1976. Tests and Measurements in Child Development: Handbook II, Vols. 1 and 2. Jossey-Bass, San Francisco.

Jones, J. A., Piper, G. W., and Matthews, V. L. 1970. A student-directed program in smoking education. Can. J. Public Health 61:253–258.

Jones, J. B., Namerow, P. B., and Philliber, S. 1982. Adolescents' use of a hospital-based contraceptive program. Family Plan. Perspect. 14:224–231.

Jones, R. 1968. A factored measure of Ellis' irrational belief system. Unpublished doctoral dissertation, Texas Technological College, Austin.

Jones, R. R., Reid, J. B., and Patterson, G. R. 1975. Naturalistic observations in clinical assessment. In: P. McReynolds (ed.), Advances in Psychological Assessment, Vol. 3. Jossey-Bass, San Francisco.

Jorgensen, S. R., King, S. L., and Torrey, B. A. 1980. Dyadic and social network influences on adolescent exposure to pregnancy risk. J. Marriage Family 42:141–155.

Judd, C. M., and Kenny, D. A. 1981. Process analysis: Estimating mediation in treatment evaluations. Eval. Rev. 5:602–619.

Kallman, W. M., and Feuerstein, M. 1977. Psychophysiological procedures. In: A. R. Ciminero, K. S. Calhoun, and H. E. Adams (eds.), Handbook of Behavioral Assessment. Wiley, New York.

Kandel, D., Single, E., and Kessler, R. C. 1976. The epidemiology of drug use among New York state high school students: Distribution, trends, and changes in rate use. Am. J. Public Health 66:43–53.

Kaplan, S. L. Nussbaum, M., Skomorowsky, P., et al., 1980. Health habits and depression in adolescence. J. Youth Adolescence 9:299–304.

Karmel, L. J., and Karmel, M. D. 1978. Measurement and Evaluation in the Schools. 2nd Ed. Macmillan, New York.

Katchadourian, H. A., and Lunde, D. T. 1975. Fundamentals of Human Sexuality. 2nd

Ed. Holt, Rinehart & Winston, New York.

Kaufmann, L. M., and Wagner, B. R. 1972. Barb: A systematic treatment technology for temper control disorders. Behav. Ther. 3:84–90.

Kaymakcalan, S. 1981. The addictive potential of cannabis. Bull. Narcotics 33:21–31.

Kazdin, A. E. 1977a. Assessing the clinical or applied importance of behavior change through social validation. Behav. Modification 1:427–452.

Kazdin, A. E. 1977b. The Token Economy: A Review and Evaluation. Plenum Press, New York.

Kazdin, A. E. 1978. Methodological and interpretive problems of single-case experimental designs. J. Consult. Clin. Psychol. 46:629–642.

Kazdin, A. E. 1979a. Situational specificity: The two-edged sword of behavioral assessment. Behav. Assess. 1:57–75.

Kazdin, A. E. 1980. Research Design in Clinical Psychology. Harper & Row, New York.

Kazdin, A. E., and Cole, P. M. 1981. Attitudes and labeling biases toward behavior modification: The effects of labels, content, and jargon. Behav. Ther. 12:56–68.

Kazdin, A. E., and Mascitelli, S. 1982. Covert and overt rehearsal and homework practice in developing assertiveness. J. Consult. Clin. Psychol. 50:250–258.

Kazdin, A. E., and Wilson, G. T. 1978. Criteria for evaluating psychotherapy. Arch. Gen. Psych. 35:407–416.

Kazdin. A. E., French, N. H., and Sherick, R. B. 1981. Acceptability of alternative treatments for children: Evaluations by inpatient children, parents, and staff. J. Consult. Clin. Psychol. 49:900–907.

Keefe, F. J., Kopel, S. A., and Gordon, S. B. 1978. A Practical Guide to Behavioral Assessment. Springer, New York.

Keenan, A. 1976. Interviewers' evaluation of applicant characteristics: Differences between personnel and non-personnel managers. J. Occupational Psychol. 49:223–230.

Kellam, S. G., Adams, R. C., Brown, C. H., and Ensminger, M. E. 1982. The long-term evolution of the family structure of teenage and older mothers. J. Marriage Family 44:539–553.

Kellam, S. G., Ensminger, M. E., and Simon, M. B. 1980. Mental health in first grade and teenage drug, alcohol, and cigarette use. Drug Alcohol Depend. 5:273–304.

Kelly, J. A. 1982. Social-Skills Training: A Practical Guide for Interventions. Springer, New York.

Kendall, P. C., and Finch, Jr., A. J. 1976. A cognitive-behavioral treatment of impulse control: A case study. J. Consult. Clin. Psychol. 44:852–857.

Kendall, P. C., and Finch, Jr., A. J. 1979. Developing nonimpulsive behavior in children: Cognitive-behavioral strategies for self-control. In: P. C. Kendall and S. D. Hollon (eds.), Cognitive-Behavioral Interventions: Theory, Research and Procedures. Academic Press, Inc., New York.

Kendall, P. C., and Hollon, S. D. (eds.). 1979. Cognitive-Behavioral Interventions: Theory, Research, and Procedures. Academic Press, New York.

Kendall, P. C., and Hollon, S. D. 1981a. Assessing self-referent speech: Methods in the measurement of self-statements. In: P. C. Kendall and S. D. Hollon (eds.), Assessment Strategies for Cognitive-Behavioral Interventions. Academic Press, New York.

Kendall, P. C., and Hollon, S. D. (eds.) 1981b. Assessment Strategies for Cognitive-Behavioral Interventions. Academic Press, New York.

Kendall, P. C., and Korgeski, G. 1979. Assessment and cognitive-behavioral interventions. Cognit. Ther. Res. 3:1–22.

Kendall, P. C., and Wilcox, L. E. 1980. Cognitive-behavioral treatment for impulsivity: Concrete versus conceptual training in non-self-controlled problem children. J. Consult. Clin. Psychol. 48:80–91.

Kendall, P. C., Deardorff, P. A., and Finch, Jr., A. J. 1977. Empathy and socialization in first and repeat juvenile offenders and normals. J. Abnorm. Child Psychol. 5:93–97.

Kenney, A. M., Forrest, J. D., and Torres, A. 1982. Storm over Washington: The parental notification proposal. Family Plan. Perspect. 14:185–197.

Kent, R. N., O'Leary, K. D., Dietz, A., and Diament, C. 1979. Comparison of observational recordings in vivo, via mirror, and via television. J. Appl. Behav. Anal. 12:517–522.

Kifer, R. E., Lewis, M. A., Green, D. R., and Phillips, E. L. 1974. Training predelinquent youths and their parents to negotiate conflict situations. J. Appl. Behav. Anal. 7:357–364.

Kirby, D. 1980. The effects of school sex education programs: A review of the literature. J. School Health 50:559–563.

Kirby, D., and Alter, J. 1980. The experts rate important features and outcomes of sex education programs. J. School Health, 50:497–502.

Kirkland, K. D., and Thelen, M. H. 1977. Uses of modeling in child treatment. In: B. B. Lahey and A. E. Kazdin (eds.), Advances in Clinical Child Psychology, Vol. 1. Plenum Publishing, New York.

Kirkpatrick, D. L. 1977. Determining training needs: Four simple and effective approaches. Train. Devel. J. 31:22–25.

Kirn, A. G., and Kirn, M. O'D. 1978. Life Work Planning. 4th Ed. McGraw-Hill, New York.

Kirschenbaum, D. S. 1979. Social competence intervention and evaluation in the inner city: Cincinnati's social skills development. J. Consult Clin. Psychol. 47:778–780.

Klein, D. C., and Goldston, S. E. 1977. Primary Prevention: An Idea Whose Time Has Come. U.S. Government Printing Office, Washington, DC.

Klemke, L. W. 1982. Exploring juvenile shoplifting. Sociol. Soc. Res. 67(1):59–75.

Klos, D. S., and Paddock, J. R. 1978. Relationship status: Scales for assessing the vitality of late adolescents' relationships with their parents. J. Youth Adolescence 7:353–369.

Kobasa, S. C., Maddi, S. R., and Puccetti, M. C. 1982. Personality and exercise as buffers in the stress-illness relationship. J. Behav. Med. 5:391–404.

Koenig, M. A., and Zelnik, M. 1982. The risk of premarital first pregnancy among metropolitan-area teenagers: 1976 and 1979. Family Plan. Perspect. 14:239–247.

Koepsell, T. D., Weiss, N. S., Thompson, D. J., and Martin, D. P. 1980. Prevalence of prior hysterectomy in the Seattle-Tacoma area. Am. J. Public Health 70:40–47.

Kohlberg, L. 1976. Moral stages and moralization: The cognitive-developmental approach. In: T. Lickona (ed.), Moral Development and Behavior. Holt, Rinehart, & Winston, New York.

Kolko, D. J., Dorsett, P. G., and Milan, M. A. 1981. A total-assessment approach to the evaluation of social skills training: The effectiveness of an anger control program for adolescent psychiatric patients. Behav. Assess. 3:383–402.

Konopka, G. 1973. Requirements for healthy development of adolescent youth. Adolescence 8:291–316.

Korda, M. 1977. Success! Random House, New York.

Korte, C. 1980. Urban-nonurban differences in social behavior and social psychological models of urban impact. J. Soc. Issues 36:29–51.

Kovar, M. G. 1978. Adolescent Health Status and Health-Related Behavior. National Center for Health Statistics, Washington, DC.

Kovar, M. G. 1979. Some indicators of health-related behavior among adolescents in the United States. Public Health Rep. 94:109–118.

Kratochwill, T. R. 1978. Foundations of time-series research. In: T. Kratochwill (ed.), Single Subject Research: Strategies for Evaluating Change. Academic Press, New York.

Kraus, L. M. 1980. Therapeutic strategies with adolescents. Soc. Casework 61:313–316.

Kreuter, M. W., and Christenson, G. M. 1981. School health education: Does it cause an effect? Health Educ. Q. 8:43–56.

Kutash, I. L., Schlesinger, L. B., and Associates. 1980. Handbook on Stress and Anxiety: Contemporary Knowledge, Theory, and Treatment. Jossey-Bass, San Francisco.

Labbe´, E. E., and Williamson, D. A. 1982. Behavioral treatment of two psychosomatic disorders in children and adolescents. Behav. Med. Adv. 5:2–5.

Lang, K. A. 1978. Suggestions for counseling women who want to enter a nontraditional occupation. J. Employment Counsel. 15: 180–187.

Lang, P. J. 1977. Physiological assessment of anxiety and fear. In: J. D. Cone and R. P. Hawkins (eds.), Behavioral Assessment: New Directions in Clinical Psychology. Brunner/Mazel, New York.

Lange, A. J., and Jakubowski, P. 1976. Responsible Assertive Behavior: Cognitive/ Behavioral Procedures for Trainers. Research Press, Champaign, IL.

Langford, R. W. 1981. Teenagers and obesity. Am. J. Nursing 81:556–559.

Lasch, C. 1977. Haven in a Heartless World: The Family Besieged. Basic Books, New York.

Lazarus, R. S. 1966. Psychological Stress and the Coping Process. McGraw-Hill, New York.

Lazarus, R. S. 1972. Behavior Therapy and Beyond. McGraw-Hill, New York.

Lazarus, R. S., and Launier, R. 1978. Stress-related transactions between person and environment. In: L. A. Pervin and M. Lewis (eds.), Perspectives in Interactional Psychology. Plenum Publishing, New York.

Lazarus, R. S., Averill, J. R., and Opton, Jr., E. M. 1974. The psychology of coping: Issues of research and assessment. In: G. V. Coelho, D. A. Hamburg, and J. E. Adams (eds.), Coping and Adaptation. Basic Books, New York.

LeBoeuf, M. 1979. Working Smart: How To Accomplish More in Half the Time. McGraw-Hill, New York.

Lefcourt, H. M. 1976. Locus of Control: Current Trends in Theory and Research. Lawrence Erlbaum Associates, Hillsdale, NJ.

Leon, G. R. 1979. Thoughts on a cognitive child behavior therapy. Child Behav. Ther. 1:3–4.

Levine, S. M., and Pearson, L. M. 1979. Responsiveness of pre- and nondelinquents to incentive aspects of a reinforcing event. Percept. Motor Skills 49:715–720.

Levis, D. J., and Plunkett, W. J. 1979. The use of subjective magnitude estimation technique to validate procedures for pre-selecting ''phobic'' subjects. Behav. Assess. 1:191–201.

Lieberoff, A. J. 1978. Good Jobs, High Paying Opportunities. Working for Yourself or for Others. Prentice-Hall, Englewood Cliffs, NJ.

Light, K. C. 1981. Cardiovascular responses to effortful active coping: Implications for the role of stress in hypertension development: Young Psychophysiologist Award Address, 1980. Psychophysiology 18:216–225.

Lindemann, C. 1974. Birth Control and Unmarried Young Women. Springer, New York.

Litt, I. F., Cuskey, W. R., and Rudd, S. 1980. Identifying adolescents at risk for noncompliance with contraceptive therapy. J. Pediatr. 96:742–745.

Little, V. L., and Kendall, P. C. 1979. Cognitive-behavioral interventions with delinquents: Problem solving, role-taking, and self-control. In: P. C. Kendall and S. D. Hollon (eds.), Cognitive-Behavioral Interventions: Theory, Research and Procedures. Academic Press, Inc., New York.

Lloyd, M. E. 1983. Selecting systems to measure client outcome in human service agencies. Behav. Assess. 5:55–70.

Lockwood, A. 1978. The effects of values clarification and moral development criteria. Rev. Educ. Res. 48:325–364.

Loewenstein, S. F. 1980. Understanding lesbian women. Soc. Casework 61:29–38.

Looft, W. R. 1976. Egocentrism and social interaction in adolescence. Adolescence 6:485–494.

Lowe, M. R., and Cautela, J. R. 1978. A self-report measure of social skill. Behav. Ther. 9:535–544.

Luker, K. 1975. Taking Chances: Abortion and the Decision Not To Contracept. University of California Press, Berkeley, CA.

Luker, K. 1977. Contraceptive risk taking and abortion: Results and implications of a San Francisco Bay Area study. Stud. Family Plan. 8:190–196.

Luria, A. R. 1961. The Role of Speech in the Regulation of Normal and Abnormal Behavior. Liveright, New York.

Maher, B. A. 1966. Principles of Psychopathology. McGraw-Hill, New York.

Mahoney, E. R. 1979. Sex education in the public schools: A discriminant analysis of characteristics of pro and anti individuals. J. Sex Res. 15:264–275.

Mahoney, M. J. 1974. Cognition and Behavior Modification. Ballinger, Cambridge, MA.

Mahoney, M. J. 1978. Experimental methods and outcome evaluation. J. Consult. Clin. Psychol. 46:660–672.

Mahoney, M. J. 1979. Cognitive issues in the treatment of delinquency. In: J. S. Stumphauzer (ed.), Progress in Behavior Therapy with Delinquents. Charles C Thomas, Springfield, IL.

Mahoney, M. J., and Arnkoff, D. B. 1979. Self-management. In: O. F. Pomerleau and J. P. Brady (eds.), Behavioral Medicine: Theory and Practice. Williams & Wilkins, Baltimore.

Mahoney, M. J., and Thoresen, C. E. 1974. Self-Control: Power to the Person. Wadsworth, Belmont, CA.

Maisto, S. A., and Caddy, G. R. 1981. Self-control and addictive behavior: Present status and prospects. Int. J. Addictions 16:109–133.

Manaster, G. J. 1977. Adolescent Development and the Life Tasks. Allyn & Bacon, Boston.

Marano, H. 1977. Can certain semen seed cervix CA? Hospital Trib. 11:1, 14.

Marlatt, G. A., and Gordon, J. 1980. Determinants of relapse: Implications for the maintenance of behavior change. In: P. O. Davidson and S. M. Davidson (eds.), Behavioral Medicine: Changing Health Lifestyles. Brunner/Mazel, New York.

Marsh, D. T., Serafica, F. C., and Barenboim, C. 1980. Effect of perspective-taking training on interpersonal problem solving. Child Devel. 51:140–145.

Martin, G. A., and Worthington, Jr., E. L. 1982. Behavioral homework. In: M. Hersen, R. M. Eisler, and P. M. Miller (eds.), Progress in Behavior Modification, Vol. 13. Academic Press, New York.

Martin, R. 1975. Legal Challenges to Behavior Modification: Trends in Schools, Corrections, and Mental Health. Research Press, Champaign, IL.

Mash, E. J., and Terdal, L. G. (eds.). 1976. Behavior Therapy Assessment. Springer, New York.

Masters, S., Garfinkel, I., and Bishop, J. 1978. Benefit-cost analysis in program evaluation. J. Soc. Serv. Res. 2:79–93.

Masters, W. H., Johnson, V. E., and Kolodny, R. C. 1982. Human Sexuality. Little, Brown, Boston.

Mathews, R. M., Whang, P. L. and Fawcett, S. B. 1980. Development and validation of an occupational skills assessment instrument. Behav. Assess. 2:71–85.

Matson, J. L., Esveldt-Dawson, K., Andrasik, F., et al. 1980. Direct observational and generalization effects of social skills training with emotionally disturbed children. Behav. Ther. 11:522–531.

Matthews, K. A. 1979. Efforts to control by children and adults with the Type A coronary-prone behavior pattern. Child Devel. 50:842–847.

Matthews, K. A., and Angulo, J. 1980. Measurement of the Type A behavior pattern in children: Assessment of children's competitiveness, impatience-anger, and aggression. Child Devel. 51:466–475.

McAlister, A. L. 1979. Tobacco, alcohol, and drug abuse: Onset and prevention. In: Healthy People, Background Papers, 1979 [DHEW (PHS) Publication No. 79–550–71A]. U.S. Government Printing Office, Washington, DC.

McAlister, A. L. 1981. Social and environmental influences on health behavior. Health Educ. Q. 8:25–30.

McAlister, A. L., Perry, C., Killen, J., et al. 1980. Pilot study of smoking, alcohol and drug abuse prevention. Am. J. Public Health 70:719–721.

McAlister, A. L., Perry, C., and Maccoby, N. 1979. Adolescent smoking: Onset and prevention. Pediatrics 63:650–658.

McCandless, B. R., and Coop, R. H. 1979. Adolescents: Behavior and Development. 2nd ed. Holt, Rinehart, & Winston, New York.

McCarthy, J., and Radish, E. S. 1982. Education and childbearing among teenagers. Family Plan. Perspect. 14:154–155.

McClure, L. F., Chinsky, J. M., and Larcen, S. W. 1978. Enhancing social problem-solving performance in an elementary school setting. J. Educ. Psychol. 4:504–513.

McClure, W. J. 1978. Effectively counseling the shy minority client. J. Employment Counsel. 15:150–156.

McCoy, C. B., and Watkins, V. Mc. 1980. Drug use among urban ethnic youth: Appalachian and other comparisons. Youth Soc. 12:83–106.

McCullough, J. P., Huntsinger, G. M., and Nay, W. R. 1977. Case study: Self-control treatment of aggression in a 16-year-old male. J. Consult. Clin. Psychol. 45:322–331.

McFall, M. E., Winnett, R. L., Bordewick, M. C., and Bornstein, P. H. 1982. Nonverbal components in the communication of assertiveness. Behav. Modif. 6:121–140.

McFall, R. M. 1982. A review and reformulation of the concept of social skills. Behav. Assessment, 4(1). 1–33.

McGee, D. W. 1981. Sharpen students' job seeking skills with employment applications and role played interviews. Teaching Except. Child. 13:152–155.

McGovern, T. V. 1976. Assertion training for job interviewing and management/staff development. In: A. J. Lange and P. Jakubowski (eds.), Responsible Assertive Behavior: Cognitive/Behavioral Procedures for Trainers. Research Press, Champaign, IL.

McKay, M., Davis, M., and Fanning, P. 1981. Thoughts and Feelings: The Art of Cognitive Stress Intervention. New Harbinger, Richmond, CA.

Mechanic, D., and Cleary, P. D. 1980. Factors associated with the maintenance of positive health behavior. Prevent. Med. 9:805–814.

Mecklenburg, M. 1982. Should the government tell? San Diego Trib. April 13.

Meichenbaum, D. 1975. A self-instructional approach to stress management: A proposal for stress inoculation training. In: C. D. Spielberger and I. G. Sarason (eds.), Stress and Anxiety, Vol. 1. Hemisphere, Washington, DC.

Meichenbaum, D. 1977. Cognitive-Behavior Modification: An Integrative Approach. Plenum Publishing, New York.

Meichenbaum, D. 1978. Teaching children self-control. In: B. Lahey and A. Kazdin (eds.), Advances in Child Clinical Psychology, Vol. 2. Plenum Publishing, New York.

Meichenbaum, D., and Asarnow, J. 1979. Cognitive-behavioral modification and metacognitive development: Implications for the classroom. In: P. C. Kendall and S. D. Hollon (eds.), Cognitive-Behavioral Interventions: Theory, Research and Procedures. Academic Press, New York.

Meichenbaum, D., and Jaremko, M. E. (eds.). 1983. Stress Reduction and Prevention. Plenum Publishing, New York.

Meichenbaum, D., and Novaco, R. 1978. Stress inoculation: A preventative approach. In: C. D. Spielberger and I. G. Sarason (eds.), Stress and Anxiety, Vol. 5. Hemisphere, Washington, DC.

Meichenbaum, D., Henshaw, D., and Himel, N. 1982. Coping with stress as a problem-solving process. In: W. Krohne and L. Laux (eds.), Achievement, Stress and Anxiety. Hemisphere, Washington, DC.

Meichenbaum, D., Turk, D., and Burstein, S. 1975. The nature of coping with stress. In: I. Sarason and C. Spielberger (eds.), Stress and Anxiety, Vol. 1. Hemisphere, Washington, DC.

Mercer, R. C., and Loeschi, L. C. 1979. Audio tape ratings: Comments and guidelines. Psychotherapy: Theory, Res. Practice 16:79–85.

Merki, D. J., Creswell, W. H., Stone, D. B., et al. 1968. The effects of two educational methods and message themes on rural youth smoking behavior. J. School Health 38:448–454.

Meyer, A. J., Nash, J. D., McAlister, A. L., et al. 1980. Skills training in a cardiovascular health education campaign. J. Consult. Clin. Psychol. 48:129–142.

Meyers, F. H. 1979. Drug use among adolescents. In: R. T. Mercer (ed.), Perspectives on Adolescent Health Care. Lippincott, Philadelphia.

Michelson, L., and Wood, R. 1980. Behavioral assessment and training of children's social skills. In: M. Hersen, R. M. Eisler, and P. M. Miller (eds.), Progress in Behavior Modification, Vol. 9. Academic Press, New York.

Mikhail, A. 1981. Stress: A psychophysiological conception. J. Human Stress 7:9–15.

Miller, W. R., and Lief, H. I. 1979. The Sex Knowledge and Attitude Test (SKAT). J. Sex Marital Ther. 5:282–287.

Mills, C. M., and Walter, T. L. 1977. A behavioral employment intervention program for reducing juvenile delinquency. Behav. Ther. 8:270–272.

Mindick, B., and Oskamp, S. 1979. Longitudinal predictive research: An approach to methodological problems in studying contraception. J. Popul. 2:259–276.

Minkin, N., Braukmann, C. J., Minkin, B. L., et al. 1976. The social validation and training of conversational skills. J. Appl. Behav. Anal. 9:127–139.

Minor, J. H., and Minor, B. J. 1978. Value conflict resolution: A training model for counselors of minority clients. J. Employment Counsel. 15:164–170.

Mischel, W., and Mischel, H. 1976. A cognitive social learning approach to morality and self regulation. In: T. Lickona (ed.), Moral Development and Behavior: Theory, Research, and Social Issues. Holt, Rinehart, & Winston, New York.

Mischel, W., and Patterson, C. J. 1976. Substantive and structural elements of effective plans for self-control. J. Personality Soc. Psychol. 34:942–950.

Mitchell, J. J. 1976. Adolescent intimacy. Adolescence 11:275–280.

Moe, K. O., and Zeiss, A. M. 1982. Measuring self-efficacy expectations for social skills: A methodological inquiry. Cognit. Ther. Res. 6:191–205.

Moore, D. R., Chamberlain, P., and Mukai, L. H. 1979. Children at risk for delinquency: A follow-up comparison of aggressive children and children who steal. J. Abnorm. Psychol. 7:345–355.

Moore, K. A., and Waite, L. J. 1977. Early childbearing and educational attainment. Family Plan. Perspect. 9:220–225.

Moos, R. 1974. Family, Work and Group Environment Scales and Manual. Consulting Psychologists Press, Palo Alto, CA.

Mott, F. L., and Maxwell, N. L. 1981. School-age mothers: 1968 and 1979. Family Plan. Perspect. 13:287–292.

Mungas, D. M., and Walters, H. A. 1979. Pretesting effects in the evaluation of social skills training. J. Consult. Clin. Psychol. 47:216–218.

Murphy, L. B. 1962. The Widening World of Childhood. Basic Books, New York.

Mussen, P. H. 1963. The Psychological Development of the Child. Prentice-Hall, Inc., Englewood Cliffs, NJ.

Mussen, P. H., Conger, J. J., Kagan, J., and Geiwitz, J. 1979. Psychological development: A life-span approach. Harper & Row, New York.

Muuss, R. E. 1968. Theories of Adolescence. Random House, New York.

Nader, P. R., Perry, C., Maccoby, N., et al. 1982. Adolescent perceptions of family health behavior: A tenth grade educational activity to increase family awareness of a community cardiovascular risk reduction program. J. School Health 52:372–377.

Namerow, P. B., and Jones, J. E. 1982. Ethnic variation in adolescent use of a contraceptive service. J. Adolescent Health Care 3:165–172.

National Cancer Institute. 1977. Cigarette Smoking among Teenagers and Young Women. U.S. Government Printing Office, Washington, DC.

National Center for Health Statistics. 1974. Final natality statistics, 1970. Monthly Vital Stat. Rep. 22: Supplement.

National Center for Health Statistics. 1977. Teenage childbearing: United States, 1966–75. Monthly Vital Stat. Rep. 26:1–15.

National Center for Health Statistics. 1978. Wanted and unwanted childbearing in the United States, 1968, 1969, and 1972 national natality surveys. Vital Health Stat. Series 21, No. 32.

National Center for Health Statistics. 1979a. Advance report: Final natality statistics, 1977. Monthly Vital Stat. Rep. 27:1–27.

National Center for Health Statistics. 1979b. Final marriage statistics, 1977: Advance report. Monthly Vital Stat. Rep. 28:1–7.

National Center for Health Statistics. 1980. Health, United States, 1979. U.S. Government Printing Office, Washington, DC.

National Center for Health Statistics. 1981. Advance report of final natality statistics, 1979. Monthly Vital Stat. Rep. 30(b):1–9.

National Center for Health Statistics. 1982a. Teenage Childbearing: United States, 1976–79. National Center for Health Statistics, Hyattsville, MD.

National Center for Health Statistics, United States Public Health Service, 1982b. Monthly Vital Stat. Rep. 30:No. 10.

National Center for Health Statistics. 1983. Births, marriages, divorces, and deaths. Monthly Vital Stat. Rep. 31:1–12.

National Institute of Mental Health. 1979. Developing a Sense of Competence in Young Children. Division of Scientific and Public Information, National Institute of Mental Health, Rockville, MD.

Nelson, R. O. 1980. The use of intelligence tests within behavioral assessment. Behav. Assess. 2:417–423.

Nelson, R. O., and Hayes, S. C. 1979. Some current dimensions of behavioral assessment. Behav. Assess. 1:1–16.

New York State Department of Health. 1980. Quarterly Vital Statistics Review. New York State Department of Health, Mortality Statistics Branch, Division of Vital Statistics, Albany, NY.

NiCarthy, G. 1981. Assertion Skills for Young Women. New Directions for Young Women, Tucson, AZ.

97th Congress, 1st Session, Senate of the United States. 1981. S.1090: To Amend the Public Health Service Act to Support Services and Research Relating to Adolescent Pregnancy and Parenthood. U.S. Government Printing Office, Washington, DC.

Norman, E., and Mancuso, A. 1980. Women's Issues and Social Work Practice. F. E. Peacock, Itasca, IL.

Nowicki, S., and Strickland, B. R. 1973. A locus of control scale for children. J. Consult. Clin. Psychol. 40:148–154.

Nuehring, E., and Markle, G. E. 1974. Nicotine and norms: The re-emergence of a deviant behavior. Soc. Problems 21:513–526.

Nye, G. S. 1980. Patient confidentiality and privacy: The federal initiative. Am. Orthopsych. Assoc. 50:649–658.

Oettinger, K. B. 1979. "Not with My Daughter": Facing Up to Adolescent Pregnancy. Prentice-Hall, Englewood Cliffs, NJ.

Offer, D., and Howard, K. I. 1972. An empirical analysis of the Offer Self-Image Questionnaire for Adolescents. Arch. Gen. Psych. 27:529–533.

Offer, D., Marohn, R. C., and Ostrov, E. 1979. The Psychological World of the Juvenile Delinquent. Basic Books, New York.

Offer, D., Ostrov, E., and Howard, K. I. 1977. The self-image of adolescents: A study of four cultures. J. Youth Adolescence 6:265–280.

Offer, D., Ostrov, E., and Howard, K. I. 1981a. The Adolescent: A Psychological Self-Portrait. Basic Books, New York.

Offer, D., Ostrov, E., and Howard, K. I. 1981b. The mental health professional's concept of the normal adolescent. AMA Arch. Gen. Psych. 38(2):149–153.

Office of Drug Abuse Policy. 1978. Report Prepared by the White House Committee on Drug Abuse for the President, 1978. U.S. Government Printing Office, Washington, DC.

O'Leary, K. D. 1980. Pills or skills for hyperactive children. J. Appl. Behav. Anal. 13:131–204.

O'Leary, K. D., Poulos, R. W., and Devine, V. T. 1972. Tangible reinforcers: Bonuses or bribes. J. Consult. Clin. Psychol. 38:1–8.

Ollendick, T. H., and Hersen, M. 1979. Social skills training for juvenile delinquents. Behav. Res. Ther. 17:547–554.

Olson, D. H., Russell, C. S., and Sprenkle, D. H. 1979. Circumplex model of marital and family systems II: Empirical studies and clinical intervention. In: J. Vincent (ed.), Advances in Family Intervention, Assessment, and Theory. JAI Press, Greenwich, CT.

Olson, D. H., Sprenkle, D. H., and Russell, C. S. 1979. Circumplex model of marital and family systems. I: Cohesion and adaptability dimensions, family types, and clinical applications. Family Process 18:3–28.

Olson, L. 1980. Social and psychological correlates of pregnancy resolution among adolescent women: A review. Am. J. Orthopsych. 50:432–445.

O'Rourke, T. W. 1980. Methodological considerations to improve anti-smoking research. J. Drug Educ. 10:159–171.

Osborn, S. M., and Harris, G. G. 1975. Assertive Training for Women. Charles C Thomas, Springfield, IL.

Panel on Youth of the President's Science Advisory Committee. 1974. Youth: Transition to Adulthood. University of Chicago Press, Chicago.

Patterson, G. R. 1982. A Social Learning Approach, Vol. 3: Coercive Family Process. Castalia, Eugene, OR.

Patterson, G. R., and Cobb, J. A. 1971. A dyadic analysis of "aggressive" behaviors. In: J. P. Hill (ed.), Minnesota Symposia on Child Psychology, Vol. 5. University of Minnesota Press, Minneapolis, MN.

Patterson, G. R., Reid, J. B., Jones, R. R., and Conger, R. E. 1975. A Social Learning Approach to Family Intervention, Vol. 1: Families with Aggressive Children. Castalia, Eugene, OR.

Payton, C. R. 1981. Substance abuse and mental health: Special prevention strategies needed for ethnics of color. Public Health Rep. 96:20–25.

PCP: You Never Know. 1980. Harper & Row, Criminal Justice Media, Hagerstown, MD. (film).

Pecora, P. J., and Gingerich, W. G. 1981. Worker roles and knowledge utilization in group child care: First findings. Child Welfare 60:221–232.

Pelletier, K. R. 1977. Mind as Healer, Mind as Slayer. Dell, New York.

Peng, S. S. 1977. An Assessment of Job Training Programs in American High Schools. Center for Educational Research and Evaluation, Research Triangle Park, NC.

Perlman, S. B., Klerman, L. V., and Kinard, E. M. 1981. The use of socio-economic data to predict teenage birth rates: An exploratory study in Massachusetts. Public Health Rep. 96:335–341.

Perry, M. A., and Furukawa, M. J. 1980. Modeling methods. In: F. H. Kanfer and A. P. Goldstein (eds.), Helping People Change: A Textbook of Methods. 2nd Ed. Pergamon Press, New York.

Peters, D. L., and Sibbison, V. 1980. Considerations in the assessment of community child care needs. Residential Commun. Child Care Admin. 1:407–420.

Phillips, E. L. 1968. Achievement Place: Token reinforcement procedures in a home-style rehabilitation setting for "pre-delinquent" boys. J. Appl. Behav. Anal. 1:213–223.

Piaget, J. 1967. Six Psychological Studies. Vintage Press, New York.

Piaget, J. 1972. Intellectual evolution from adolescence to adulthood. Human Development 15:1–12.

Pinney, J. M. 1979. The largest preventable cause of death in the United States. Public Health Rep. 94:107–108.

Piper, G. W., Jones, J. A., and Matthews, V. L. 1970. The Saskatoon smoking project: The model. Can. J. Public Health 61:503–508.

Piper, G. W., Jones, J. A., and Matthews, V. L. 1974. The Saskatoon smoking project: Results of the second year. Can. J. Public Health 65:127–129.

Plant, M. A. 1976. Is illegal drug taking a problem? In: J. Madden, R. Walker, and W. Kenyon (eds.), Alcohol and Drug Dependence: A Multi-disciplinary Approach. Penguin Press, New York.

Plant, M. A. 1980. Drugtaking and prevention: The implications of research for social policy. Br. J. Addictions 75:245–254.

Platt, J. J., and Spivak, G. 1972. Social competence and effective problem-solving thinking in psychiatric patients. J. Clin. Psychol. 28:3–5.

Platt, J. J., and Spivak, G. 1975. Manual for the Means-Ends Problem-Solving Procedure (MEPS). Hahnemann Community Mental Health/Mental Retardation Center, Philadelphia.

Pocs, D., Godow, A., Tolone, W., and Walsh, R. 1977. Is there sex after 40? Psychol. Today 11:54–56,87.

Polster, R. A., Lynch, M. A., and Pinkston, E. M. 1981. Reaching underachievers. In: S. P. Schinke (ed.), Behavioral Methods in Social Welfare. Aldine Publishing, Hawthorne, NY.

Population Reference Bureau. 1980. Intercom: Int. Popul. News 8(1):1–12.

Presser, H. B., and Baldwin, W. 1980. Child care as a constraint on employment: Prevalence, correlates, and bearing on the work and fertility nexus. Am. J. Sociol. 85:1202–1213.

Prinz, R. J., and Kent, R. N. 1978. Recording parent-adolescent interactions without the use of frequency or interval-by-interval coding. Behav. Ther. 9:602–604.

Protinsky, H., Sporakowski, M., and Atkins, P. 1982. Identity formation: Pregnant and non-pregnant adolescents. Adolescence 17:73–80.

Rabichow, H. G. 1980. Dilemmas in agency practice. In: J. Mishne (ed.), Psychotherapy and Training in Clinical Social Work. Gardner Press, New York.

Rabinowitz, H. S., Spero, J. R., Grenn, S. J., and Insera, M. T. 1979. A health careers program to improve employability of low-achieving youth. J. Employment Counsel. 16:197–227.

Rabkin, R. 1970. Inner and Outer Space. W.W. Norton, New York.

Radelet, M. L. 1981. Health beliefs, social networks, and tranquilizer use. J. Health Soc. Behav. 22:165–173.

Radius, S. M., Dielman, T. E., Becker, M. H., et al. 1980a. Adolescent perspectives on health and illness. Adolescence 15:375–384.

Radius, S. M., Dielman, T. E., Becker, M. H., et al. 1980b. Health beliefs of the school-aged child and their relationship to risk-taking behaviours. Int. J. Health Educ. 23:3–11.

Rappaport, B. M. 1981. Helping men ask for help. Public Welfare 39:22–27.

Rappoport, L., 1972. Personality Development, The Chronology of Experience. Scott, Foresman, Glenview, IL.

Rathus, S. A. 1973. A 30-item schedule for assessing assertive behavior. Behav. Ther. 4:398–406.

Reardon, R. C., Hersen, M., Bellack, A. S., and Foley, J. M. 1979. Measuring social skill in grade school boys. J. Behav. Assess. 1:87–105.

Redd, W. H., and Andersen, G. V. 1981. Conditioned aversion in cancer patients. Behav. Ther. 4:3–4.

Redican, K. J., Olsen, L. K., Stone, D. B., and Wilson, R. W. 1979. Cigarette smoking attitudes of lower socioeconomic sixth grade students. J. Drug Educ. 9:55–65.

Reed, J. (ed.). 1977. Resumes That Get Jobs. ARCO Publishing Co., New York.

Reid, D. 1982. School sex education and the causes of unintended teenage pregnancies—A review. Health Educ. J. 41:4–11.

Reid, W. J., and Smith, A. D. 1981. Research in Social Work. Columbia University Press, New York.

Reppucci, N. D. 1977. Implementation issues for the behavior modifier as institutional change agent. Behav. Ther. 8:594–605.

Reppucci, N. D., and Saunders, J. T. 1974. Social psychology of behavior modification: Problems of implementation in natural settings. Am. Psychol. 29:649–660.

Resnik, H. S. 1980. Drug Abuse Prevention for Low-Income Communities: Manual for Program Planning. National Institute on Drug Abuse, Rockville, MD.

Rinn, R. C., and Markle, A. 1979. Modification of social skill deficits in children. In: A. S. Bellack and M. Hersen (eds.), Research and Practice in Social Skills Training. Plenum Publishing, New York.

Rinn, R. C., and Vernon, J. C. 1975. Process evaluation of outpatient treatment in a community mental health center. J. Ther. Exp. Psych. 6:5–11.

Risley, T. R. 1975. Certify procedures for people. In: W. S. Wood (ed.), Issues in Evaluating Behavior Modification. Research Press, Champaign, IL.

Robin, A. L. 1981. A controlled evaluation of problem-solving communication training with parent-adolescent conflict. Behav. Ther. 12:593–609.

Robin, A. L. Parent-adolescent conflict: A skill training approach. In: D. P. Rathjen and J. P. Foreyt (eds.), Developing Social Competence: Programs for Children and Adults. Plenum Publishing, New York. In press.

Robin, A. L., Kent, R., O'Leary, K. D., et al. 1977. An approach to teaching parents and adolescents problem-solving communication skills. Behav. Ther. 8:639–643.

Robinson, B. E., and Barret, R. L. 1982. Issues and problems related to the research on teenage fathers: A critical analysis. J. School Health 52:596–600.

Roesler, T., and Deisher, R. W. 1972. Youthful male homosexuality. J. Am. Med. Assoc. 219:1018–1022.

Roff, M. Childhood social interactions and young adult bad conduct. J. Abnorm. Soc. Psychol. 63:333–337.

Roff, M. 1977. Long-term follow-up of juvenile and adult delinquency with samples differing in some important respects: Cross-validation within the same research program. In: J. Strauss, M. Babigian, and M. Roff (eds.), The Origins and Course of Psychopathology. Plenum Publishing, New York.

Rogel, M. J., Zuehlke, M. E., Petersen, A. C., et al. 1980. Contraceptive behavior in adolescence: A decision-making perspective. J. Youth Adolescence 9:491–506.

Rogers, C. R. 1957. The necessary and sufficient conditons of therapeutic personality change. J. Consult. Psychol. 212:95–103.

Rogers, D. 1972. The Psychology of Adolescence. Appleton-Century-Crofts, New York.

Rogers, D. 1977. Issues in Adolescent Psychology. 3rd Ed. Prentice-Hall, Englewood Cliffs, NJ.

Room, R. 1981. The cast for a problem prevention approach to alcohol, drug, and mental problems. Public Health Rep. 96:26–33.

Roosa, J. B. 1973. SOCS (Situation, Options, Consequences, Simulation): A technique for teaching social interaction. Paper presented at the Annual Meeting of the American Psychological Association, Montreal.

Rose, S. 1981. Cognitive behavioural modification in groups. Int. J. Behav. Soc. Work Abstr. 1:27–37.

Rosen, R. H. 1980. Adolescent pregnancy decision-making: Are parents important? Adolescence 15:44–54.

Rosen, R. H., and Ager, J. W. 1981. Self-concept and contraception: Pre-conception decision-making. Popul. Envir. 4:11–23.

Rosen, R. H., Benson, T., and Stack, J. M. 1982. Help or hindrance: Parental impact on pregnant teenagers' resolution decisions. Family Relations 31:271–280.

Rosenbaum, D. E. 1981. Health secretary against sex education programs. Seattle Post Intell.

Rosenthal, T., and Bandura, A. 1978. Psychological modeling: Theory and practice. In: S. L. Garfield and A. E. Bergin (eds.), Handbook of Psychotherapy and Behavior Change: An Empirical Analysis. 2nd ed. Wiley, New York.

Roskies, E., and Lazarus, R. S. 1980. Coping theory and the teaching of coping skills. In: P. O. Davidson and S. M. Davidson (eds.), Behavioral Medicine: Changing Health Lifestyles. Brunner/Mazel, New York.

Ross, A. O. 1980. Psychological Disorders of Children: A Behavioral Approach to Theory, Research, and Therapy. 2nd Ed. McGraw-Hill, New York.

Ross, D. M., and Ross, S. A. 1976. Hyperactivity: Research, Theory, and Action. Wiley, New York.

Ross, S. 1979. The Youth Values Project. The Population Institute, Washington, DC.

Rothenberg, P. B. 1980. Communication about sex and birth control between mothers and their adolescent children. Popul. Envir. 3:35–50.

Rothman, J. 1980. Social R & D: Research and Development in the Human Services. Prentice-Hall, Englewood Cliffs, NJ.

Rothstein, A. A. 1978. Adolescent males, fatherhood, and abortion. J. Youth Adolescence 7:203–214.

Rothstein, M., and Jackson, D. N. 1980. Decision making in the employment interview: An experimental approach. J. Appl. Psychol. 65:271–283.

Rotter, J. 1966. Generalized expectancies for internal versus external control of reinforcement. Psychol. Monogr. 80(1, Whole No. 69).

Roush, G. C., Thompson, W. D., and Berberian, R. M. 1980. Psychoactive medicinal and nonmedicinal drug use among high school students. Pediatrics 66:709–715.

Rozensky, R. H., and Bellack, A. 1974. Behavior change and individual differences in self-control. Behav. Res. Ther. 12:267–268.

Rubenstein, J. J., Watson, F. G., Drolette, M. E., and Rubenstein, H. S. 1976. Young adolescents' sexual concerns. Adolescence 11:487–496.

Rusch, R. F., Weithers, J. A., Menchetti, B. M., and Schutz, R. P. 1980. Social validation of a program to reduce topic repetition in a nonsheltered setting. Educ. Train. Ment. Retard. 15:208–215.

Russell, C. S. 1980. A methodological study of family cohesion and adaptability. J. Marital Family Ther. 6:459–470.

Russell, D., Peplau, L. A., and Ferguson, M. L. 1978. Developing a measure of loneliness. J. Personality Assess. 42:290–294.

Saluter, A. F. 1979. Marital status and living arrangements: March 1978. Current Popul. Rep. Series P-20 (No. 338), May.

Sandifer, B. A., and Hollandsworth, Jr., J. G. 1978. Job-Interview Skills Training: A Workshop Model. Research and Curriculum Unit for Vocation-Technical Education, College of Education, Mississippi State, MS.

Santrock, J. W. 1981. Adolescence, an Introduction. William C. Brown, Dubuque, IA.

Sarason, I. G., and Sarason, B. R. 1981. Teaching cognitive and social skills to high school students. J. Consult. Clin. Psychol. 49:908–918.

Savin-Williams, R. C., and Jaquish, G. A. 1981. The assessment of adolescent self-esteem: A comparison of methods. J. Personality 49:324–336.

Scales, P. 1979. The context of sex education and the reduction of teen-age pregnancy. Child Welf. 58:263–273.

Schaffer, D., Pettigrew, A., Wolkind, S., and Zajicek, E. 1978. Psychiatric aspects of pregnancy in schoolgirls: A review. Psychol. Med. 8:-119–130.

Schinke, S. P. 1978. Teenage pregnancy: The need for multiple casework services. Soc. Casework 59:406–410.

Schinke, S. P. 1979. Evaluating social work practice: A conceptual model and example. Soc. Casework 60:195–200.

Schinke, S. P. (ed.). 1981a. Behavioral Methods in Social Welfare. Aldine Publishing, Hawthorne, NY.

Schinke, S. P. 1981b. Ethics, In: R. M. Grinnell, Jr. (ed.), Social Work Research and Evaluation. F. E. Peacock, Itasca, IL.

Schinke, S. P. 1981c. Interpersonal-skills training with adolescents. In: M. Hersen, R. M. Eisler, and P. M. Miller (eds.), Progress in Behavior Modification, Vol. 11. Academic Press, New York.

Schinke, S. P. 1981d. Culturally Syntonic Prevention. Paper presented at the meeting of the University of Washington Alcohol and Drug Abuse Institute. September. Seattle, WA.

Schinke, S. P. 1982. A school-based model for teenage pregnancy prevention. Soc. Work Educ. 4:34–42.

Schinke, S. P. 1983. Data-based practice. In: A. Rosenblatt and D. Waldfogel (eds.), Handbook of Clinical Social Work. Jossey-Bass, San Francisco. In press.

Schinke, S. P. 1983a. Preventing teenage pregnancy. In: M. Hersen, R. M. Eisler, and P. M. Miller (eds.), Progress in Behavior Modification, Vol. 13. Academic Press, New York. In press.

Schinke, S. P. 1983b. The clinical context of aversion therapy. In: W. H. Butterfield (ed.), Aversion Conditioning and Behavior Therapy. Springer, New York. In press.

Schinke, S. P., and Blythe, B. J. 1981. Cognitive-behavioral prevention of children's smoking. Child Behav. Ther. 4:25–42.

Schinke, S. P., and Gilchrist, L. D. 1977. Adolescent pregnancy: An interpersonal skill training approach to prevention. Soc. Work Health Care 3:159–167.

Schinke, S. P., and Gilchrist, L. D. Primary prevention of tobacco smoking. J. School Health. In press.

Schinke, S. P., and Olson, D. G. 1982. Home-based remediation of subacute sclerosing panencephalitis. Educ. Treatment Child. 5:261–269.

Schinke, S. P., and Rose, S. D. 1976. Interpersonal skill training in groups. J. Counsel. Psychol. 23:442–448.

Schinke, S. P., and Schilling, R. F. 1980. Needs assessment and child care staff training. Child Care Q. 9:73–81.

Schinke, S. P., and Smith, T. E. 1979. A videotape character generator for training and research. Behav. Engin. 5:101–104.

Schinke, S. P., and Wong, S. E. 1977. Coding group home behavior with a continuous real-time recording device. Behav. Engin. 4:5–9.

Schinke, S. P., Blythe, B. J., and Gilchrist, L. D. 1981. Cognitive-behavioral prevention of adolescent pregnancy. J. Counsel. Psychol. 28:451–454.

Schinke, S. P., Blythe, B. J., Gilchrist, L. D., and Burt, G. A. 1981. Primary prevention of adolescent pregnancy. Soc. Work Groups 4:121–135.

Schinke, S. P., Gilchrist, L. D., and Blythe, B. J. 1980. Role of communication in the prevention of teenage pregnancy. Health Soc. Work 5:54–59.

Schinke, S. P., Gilchrist, L. D., Lodish, D., and Bobo, J. 1983. Strategies for prevention research in service environments. Eval. Rev. 7:126–136.

Schinke, S. P., Gilchrist, L. D., and Small, R. W. 1979a. Preventing unwanted adolescent pregnancy: A cognitive-behavioral approach. Am. J. Orthopsych. 49:81–88.

Schinke, S. P., Gilchrist, L. D., and Smith, T. E. 1980. Increasing the economic self-sufficiency of teenage mothers. In: S. J. Bahr (ed.), Economics and the Family. D. C. Heath, Lexington, MA.

Schinke, S. P., Gilchrist, L. D., Smith, T. E., and Wong, S. E. 1978. Improving teenage mothers' ability to compete for jobs. Soc. Work Res. Abstr. 14:25–29.

Schinke, S. P., Gilchrist, L. D., Smith, T. E., and Wong, S. E. 1979b. Group interpersonal skills training in a natural setting: An experimental study. Behav. Res. Ther. 17:149–154.

Schnoll, S. 1978. Drug abuse in today's adolescent. Paper presented to the Symposium on Drug Abuse in Adolescents, New York.

Schrader, C. 1979. Behavioral group therapy with adolescents: A review and pilot program. In: D. Upper and S. M. Ross (eds.), Behavioral Group Therapy, 1979: An Annual Review. Research Press, Champaign, IL.

Schwartz, G. E. 1978. Psychobiological foundations of psychotherapy and behavior change. In: S. L. Garfield and A. E. Bergin (eds.), Handbook of Psychotherapy and Behavior Change: An Empirical Analysis. 2nd Ed. Wiley, New York.

Schwartz, R. M., and Gottman, J. M. 1976. Toward a task analysis of assertive behavior. J. Consult Clin. Psychol. 44:910–920.

Schwitzgebel, R. L. 1967. Short-term operant conditioning of adolescent offenders on socially relevant variables. J. Abnorm. Psychol. 72:134–142.

Seaman, B., and Seaman, G. 1977. Women and the Crisis of Sex Hormones. Rawson, New York.

Selye, H. 1974. Stress without Distress. Lippincott & Crowell, New York.

Serdahely, W. J. 1980. A factual approach to drug education and its effects on drug consumption. J. Alcohol Drug Educ. 26:63–68.

Shafer, D., Pettigrew, A., Wolkind, S., and Zajicek, E. 1978. Psychiatric aspects of pregnancy in schoolgirls: A review. Psychol. Med. 8:119–130.

Shapiro, C. H. 1980. Sexual learning: The short-changed adolescent male. Soc. Work 25:489–493.

Shapiro, C. H. 1981. Adolescent Pregnancy Prevention—School-Community Cooperation. Charles C Thomas, Springfield, IL.

Shapiro, C. H., Eggleston, A., and Kenworthy, R. 1979. Adolescent Pregnancy Prevention: A Team Approach. New York State College of Human Ecology, Cornell University, Ithaca, NY.

Shedd, C. (ed.). 1978. You Are Somebody Special. McGraw-Hill, New York.

Shelton, J. L., and Levy, R. L. 1981. Behavioral Assignments and Treatment Compliance: A Handbook of Clinical Strategies. Research Press, Champaign, IL.

Shepard, D. S., and Thompson, M. S. 1979. First principles of cost-effectiveness analysis in health. Public Health Rep. 94:535–543.

Shore, M. F. 1977. Evaluation of a community-based clinical program for antisocial youth. Evaluation 4:104–107.

Shornack, L. L., and Shornack, E. M. 1982. The new sex education and the sexual revolution: A critical view. Family Relations 31:531–544.

Shostrum, E. L. 1972. Man, the Manipulator. Bantam Books, New York.

Should parents be notified? Proposed teen contraceptive rule draws fire. 1982. Intercom March: 3 (Population Reference Bureau, Washington, DC.)

Shure, M. B. 1979. Training children to solve interpersonal problems: A preventive mental health program. In: R. F. Muñoz, L. R. Snowden, and J. G. Kelly (eds.), Social and Psychological Research in Community Settings. Jossey-Bass, San Francisco.

Shure, M. B. 1981. Social competence as a problem-solving skill. In: J. D. Wine & M. D. Smye (eds.), Social Competence. Guilford, New York.

Shure, M. B., and Spivack, G. 1970. Cognitive Problem Solving Skills, Adjustment, and Social Class (Research and Evaluation Report No. 22). Department of Mental Health Services, Hahnemann Community Mental Health/Mental Retardation Center, Philadelphia.

Shure, M. B., and Spivack, G. 1972. Means-end thinking, adjustment, and social class among elementary school-aged children. J. Consult. Clin. Psychol. 38:348–353.

Shure, M. B., and Spivack, G. 1978. Problem-Solving Techniques in Child-Rearing. Jossey-Bass, Inc., San Francisco.

Shute, R. E., St. Pierre, R. W., and Lubell, E. G. 1981. Smoking awareness and practices of urban pre-school and first-grade children. J. School Health 51:347–351.

Siegel, J. M., and Leitch, C. J. 1981. Assessment of the Type A behavior pattern in adolescents. Psychosom. Med. 43:45–56.

Silber, E., Hamburg, D. A., Coelho, G. V., et al. 1961. Adaptive behavior in competent adolescents. Arch. Gen. Psych. 5:354–365.

Simmons, R. G., Rosenberg, F., and Rosenberg, M. 1973. Disturbance in the self-image at adolescence. Am. Sociol. Rev. 38:553–568.

Simonds, J. D. 1980. Specific drug use and violence in delinquent boys. Am. J. Drug Alcohol Abuse 7:305–322.

Single, E., Kandel, D., and Faust, R. 1975. Patterns of multiple drug use in high school. J. Health Soc. Behav. 15:344–357.

Skinner, B. F. 1953. Science and Human Behavior. Macmillan, New York.

Sklar, L. S., and Anisman, H. 1981. Stress and cancer. Psychol. Bull. 89:369–406.

Smart, M. S., Smart, R. C., and Smart, L. S. (eds.). 1978. Adolescents: Development and Relationships. 2nd Ed. Macmillan, New York.

Smith, P. B., and Gorry, G. A. 1980. Evaluating sex education programs. J. Sex Educ. Ther. 6:17–23.

Smith, P. B., Nenney, S. W., Mumford, D. M., and Kaufman, R. H. 1982. Selected family planning and general health profiles in a teen health clinic. J. Adolescent Health Care 2:267–272.

Smith, P. B., Weinman, M. L., and Mumford, D. M. 1982. Social and affective factors associated with adolescent pregnancy. J. School Health 52:90–93.

Smith, R. E. 1980. Development of an integrated coping response through cognitive-affective stress management training. In: I. G. Sarason and C. D. Spielberger (eds.), Stress and Anxiety, Vol. 7. Hemisphere, Washington, DC.

Smith, R. E., Sarason, I. G., and Sarason, B. R. 1978. Psychology: The Frontiers of Behavior. Harper & Row, New York.

Snyder, J. J., and White, M. J. 1979. The use of cognitive self-instruction in the treatment of behaviorally disturbed adolescents. Behav. Ther. 10:227–235.

Solkoff, N. 1981. Children of survivors of the Nazi Holocaust: A critical review of the literature. Am. J. Orthopsych. 51:29–42.

Sommer, R., and Sommer, B. B. 1980. A Practical Guide to Behavioral Research. Oxford, New York.

Sorensen, R. C. 1973. Adolescent Sexuality in Contemporary America: Personal Values and Sexual Behavior Ages Thirteen to Nineteen. World, New York.

Spitzzeri, A., and Jason, L. A. 1979. Prevention and treatment of smoking in school age children. J. Drug Educ. 9:315–326.

Spivack, G., and Swift, M. 1967. Devereux Elementary School Behavior Rating Scale. The Devereux Foundation, Devon, PA.

Spivack, G., Platt, J. J., and Shure, M. B. 1976. The Problem-Solving Approach to Adjustment. Jossey-Bass, San Francisco.

Spoth, R. 1980. Using a differential stress reduction model with substance abusers: Matching treatment presentation with locus of control. Behav. Anal. Modif. 4:188–200.

Stanat, K. W., and Reardon, P. 1977. Job Hunting Secrets and Tactics. Westwind Press, Milwaukee, WI.

Steinberg, L. D., Greenberger, E., Jacobi, M., and Garduque, L. 1981. Early work experience: A partial antidote for adolescent egocentrism. J. Youth Adolescence 10:141–157.

Stokes, T. F., and Baer, D. M. 1977. An implicit technology of generalization. J. Appl. Behav. Anal. 10:349–367.

Stokols, D. 1979. A congruence analysis of human stress. In: I. G. Sarason and C. D. Spielberger (eds.), Stress and Anxiety, Vol. 6. Hemisphere, Washington, DC.

Stolz, S. B., and Associates. 1978. Ethical Issues in Behavior Modification. Jossey-Bass, San Francisco.

Stone, L. J., and Church, J. 1975. Adolescence as a cultural invention. In: A. H. Esman (ed.), The Psychology of Adolescence, Essential Readings. International Universities Press, New York.

Strain, P. S., and Ezzell, D. 1978. The sequence and distribution of behavioral disordered adolescents' disruptive/inappropriate behaviors: An observational study in a residential setting. Behav. Modification 2:403–425.

Strober, M. 1979. The structuring of interpersonal relations in schizophrenic adolescents: A decentering analysis of thematic apperception test stories. J. Abnorm. Child Psychol. 7:309–316.

Stuart, R. B. 1970. Trick or Treatment: How and When Psychotherapy Fails. Research Press, Champaign, IL.

Stuart, R. B., Tripodi, T., Jayaratne, S., and Camburn, D. 1979. An experiment in social engineering in serving the families of predelinquents. J. Abnorm. Child Psychol. 4:243–261.

Sulzer-Azaroff, B., and Mayer, G. R. 1977. Applying Behavior-Analysis Procedures with Children and Youth. Holt, Rinehart & Winston, New York.

Sutton-Simon, K. 1981. Assessing belief systems: Concepts and strategies. In: P. C. Kendall and S. D. Hollon (eds.), Assessment Strategies for Cognitive-Behavioral Interventions. Academic Press, New York.

Swan, R. W. 1980. Sex education in the home: The U.S. experience. J. Sex Educ. Ther. 6:3–10.

Teasdale, J. D. 1979. Behaviour therapy and modification. Br. J. Criminol. 19:323–332.

Teenage Turn-on: Drinking and Drugs. 1978. McGraw-Hill Films, Highstown, NJ (film).

Tennant, Jr., F. S., Weaver, S. C., and Lewis, C. E. 1973. Outcomes of drug education: Four case studies. Pediatrics 52:246–251.

Tennov, B. 1975. Psychotherapy: The Hazardous Cure. Abelard-Schuman, New York.

Tepper, S. S., and Barnard, G. 1977. Choices. Rocky Mountain Planned Parenthood, Denver, CO.

Teri, L. 1982. Depression in adolescence: Its relationship to assertion and various aspects of self-image. J. Clin. Child Psychol. 11:101–106.

Tessler, R., and Sushelsky, L. 1978. Effects of eye contact and social status on the perception of a job applicant in an employment interviewing situation. J. Vocational Behav. 13:338–347.

Tharp, R. G., and Wetzel, R. J. 1969. Behavior Modification in the Natural Environment. Academic Press, New York.

Thomas, E. J. 1978. Generating innovation in social work: The paradigm of developmental research. J. Soc. Serv. Res. 2:114.

Thornburg, H. D. 1981a. Adolescent sources of information on sex. J. School Health 51:274–277.

Thornburg, H. D. 1981b. The amount of sex information learning obtained during early adolescence. J. Early Adolescence 1:171–183.

Tietze, C. 1978. Teenage pregnancies: Looking ahead to 1984. Fam. Plan. Perspect. 10:205–207.

Topper, M. D. 1981. The drinker's story: An important but often forgotten source of data. J. Stud. Alcohol Suppl. 9:73–86.

Toseland, R. W. 1981. Choosing an appropriate research method. In: R. M. Grinnell, Jr. (ed.), Social Work Research and Evaluation. F. E. Peacock, Itasca, IL.

Trower, P. 1978. Skills training for adolescent social problems: A viable treatment alternative? J. Adolescence 1:319–329.

Trower, P. 1980. Situational analysis of the components and processes of socially skilled and unskilled persons. J. Consult. Clin. Psychol. 48:327–329.

Trower, P., Bryant, B., Argyle, M., and Marzillier, J. 1978. Social Skills and Mental Health. University of Pittsburgh Press, Pittsburgh, PA.

Trussell, J., and Menken, J. 1978. Early childbearing and subsequent fertility. Family Plan. Perspect. 10:209–218.

Tucker, D. H., and Rowe, P. M. 1977. Consulting the application form prior to the interview: An essential step in the selection process. J. Appl. Psychol. 62:283–287.

Tudor, C. G., Peterson, D. M., and Elifson, K. W. 1980. An examination of the relationship between peer and parental influences and adolescent drug use. Adolescence 15:783–798.

Tukey, J. W. 1977. Exploratory Data Analysis. Addison-Wesley Publishing, Reading, MA.

Turkat, I. D., and Feuerstein, M. 1978. Behavior modification and the public misconception. Am. Psychol. 33:194.

Turkat, I. D., and Forehand, R. 1980. The future of behavior therapy. In: M. Hersen, R. M. Eisler, and P. M. Miller (eds.), Progress in Behavior Modification, Vol. 9. Academic Press, New York.

Turkat, I. D., Harris, F. C., and Forehead, R. 1979. An assessment of the public reaction to behavior modification. J. Behav. Ther. Exp. Psych. 10:101–103.

Twentyman, C. T., Gibralter, J. C., and Inz, J. M. 1979. Multimodal assessment of rehearsal treatments in an assertion training program. J. Counsel. Psychol. 26:384–389.

Twentyman, C. T., and Zimering, R. T. 1979. Behavioral training of social skills: A critical review. In: M. Hersen, R. M. Eisler, and P. M. Miller (eds.), Progress in Behavior Modification, Vol. 7. Academic Press, New York.

Ullman, L. P., and Krasner, L. 1969. A Psychological Approach to Abnormal Behavior. Prentice-Hall, Inc., Englewood Cliffs, NJ.

United States Bureau of the Census. 1980. Families maintained by female householders 1970–1979. Current Popul. Rep. P-23.

United States Department of Health and Human Services. 1980. Promoting Health/Preventing Disease, Objectives for the Nation. Superintendent of Documents, Washington, DC.

United States Department of Justice. 1978. Uniform Crime Reports for the United States. U.S. Government Printing Office, Washington, DC.

United States Department of Labor, Bureau of Labor Statistics. 1979. Young Workers and Families: A Special Section (Special Labor Force Report 233). U.S. Department of Labor, Washington, DC.

United States Department of Labor, Bureau of Labor Statistics. 1980. Profile of the Teenage Worker (Bulletin 2039). U.S. Department of Labor, Washington, DC.

United States Department of Labor, Bureau of Labor Statistics. 1981a. Employment in Perspective: Minority Workers (Report 652). U.S. Department of Labor, Washington, DC.

United States Department of Labor, Bureau of Labor Statistics. 1981b. School and Work among Youth during the 1970's (Special Labor Force Report 241). U.S. Department of Labor, Washington, DC.

United States Department of Transportation, National Highway Traffic Safety Administration. 1977. You . . . Alcohol and Driving. U.S. Government Printing Office, Washington, DC.

United States Public Health Service, Department of Health, Education, and Welfare. 1979a. Smoking and Health: A Report of the Surgeon General. U.S. Government Printing Office, Washington, DC.

United States Public Health Service, Department of Health, Education, and Welfare. 1979b. Healthy People: The Surgeon General's Report on Health Promotion and Disease Prevention. U.S. Government Printing Office, Washington, DC.

United States Subcommittee on Health and Scientific Research of the Committee on Labor and Human Resources, 96th Congress, 1st Session. 1980. On Examination of the Use and Misuse of Valium, Librium, and Other Minor Tranquilizers. U.S. Government Printing Office, Washington, DC.

Van Hasselt, V. B., Hersen, M., Bellack, A. S., et al. 1979. Tripartite assessment of the effects of systematic desensitization in a multi-phobic child: An experimental analysis. J. Behav. Ther. Exp. Psych. 10:51–55.

Van Hasselt, V. B., Hersen, M., and Milliones, J. 1978. Social skills training for alcoholics and drug addicts: A review. Addict. Behav. 3:221–233.

Van Hasselt, V. B., Hersen, M., Whitehall, M. B., and Bellack, A. S. 1979. Social skill assessment and training for children: An evaluative review. Behav. Res. Ther. 17:413–437.

Ventura, S. J. 1977. Teenage childbearing: United States, 1966-75. Monthly Vital Stat. Rep. 26(5).

Vickers, Jr., R. R., Hervig, L. K., Rahe, R. H., and Rosenman, R. H. 1981. Type A behavior patterns and coping and defense. Psychosom. Med. 43:381–396.

Voors, A. W., Sklov, M. C., Wolf, T. M., et al. 1982. Cardiovascular risk factors in children and coronary-related behavior. In: T. J. Coates, A. C. Petersen, and C. Perry (eds.), Promoting Adolescent Health: A Dialog on Research and Practice. Academic Press, New York.

Wagner, H. 1980. Sexual behavior of adolescents. Adolescence 15:567–580.

Washington Crime Watch. 1982. Shoplifting: Nobody but Me Decides. Office of the Attorney General, Washington State, Olympia, WA.

Washington, R. O., Rindfleisch, N. J., Toomey, B., et al. 1979. The Project Report—A Report of the Ohio-Wisconsin Children's Services Training Needs Assessment Project. School of Social Work, Ohio State University, Columbus.

Wasik, B. H., and Loven, M. D. 1980. Classroom observation data: Sources of inaccuracy and proposed solutions. Behav. Assess. 2:211–227.

Watson, D., and Friend, R. 1969. Measurement of social-evaluative anxiety. J. Consult. Clin. Psychol. 33:448–457.

Watson, J. M. 1980. Solvent abuse by children and young adults: A review. Br. J. Addiction 75:27–36.

Watson, K. W. 1979. Social work and stress and personal belief. Child Welfare 58:3–12.

Watson, L. M. 1966. Cigarette smoking in school children: A study of the effectiveness of different health education methods in modifying behavior, knowledge, and attitudes. Health Bull. 24:5–12.

Watt, N. 1978. Patterns of childhood social development in adult schizophrenics. Arch. Gen. Psych. 35:160–165.

Weinberg, M. S., and Williams, C. J. 1974. Male Homosexuals: Their Problems and Adaptations. Oxford University Press, New York.

Weiner, H. 1980. Administrative responsibility for staff development. In: F. D. Perlmutter and S. Slavin (eds.), Leadership in Social Administration, pp. 230–248. Temple University Press, Philadelphia.

Welldon, D. A. 1866. Rhetoric of Aristotle. G. P. Sullivan and Sons, New York.

Werner, J. S., Phillips, E. L., Minkin, N., et al. 1975. Intervention package: An analysis to prepare juvenile delinquents for encounters with police officers. Crim. Justice & Behav. 2:55–84.

Wessberg, H. W., Mariotto, M. J., Conger, A. J., et al. 1979. Ecological validity of role plays for assessing heterosocial anxiety and skill of male college students. J. Consult. Clin. Psychol. 47:525–535.

Whaley, L. F., and Wong, D. L. 1979. Nursing Care of Infants and Children. C. V. Mosby, St. Louis.

Wheeler, K. 1977. Assertiveness and the job hunt. In: R. E. Alberti (ed.), Assertiveness: Innovations, Applications, Issues. Impact, San Luis Obispo, CA.

White, R. W. 1959. Motivation reconsidered: The concept of competence. Psychol. Rev. 66:297–333.

Whittaker, J. K. 1979. Caring for Troubled Children: Residential Treatment in a Community Context. Jossey-Bass, San Francisco.

Whittaker, J. K., and Pecora, P. J. 1981. The social "R & D" paradigm in child and youth services: Building knowledge convivially. Child. Youth Serv. Rev. 3:305–317.

Whittaker, J. K., and Small, R. W. 1977. Differential approaches to group treatment of children and adolescents. Child Youth Serv. 1:1–13.

Williams, D. Y., and Akamatsu, T. J. 1978. Cognitive self-guidance training with juvenile delinquents: Applicability and generalization. Cognitive Ther. Res. 2:285–288.

Willner, A. G., Braukman, C. J., Kirigin, K. A., et al. 1977. The training and validation of youth-preferred social behaviors of child-care personnel. J. Appl. Behav. Anal. 10:219–230.

Wilson, G. T. 1981. Expectations and substance abuse. Can basic research benefit clinical assessment and therapy? Addictive Behav. 6:221–231.

Wilson, S. J. 1978. Confidentiality in Social Work: Issues and Principles. The Free Press, New York.

Wodarski, J. S. 1981a. Group work with antisocial children. In: S. P. Schinke (ed.), Behavioral Methods in Social Welfare. Aldine Publishing, Hawthorne, NY.

Wodarski, J. S. 1981b. The Role of Research in Clinical Practice: A Practical Approach for the Human Services. University Park Press, Baltimore.

Wodarski, J. S., and Ammons, P. W. 1981. Comprehensive treatment of runaway children and their parents. Family Ther. 8:229–240.

Wodarski, J. S., Filipczak, J., McCombs, D., et al. 1979. Follow-up on behavioral intervention with troublesome adolescents. J. Behav. Ther. Exper. Psych. 10:181–188.

Wolf, M. M. 1978. Social validity: The case for subjective measurement or how applied behavior analysis is finding its heart. J. Appl. Behav. Anal. 11:203–214.

Wolf, T. M., Sklov, M. C., Wenzl, P. A., et al. 1982. Validation of a measure of Type A behavior pattern in children: Bogalusa Heart Study. Child Devel. 53:126–135.

Woolfolk, A. E., and Woolfolk, R. L. 1979. Modifying the effect of the behavior modification label. Behav. Ther. 10:575–578.

Woolfolk, A. E., Woolfolk, R. L., and Wilson, G. T. 1977. A rose by any other name. . . .: Labeling bias and attitudes toward behavior modification. J. Consult. Clin. Psychol. 45:184–191.

Wright, M. J. 1980. Measuring the social competence of preschool children. Can. J. Behav. Sci. 12:17–32.

Wrubel, J., Benner, P. and Lazarus, R. S. Social competence from the perspective of stress and coping. In: J. D. Wine and M. D. Smye (eds.), Social Competence. Guilford, New York.

Wurmser, L. 1972. Drug abuse: Nemesis of psychiatry. Int. J. Psych. 10:94–107.

Wurmser, L. 1978. The Hidden Dimension: Psychodynamics in Compulsive Drug Use. Aronson, New York.

Yankelovich, D. 1974. The New Morality: A Profile of American Youth in the 1970s. McGraw-Hill, New York.

Yates, B. T. 1979. How to improve, rather than evaluate, cost-effectiveness. Counsel. Psychol. 8:72–75.

Young, S. 1981. Aspects of social support networks among institutionalized adolescents. Adolescence 16:123–137.

Youngman, G., and Sadongei, M. 1979. Counseling the American Indian child. In: D. R. Atkinson, G. Moreten, and D. W. Sue (eds.), Counseling American Minorities: A Cross-Cultural Perspective. Wm. C. Brown, Dubuque, IA.

Zehring, J. W. 1975. Rejection shock. J. College Placement 35:34–35.

Zellman, G. L. 1982. Public school programs for adolescent pregnancy and parenthood: An assessment. Family Plan. Perspect. 14:15–21.

Zelnik, M., and Kantner, J. F. 1978. First pregnancies to women aged 15–19: 1971 and 1976. Fam. Plan. Perspect. 10:11–20.

Zelnik, M., and Kantner, J. F. 1979. Reasons for nonuse of contraception by sexually active women aged 15–19. Family Plan. Perspect. 11:289–296.

Zelnik, M., and Kantner, J. F. 1980. Sexual activity, contraceptive use and pregnancy among metropolitan-area teenagers: 1971–1979. Fam. Plan. Perspect. 12:230–237.

Zelnik, M., and Kim, Y. J. 1982. Sex education and its association with teenage sexual activity, pregnancy, and contraceptive use. Family Plan. Perspect. 14:117–126.

Zelnik, M., Kim, Y. J., and Kantner, J. F. 1979. Probabilities of intercourse and conception among U.S. teenage women, 1971 and 1976. Family Plan. Perspect. 11:177–183.

Zigler, E., and Trickett, P. K. 1978. IQ, social competence, and evaluation of early childhood intervention programs. Am. Psychol. 33:789–798.

Zober, M. A. 1980. A systematic perspective on the staff development and training evaluation process. Arete 6:51–70.

Zukerman, E. 1979. Changing Directions in the Treatment of Women: A Mental Health Bibliography. National Institute of Mental Health, Rockville, MD.

Author Index

Subject Index

DATE DUE